COSMOPOLITAN BELONGINGNESS
AND WAR

COSMOPOLITAN BELONGINGNESS AND WAR

ANIMALS, LOSS, AND SPECTRAL-POETIC MOMENTS

MATTHEW LEEP

Cover image: Thomas Smillie, cyanotype, 1890. Smithsonian Institute Archives.

Published by State University of New York Press, Albany

© 2021 State University of New York

All rights reserved.

Printed in the United States of America

No part of this book may be used or reproduced in any manner without written permission. No part of this book may be stored in a retrieval system or transmitted in any form or by any means including electronic, electrostatic, magnetic tape, mechanical, photocopying, recording, or otherwise without the prior permission in writing of the publisher.

For information, contact State University of New York Press, Albany, NY
www.sunypress.edu

Library of Congress Cataloging-in-Publication Data

Names: Leep, Matthew, author.
Title: Cosmopolitan belongingness and war : animals, loss, and spectral-poetic moments / Matthew Leep.
Other titles: Animals, loss, and spectral-poetic moments
Description: Albany : State University of New York Press, [2021] | Includes bibliographical references and index.
Identifiers: LCCN 2020024816 | ISBN 9781438482439 (hardcover : alk. paper) | ISBN 9781438482446 (pbk. : alk. paper) | ISBN 9781438482453 (ebook)
Subjects: LCSH: Iraq War, 2003–2011—Casualties. | Animal welfare—Moral and ethical aspects—Iraq. | Cosmopolitanism. | Human-animal relationships—Political aspects. | War and society. | Derrida, Jacques.
Classification: LCC DS79.767.C37 L44 2021 | DDC 956.7044/31—dc23
LC record available at https://lccn.loc.gov/2020024816

10 9 8 7 6 5 4 3 2 1

To the lost

Contents

List of Poems ix

List of Illustrations xi

Acknowledgments xiii

Introduction: Cosmopolitan Elegies 1

Chapter 1 Spectral Cosmopolitanism 19

Chapter 2 Stray Hearts, Vectors: The Wandering Dogs of Iraq 45

Chapter 3 Caged Cosmopolitanism: Menagerie Moments of War 65

Chapter 4 Black Sheep: ISIS and the Smoke of Qayyarah 83

(In)Conclusion(s): Spectral-Poetic Proximities 99

Notes 107

Works Cited 135

About the Author 153

Index 155

Poems

Alone Ghosts	7
Qarqar	19
Remember That	26
Wolf-Time	37
A Promise, a Threat	48
Clusters	50
Tangled	51
Delta	54
Palm Cloak	57
Raven's Coat	58
Nightpsalm, Rusted	68
Absential	71
Birdflowers	72
Breath	73
Rememberkey	77
Notes, Cinders	79
Hourglass	79
Burned Compass	86

Recognition	92
Find Me	92
Moonpaths	94

Illustrations

Figure 2.1	Stray Dog in a Cage	55
Figure 2.2	Camp Slayer Vector Control	56
Figure 3.1	Hope and Riley	66
Figure 3.2	A Note for Looters	75
Figure 4.1	Qayyarah Oil Field Fires	88
Figure 4.2	Qayyarah Oil Smoke	89
Figure 4.3	Mine Dog in Qayyarah	95

Acknowledgments

I am grateful to the anonymous reviewers for their constructive comments and kind words. Many thanks are owed to Michael Rinella at SUNY Press for his support, confidence, and guidance. I offer my deep appreciation to my parents and sisters for their encouragement. I offer thanks to Walden Pond, Corniche Beirut and the Mediterranean Sea, Lake Superior, and Bahía Honda. Jeremy Pressman deserves a special mention for his assistance on a variety of projects. I am forever thankful for Moszka, a wanderer—my heart. I am grateful for the lifelong friendship of Adrian Butler (LA is infinite). I have been privileged to work with my colleagues and students at WGU. A special thanks to Kate Warrington and DJ Bradley for their kindness and support for my work. In no particular order, thanks also to the following individuals or groups for their inspiration, feedback, kind words, or other forms of support: Donna Lee Van Cott, Bangkok street dogs, Eileen Nizer, Sneha Subramanian Kanta, Shawn Berman, the folks at my synagogue, Congregation Sinai, Rafi Youatt, Cyrus (Ernie) Zirakzadeh, Bryan Benson, Jamie Mayerfeld, Christian Hunold, Jennifer Sterling-Folker, Doug Kriner, Susan Howe, Katherine Douglas, Cheryl Hall, Lee Jones, the ibises of Silver Sands and Hammonasset, Barry Sharpe, Bill Kakenmaster, and Garry Clifford. I also thank you, reader, for your engagement. Most of all, thanks to Alise. Your compassion for the world compels me to engage it differently, more deeply. I am forever indebted to you in far too many ways to list here. Amidst these red frogs and dune deer, I follow your heart to an oropendola's dream.

An earlier version of chapter 2 was originally published by Sage Publications as "Stray Dogs, Post-Humanism and Cosmopolitan Belongingness: Interspecies Hospitality in Times of War," in *Millennium: Journal of International Studies* 47, no. 1 (September 2018). The appearance of US Department of Defense visual information does not imply or constitute DoD endorsement.

Introduction

Cosmopolitan Elegies

Naming assures a kind of longevity and survival, writes Jacques Derrida.[1] After war, the names of the lost might persist in documents, on monuments, and in memories.[2] The Iraq War, like every war, has resulted in the loss of so many soldiers, civilians, and (often nameless) animals.[3] The nameless lost animals are often neglected or maintained in abstractions, disciplined and distant. The losses, tallied or unrecorded, are untethered from the lived moments of life and death. Who are these animal others? Who are we when we imagine their voices?

Derrida claims that "we owe ourselves to death" (*nous nous devons à la mort*).[4] These losses in Iraq move toward us, withdrawing and escaping, appearing within the nowhere space of the poem—an elegiac space for the animal other. Perhaps we owe ourselves to these losses, to the memory of the lost, to the poetic voice of a specter. Cosmopolitans would do well to consider this voice. This voice—finding "us" within a spectral-poetic moment. Engaging this voice will likely bear little resemblance to most accounts of war. But this engagement opens us to thinking about how to live differently in and with the world. This endeavor also raises critical questions about how to write about, with, and for a multispecies world. Perhaps elegies can generate meaningful reflection on nonhuman moments of loss and our posthumanist responsibilities. In cosmopolitan elegies, we might recall the ends of worlds, our debt to the distant heart of the other, traces of unknown interiorities.

Across borders—a debt, a voice. For traditional cosmopolitans, borders and "other boundaries considered to restrict the scope of justice are irrelevant roadblocks in appreciating our responsibilities to all in the global community."[5] Cosmopolitanism is about connections with and support for distant others; it is about "the interconnectivity of the world."[6] From this traditional perspective, justice is about the living and its scope is global and temporally oriented toward the present and future. Cosmopolitan justice attends to the limited horizons of the human. But what of justice for the mostly unknown and nameless animal dead? As Derrida reminds us, "just because the dead no longer exist does not mean that we are done with specters."[7] No, the specter "asks [us] to respond or to be responsible," and there is no "demand for justice" without this responsibility to the spectral other.[8] Yet possibilities of memories from and connection to the lost are typically not central to the intellectual project of cosmopolitanism. Moreover, there is little attention to the interiority of life becoming lost to war, and only faint concern for how the lost still might move toward us, within the elegiac space of a poem. What if we subject cosmopolitanism to these spectral-poetic demands of justice?

This book aims to generate shifts in cosmopolitan thought toward an imaginative memory of the distant and often unknown animal others lost to war, toward a poetic memory of and from the other, toward the other's experience and time of loss. Put another way, this book seeks to articulate a multispecies cosmopolitanism that addresses the following questions: How might we encounter and connect to the loss of distant, mostly unknown animal others of war? How can we approach the interior life of animals lost to war? These queries stimulate cosmopolitanism to become something else, something more "posthumanist" and poetic, something less interested in telling us about justice and belonging and more conversant with animal ghosts.[9] It is a spectral-weaved cosmopolitanism embodying this impossible hope.

Cosmopolitanism—a rich philosophical tradition, a varied set of aspirations for global justice, a sense of debt to distant others across boundaries and borders—is always a kind of possibility. There is a vibrancy, fluidity, and dynamism to it. Cosmopolitanism always seems to resist closure, seems to stretch alive with voices calling from pasts and futures, pressing us about the meaning(s) of distance, connection, loss. This book anchors itself to these poetic voices, the incantational voices of animals from the Iraq War—unveiled, pursuing and interrupting us—from the past and from within ourselves. "The interactions of the living must be interrupted, the veil must be torn toward the other, the other dead *in us* though other still," writes Jacques Derrida.[10] Holding on to these voices of the lost within us involves not only expanding the boundaries of thinking about war in its multispecies entanglements but also orienting our attention toward the experience of the other, for the other (though always irreducibly other). The unknowable voice, their impossible presence, lost—*here* is a space for arrival, for interruption, for belongingness. Belongingness—a pursuit to be-with, a being-followed by and following of the poetic voice of the other. A spectral-poetic chasing of the lost, an attempt to keep company with animal ghosts.

These cosmopolitan pursuits of and by the other resonate with (and intervene in) two larger aspirations in International Relations (IR): (1) aims toward the aesthetic and sensory life of global politics, and (2) efforts toward understanding global politics as always a kind of interspecies politics.[11] This book is a cosmopolitan convergence of these aims, an elegiac turn within what we might call an interspecies-sensory focus on global politics. In summoning this sensory approach, Christine Sylvester suggests that "not everyone touches war in the same way but everyone can be touched by it," and that we need to look at war in terms of what it "feels like" to those within the space of war but also to "us as individuals."[12] As a broad conceptual starting place, I believe cosmopolitanism is suited to this reflexive and sensory task of the touch, the melancholic work of tracing the spectral other being touched by war. The task is one of self-relation and other-relation. It is an intermingled *relationing* toward the depth of distance within and between us. Within this distance is an empty space, an elegiac space for the poetic voice of the animal other. This book sets out to explore forms of connection within this space. It attempts to think of the cosmopolitan text as an elegiac space for the other, a space for listening for the poetic timbre of lost voices. This book asks how we might describe and make connection with the life and death of war rather than merely theorizing it, pre-supposing it, measuring it, or otherwise making arguments about it. It asks how to cross borders and boundaries in our own thinking, writing, feeling, and listening. In other words, it seeks to imagine a cosmopolitanism of self-reflexivity and connection to the unknown loss of life across borders, to the unknown (and always interspecies) past.[13] While there has been separate work on interspecies politics and sensory politics, this book opens them up and into each other, seeking to grasp at the distance, hoping to sense the space and time of the animal other, lost in war, finding us in poetry.[14] With this in mind, the book works to pull apart the event of war (specifically the Iraq War) in order to see and sense its interspecies moments of life and death, to connect to the loss of others, and to poetically dwell in these moments. Put somewhat differently, it sees cosmopolitanism as a kind of elegiac endeavor, as an approach to war that is attuned to the interspecies entanglements of loss, distance, and violence.[15]

A war is not only a singular event in the past but is also its mostly unknown experiential moments, which might be encountered in poetic terms, in poetic space. There is an ongoingness to the event of war; war is comprised of moments of living and dying, the often invisible and unmarked sensory details of experiences that can be sensed by us still in the textual space of a poem. We might therefore sense these small fragments of evidence without names. These moments are still there—audible traces in an imagined frequency, crackling underneath the buzz of the facts of war. How do animals, these singular lives often without names, experience becoming lost to war? And how do we come to know them or encounter them? While we might know the conditions of death, the experience of it is often impenetrable. Most experiences of war are unknown. Human survivors might tell stories of the lost, but animals cannot speak to us with these same kind of stories. They are mostly without names, without a voice, or without a language that we are used to engaging. The facts of these nonhuman losses are therefore often unknown and outside the gates of the human vocabulary of war. As I think of paths forward, I am reminded of Robert Lowell's musing about being "paralyzed by fact" and writing "something imagined, not recalled."[16] But what if there is no recording to recall, or what if there are only pieces of facts to remember? Perhaps we must imagine. The facts of loss, the memory of it, call out to our imagination, call in for connection, call for imaginative dirge-thinking. The facts, touched, become an address to and from the animal other, a sensory account of the other's address, a relational, ghostly addressing. Poetically encountering these moments of war, the ongoingness of experiencing, is one path toward a space of and for connection with the lost animal other, a movement toward their poetic voice—the other, always other—within us.[17]

This Strange Time

This book explores war in terms of spectral-poetic moments. This exploration involves an animal-centric (and poetic) approach to the experience of becoming lost (becoming so-called collateral damage). By this I mean that wartime decisions and "events" are approached and assessed in terms of how they created moments of animal injury and death. It also means that I zoom in to explore the mostly unknown experience of these moments, and also the ways in which we can "be-with" these moments. For example, I examine how U.S. decisions about the occupation of Iraq resulted in a trash collection problem in Baghdad, a seemingly trivial concern on the surface but one that created conditions for the mass killing of stray dogs. How did these street dogs experience the uncertainty of life in Baghdad? How did they experience moments of becoming lost to the violence of post-invasion life in the capital city? And how are we touched, in a ghostly way, by these experiences? *What is my responsibility to you, dog, as I write to and about you, about a war that broke you? Who was your pack? What does a coarse remembrance of your eyes, the texture of your fur, the misremembrance or nonremembrance of your experiences, your becoming "collateral damage" matter? Who am "I" with "you," your winged bark, your quelled name?* In a poem I return to you. The time of you, then, you in me, now—spectral-poetic time. "This strange time of the dead courier."[18]

Susan Howe tells us that "a poet is like an ethnographer. You open your mind and textual space to many voices, to an interplay and contradiction and complexity of voices."[19] Cosmopolitans do not all need to be poets, but poetry can open up a space to the life, loss, and voice of the other, including the animal-ghost other. The cosmopolitan text can become an offering of space for the time of the other; it can be space for the other's time folding into us within a textual dwelling. While assessing, describing, and theorizing the conditions of wartime loss are important, so too is encountering animals' experiences with war, their becoming lost to it. For this I take a poetic path, interrupting the description and assessment of violence with elegiac fragments of imagined animal experiences of becoming lost, digressions of "being-with" loss, fragments of voices merging. This poetic path toward the time of the other is what I call "spectral cosmopolitanism."[20]

Susan Howe also reminds us that poetry has "something to do with abstracting and recuperating the measure of time and memory. It's a balance of openness and closure, momentary epiphanies, human voices—unanswered questions."[21] Howe's insight here helps inform the approach I take toward the time of the other. The cosmopolitanism sketched out here is an open and ghostly invitation to be-with the unknown animal other, an invitation to the self, to you, to the others (if an invitation is possible, as Derrida might say); it is an offer to open the self to the plurality of others, always other.[22] It is about being open to the memory of human *and* animal ghost voices. It is about the time of the other, an openness to absence, a searching for the fading whispers of the silenced. These nonhuman voices remind us of the multispecies experiences of war, returning to us in the poem and urging us to remember.

To search for the other within the poem is to also excavate the other (and otherness) within the self—an excavation of fragments of the other within the spectral strata of belonging. As Derrida puts it, the memory of the spectral other, their voice and look, "are only lacunary fragments" that become "parts of us, included 'in us' in a memory which suddenly seems greater and older than us."[23] This move toward the memory of the other is a responsibility marking us as "present," as entangled, as connected reference points in space-time, continually searching. This poetic search for an unknown voice is also a moment in which a voice finds us, a finding/being found within an elegiac accounting of the moments of war. In this way we become opened to the name of the nameless other and into a sense of belongingness. Mapped by a ghost—a touch, impossible, a fragment of belongingness. Sensing the other within this opening, within this breaking of the self toward the other, we might be prompted to think war otherwise, urged to clarify the conditions of loss, and pressed to sketch out schemes of interspecies connection and protection.

Throughout this book, poetry becomes an inquiry into connections to the voice of the mostly undocumented experience of becoming lost, unspooling the event of war into its moments of animal loss. Put another way, poetic inquiry is listening to the voices of lost animals, bringing them to bear on our thinking of wartime decisions and what war "is." Poetry releases often detached notions of *connection* and *war*, a release that wounds us with a glimpse of an animal's experience of loss. In this sense, a poetic approach is a cautionary bulwark against an anthropocentric ontology of war. It is a mode of inquiry that complements and conditions the social scientific, a disruption of descriptive and explanatory strategies that softens the boundaries of what inquiry looks and feels like. Poetic attention to war *is* a kind of inquiry; it is a vulnerable means of wounding our way through inquiry, a look within and beyond social scientific questioning, solving, and resolving. It is a move toward belongingness, a belongingness that involves a recognition that we are in this (these) world(s) together, human and animal, living and lost. We belong to and with each other, wounded; we are always and already together, even at a distance. Poetic inquiry is a coming to terms with a debt of belonging. We owe ourselves to the other, to the other's death. *Nous nous devons à la mort.*

There are certain ontological concerns within this multispecies and ghostly inquiry into war. Certainly, animals "exist" within the vulturine spaces of militaries using force. As Anthony Burke observes, war (as well as other global processes) reveals how humans have "unified their life and death process on a planetary scale and extended it to other species and life forms."[24] War is undoubtedly inclusive of animals and their experiences—their thoughts, feelings, drives, hopes, and perspectives. And certainly these animals and their experiences are always irreducibly other in terms of being irreducible to the self. These animals inhere alterities and multidimensionalities; they exist in multiple kinds of separations and escapes from the human grasp. Each animal also exists in terms of a plural self-thickness as well as within an interconnected web of relations to other beings and things—humans, other animals, streets, tanks, trash, and more. A single street dog lost to the violence of the Iraq War, for instance, had multiple "layers" to their sense of being, an untranslatable existence of living and dying within dense experiential moments—an ache in a paw, the heart-sinking fright in response to gunshots, the scent of a friend's fur, the excitement of finding food scraps, the feelings of becoming lost to war. This single, singular street dog's lived realities and sense of being were also organized within and by layers of relations (and reassembled in "our" discourse about these relations)—for instance, relations to a table providing shade for a nap, to another dog, to soldiers and battles, to the bustle of a market, to pieces of trash, to the hope of finding food.

This lost street dog also "exists" and "becomes" in a spectral-poetic way; the dog can "occupy" us through a conjuration, a haunting kind of participation in our thinking of what war "is."

"Alone Ghosts"

Street-morgued
bark whispers
from dogmensch dreams
direct me to you

some version(s) of us

Street shepherds
together-grasped
departed-touched

Alone-ghosts
borrowing your language
this distant dog knowledge

to find you
(seeing me)
then

Then is now, there is here. Elegiac space for you, us—you in us. Traversing between ontological and epistemological concerns, the questions of how we might possibility "know" and "understand" what the lost animal experiences of war "are," and what the status of a lost animal "is" and how we come to "be-with" the lost, become questions of poetic imagination, spectral preoccupation, and elegiac-textual space. From this perspective, the question of what war *was* is a question of what war *is* (and still is). This question is not a matter of making animals from the past more prominent; rather, it is an inquiry that aims to unstitch any clear response to this question. A fugitive inquiry—(never quite) escaping questions of privileging and deprivileging relations of "what is" and "knowing," moving to an experience of an impossible "being-with." Such inquiry is an opening of ourselves into the world(s) and an opening of the world(s) into our hearts; it is an infinite, impossible opening, an attempt at such an opening, if one exists, in elegies. Spectral-poetic inquiry becomes a chance for connection, a ghostly offer to think war otherwise, a cosmopolitan anticipation of belongingness. Humans and animals from past, present, and future wars are each beings in the world, in us, spectrally interconnected; they are seized by us (and seize us) in the space of the poem. What the Iraq War was and still is, for example, involves the *hauntological* flow of lives and losses across time, the pluralized versions of these lives and losses, infinitely other—in the distance but "with" and "within" us. This multispecies inquiry into war is therefore plural, relational, poetic, spectral—spectral-poetic. "That is what we would be calling here a hauntology," writes Derrida.[25] "Ontology opposes it only in a movement of exorcism. Ontology is a conjuration."[26] Cosmopolitan belongingness is a spectral preoccupation.[27]

Belongingness, Cosmopolitan Islands, Spectrality

Throughout history, cosmopolitans have been interested in the idea of belonging to a world beyond the local communities and borders that we find ourselves in. This interest is not specific to cosmopolitans, but it is particularly and deeply emphasized in cosmopolitan thought.[28] The term "cosmopolitanism" comes from *cosmos*, the Greek word for world or universe, and *polites*, which means citizen. Diogenes, one of the founders of Cynic philosophy in the fifth century BCE, was reportedly the first to claim that he was a cosmopolitan—a citizen of the world.[29] Connecting himself to and with the world (cosmos), he suggested he did not belong just to a particular political community (polis); rather, he belonged to and with the *cosmopolis* (world community). Such belongingness is rooted in the idea that all of human life is somehow connected. That is, our shared humanity is an inherently binding condition. Something shared is something dreamed, something poetic, something lost. Dreams and death bind and unbind us.

Derrida notes that Diogenes's "concern was for the *human qua human*, the human before the individual, the human prior to all moral difference differentiating the human and the individual."[30] Shared humanity in some respect blurs our differences, perhaps even species differences. Diogenes and the Cynics were also said to "live like dogs" as they strove to live in accordance with nature, simply and on the streets.[31] The term "cynic" comes from the Greek *kyon*, which means "dog." Diogenes—a cosmopolitan dog, a cosmopolitan cynic. Recent politicians have stated how their enemies "died like a dog."[32] But perhaps we all live and die like dogs. We live and we *experience* death. We dream and become lost.

Derrida observes that there is "the finitude that we share with animals."[33] Suffering, death, and dreams connect us and disconnect us. Both "humans" and "animals" dream and die, but each of us differently, alone and together. Each of us, singular. As for "the animal," Derrida calls into question the use of the singular "animal" to note differences among animals in regard to experiences of dreaming, consciousness, subconsciousness, and desire. For Derrida, these experiences separate animals from each other and are also something that "brings together certain animals and what is called man."[34] Separation and connection, multiplicities of humanities and animalities. We are dreaming of a poetic belonging at the elision of cosmopolitan islands. Animals and humans, however radically different, experience dreaming, dying, and suffering. Both can experience the welcoming of each other, as irreducibly other. As Derrida tells us, hospitality, the welcoming of the other, only happens in the face of "radical alterity."[35] Togetherness is always a gamble, a risk of strange, unassimilable difference. Citizen dogs and humans of the world, the living and lost, united (impossibly) in infinite otherness, in poetic togetherness.

A spectral-poetic approach to cosmopolitanism intends to draw us into moments of violence and loss, sensitizing us to possibilities of interspecies/international interconnectedness—a binding of sorts, a being with the other, impossibly, (re)attached at a distance, listening, watching, tracing outlines of the other, blurred. Spectral cosmopolitanism is a path toward mostly forgotten moments and imagined interior lives. It is a troubled migration from the real to imagined moments, to some possibility of belonging, a path that gives shape to theory and empirics but also reroutes us around them. This is a movement toward inaccessible others, lost to political violence; it is a move toward the "island" of the other. Poetic islands.

The distant other, their life and death, is an island. Cosmopolitan belongingness is a move toward a belongingness not of the world but of islands. While cosmopolitans have a vision of a shared world, Derrida claims that "there is no world, there are only islands."[36] This remark calls out how ungraspable the other, the human or animal other, always is. In orienting ourselves toward the other, we are never positioning with precision; rather, we shift toward a belongingness of difference, toward experiences shadowed by unknowing. A poetic move toward the other brings to bear this darkness of interspecies unknowing on how we read war. We are unknowable together, at a distance but belonging with each other in the nowhere space of the poem. We belong to and with the other's experiences, finding the other becoming lost to war—the end of the other's world.

Poetry is a way to think with these shadowy island-worlds of the lost. It is a way to reflect-feel about how to be-with others in the lost moments of war, a "being-with specters" (*être-avec les spectres*) in the words of Derrida.[37] The unnoticed island-world of the other comes into view, however hazy and inexact, within this poetic space. The cosmopolitan text, then, becomes this spectral-poetic space of and for island translations of mostly unseen moments of war, moments of becoming lost. This space is a path toward the lost other, toward the self, toward this dark island vulnerability of togetherness.

Again, when Derrida calls attention to animals' experiences of vulnerability and suffering, we might keep in mind his interest in islands as a way to acknowledge our inability to tap into their experiences, even though we share many traits. In considering Jeremy Bentham's question about "whether animals can suffer," Derrida refers to the ability of animals to suffer as a "nonpower" or "a possibility without power."[38] This nonpower is a "means of thinking [about] the finitude that we share with animals . . . to the experience of compassion, to the possibility of sharing the possibility of this nonpower, the possibility of this impossibility, the anguish of this vulnerability."[39] It is obvious that animals suffer, but it is an impossibility to fully grasp their experiences of vulnerability and suffering, even though it is necessary to compassionately reflect on them and build toward a politics of interspecies responsibility.[40] It is this "vulnerable suffering," this "compassion in impotence and not from power that we must start when we want to think the animal and its relation to man."[41] Ungraspable suffering, attempting to reach islands, poetically, is a means of receiving the lost other, a way to "commemorate amnesia" and be found, to know through unknowing, to be-with.[42] Derrida's remarks on vulnerability are important markers for thinking with an intensity of compassion and responsibility.[43] We might also think of a *poetic* intensity of compassion, of a poetic dreaming of closing distance and vulnerable togetherness, a poetic thinking "about what is meant by . . . being-with, being-before, being-behind, being-after, being and following, being followed or being following, there where *I am*, in one way or another, but unimpeachably, *near* what they call the animal."[44] Cosmopolitanism involves imagining possibilities of being-with the lost animals in times of war, dreaming of following after their moments before us, being *near* and *with* their vulnerable experiences of becoming lost. These lost animals have "been there before me who is (following) after [them]. *After* and *near* . . . and *with*."[45] In reading the mostly nonexistent records of their experiences, I sketch elegies for spectral animal others, looking toward them and their moments of living and dying, following, perhaps falling from their memories. *Toward your poetic voice, watching the ash fall. Moving toward you, learning how to be with you, impossibly*. We are always islands.

This imaginative recording of loss, this seeking to listen to ghosts, to belong to and with them, is the kind of cosmopolitanism that I propose in this book—a spectral cosmopolitanism. The literature on cosmopolitanism is far too expansive to posit any concise summary of its goals, arguments, and ambitions. But generally speaking, cosmopolitans often think about political life in terms of arguments for and against certain types of global responsibilities and courses of actions that are intended to support the "good life" (i.e., emotional and material security, the capability to flourish, etc.) for distant others.[46] There is neither a singular "responsibility" nor a monolithic "good life," but there is some generalized commitment to be responsible to the distant other, to support a good life for them, across any and all borders. But we might also consider a responsibility to the lost, a kind of spectral responsibility. The margins of the living and possibilities of the good life are marked by loss, the moments of animal voices unheard. These voices, I argue, become audible in an imagined poetic accounting, prompting us to listen with intention, to consider loss as something with us, perhaps part of us. These voices, in elegiac space, ask what we could have done, what we might still do. Pragmatics, imagination, poetry, and loss sink into each other; they become interweaving threads in a spectral move to give attention to and become closer to the lost. Cosmopolitan writing and thinking becomes reaching, becomes movement toward a space for speaking to and listening to distant and lost animal others, a space that is, as Derrida puts it, an "empty place, always, in memory of the hope" that "is the very place of spectrality."[47]

"Spectrality" of course takes on different meanings throughout Derrida's texts; it certainly is not always or exclusively about the loss of others or about a kind of space for the lost. Derrida refers, for example, to "the chance of spectrality" as a risk that undergirds the hospitable encounter, the visit from and welcome to the other who cannot be reduced to "'real' qualities, attributes, or properties" of "a living person."[48] But we can, I think, productively imagine spectrality in terms of the lost whom are with and within us, and in terms of elegiac space, a nowhere space. We might also think of spectrality in relation to responsibility, as an infinite demand from and for the lost that exceeds any possible response. This spectral responsibility is a kind of ghostly justice that circles in proximity to Derrida's "situat[ing] justice, the justice which exceeds but also requires the law, in the direction of the act of memory, of resistance to forgetting."[49] We might still listen to the lost and be haunted by them, productively, pragmatically, poetically.

Cosmopolitanism, War, and Loss

And we might listen to the lost voices and moments of wartime violence. Such listening is missing in the cosmopolitan literature about war. The IR and political theory literatures have certainly moved beyond the stale and outdated conflation of cosmopolitanism with cosmopolitan-like rhetoric used to justify wars based on ethnocentric universalism and global imperialism.[50] However, there is relatively little cosmopolitan attention to war—that is, attention to the moments of it, the particular experiences of it, and responsibilities in relation to these moments and experiences of loss. More broadly, there is a cosmopolitan reticence on the issue of wartime death and so-called collateral damage, and the ways in which imagining the life and death of war could inform how we think about war. The relatively little work on cosmopolitanism and war focuses primarily on "just war" theory, some of which engages questions about the loss of innocent life (but not animal life). While cosmopolitan arguments about just war point toward the transformative potential of borderless responsibilities, this work is often stuck within a reductive framework in which life and death is mostly unknown, is abstracted to the point where there is no experience of war, only theoretical claims about its justness. For example, Cécile Fabre's cosmopolitan just war approach includes an argument that claims civilians can justifiably be directly targeted and killed if doing so would stymie "evil." In one instance she writes that it would have been permissible for German civilians to be targeted directly during World War II, not because they were German, but if "their being German would have made it contingently more likely that the Nazis would have given in."[51] In this account, targeting civilians is worth it if it reduces the odds of an evil force remaining in power. Of course these calculations of loss can never be precise, though Fabre seems to treat them as if they could be for the purpose of theory.[52] That said, there is some value in Fabre's thinking, as such perspectives within cosmopolitanism can be helpful in pushing our thinking about certain tensions in decision making in war.

Still, it is difficult to reconcile targeting civilians with cosmopolitanism. But Fabre argues that targeting civilians can be a cosmopolitan, justifiable practice because "what matters when deciding whether or not to target civilians is not the latter's membership in our community, the enemy's, or indeed a neutral third party's; rather, it is the degree to which the attack will succeed in forestalling that evil."[53] In other words, for Fabre, if targeting civilians is not about identity or group membership itself, and is done to stop evil, it is therefore a justifiably cosmopolitan practice. She also notes how "bombing densely populated areas" can be justified because communal membership itself is not a criterion for bombing; group membership "matters only to the extent that it maximizes or minimizes just combatants' and belligerents' chances of winning their just war justly."[54]

In many respects, Fabre's argumentation, while novel in certain ways, is not unique in terms of its approach to thinking about killing. It aligns well with cosmopolitans within or related to the analytic philosophy tradition. Indeed, Fabre's work is representative of how many just war theorists conceptualize and write about killing in war. There is a valuation, a "proportionality calculus," as Fabre writes, where some lives count more than others (or particular lives are worth losing under certain conditions). But who are these lives? How do they become decoupled from, or masked within, our theorizing of them? Disciplinary norms, the language of abstracting death, the seemingly icy discourse of just war—there is certainly some value in all of this. But it is still striking, especially for a cosmopolitan approach, to prize theoretical precision while papering over the painful and violent experience of war. There are no moments of war, just abstractions and arguments about it. Experience is stripped away, and what remains is a lifeless/deathless, albeit potentially clarified, moral-analytic calculus—a clean view of the conditions of permissible killing. Fabre's arguments offer some insights into wartime decision making; however, this sort of theorizing renders experience almost entirely invisible, displacing it with the precision of abstraction. There are no warm or cold bodies—just body counts and the calculus of killing. In contrast, I think of Robin May Schott's argument that approaches to war often need less abstraction and calculation and more attention to the experience of war; such approaches might produce new narratives and discourses that provide or make way for the moments of the other.[55]

Part of the cosmopolitan task of this book is thinking toward possibilities of glimpsing the experience of the lost others, thinking and writing toward a "being-with" the lost. I think poetry is a way to adapt to this impossible enterprise. Distance and distancing are always at work in theory, in thinking, and in writing; war-writing inevitably involves spatial, temporal, and conceptual gaps between us. For many, war happens in a place faraway, years ago, and mostly to people and animals we never knew. For cosmopolitans and other IR scholars, war is something to be theorized and explained, at a distance. From and with distance, we (that is, scholars) write about war to advance knowledge and understanding. In this way, war and the experience of it are controlled—conceptualized in (and on the) terms of theory and empirics. But these terms often have a distancing effect, closing us off from the other, from the past, from connection—a kind of doubling of distance. But it seems distance is precisely what cosmopolitans should be poised to push against, seeking to at least somehow fill in the blankness, to hold it, or to see in distance an opening. Perhaps within this opening we can inscribe into distance something poetic for the other. Theories of justice and war occasionally feel like celebratory flags waived at or over the dead, from a distance. Perhaps the poem—a cosmopolitan elegy—can be something else, something for the lost, something with you, always distant.

Critics might see this kind of cosmopolitanism as overly sentimental. To think of the cosmopolitan text as an elegiac space for lost animal others, it might be argued, is to engage in mawkish behavior. It might be seen as a departure from pressing human concerns. Tobias Menely suggests that such criticisms are a crude rejection of the important affective solidarities that sentimentality seeks to create. In devaluing sentimentality, he argues that the critic's notion of sentimentality seeks to define and police the boundaries of emotional and political attachments.[56] And this devaluation "has accomplished the crucial cultural work of guarding the border of human community, a border disrupted by the cross-species sympathies."[57] War always touches and destroys nonhuman life. With poetry, our relation to this touch and destruction troubles the cool distance we often seek to produce and maintain. Poetic sympathy is not an aesthetically hollow or decorative detour around pressing issues; rather, it is a disruption of the generalizable-theoretical impulse that too often papers over the blood of the past and the meaning of it as it seeps into the present. This blood says something to you, me, and us; it says something about a shared-but-disconnected history and histories to come. It colors our uncertain futures. And blood is all too real. It is a record of displacement and removal. It is a record of the lost. Poetry is a commitment to blood.

Susan Howe's commitment to poetry revolves around the notion that "if history is a record of survivors, poetry shelters other voices."[58] This book hopes to attend to these other voices, the poetic voice of lost animals. It hopes to reorient cosmopolitanism to the unknown spectral others. So much is never known, and there is a certain violence encoded within this never-known. The islands of animal others—always missed. The meaning of war for animals often seems extralinguistic and undecodable, residing problematically in our imagination, or, even more troublesome, outside of it. This is particularly the case for temporally and spatially distant animals. Animals certainly possess languages, though philosophical traditions have deprived animals of such languages—"or more precisely" they have been deprived of the ability to respond, as Derrida notes.[59] Poetically engaging with this response is one way to connect with and understand lost animals, a way to envision them as actively responding to the world around them and us. Poetry is a record of otherness. It is a record of poetic voices of animal others, merging and moving into us, confronting our separations.

Plan of the Book

Chapter 1, "Spectral Cosmopolitanism," details the book's core ideas about cosmopolitanism, war, animals, loss, poetry, and spectral-poetic moments.

In developing these ideas, I will turn to the work of Jacques Derrida, one of the most interesting philosophers of the twentieth century.[60] Derrida's sprawling insights on human–animal relations, ethology, loss, justice, and spectrality open up intriguing possibilities for thinking about war, particularly its animal experiences and our relation to the loss of animals. As I develop a spectral cosmopolitan account of war, I focus on a particular notion of "moments" of war and the relation of "spectral-poetic moments" to an elegiac space of belongingness. This focus on spectral-poetic moments is a summons to re-feel the ways in which war unsettles time. It is an invitation into an inheritance of loss that might unsettle our sense of the timelines between us, perhaps shift our thinking of the experience of loss as a weight, a spectral debt, flickering from the past into the impossible togetherness of the present(s) and future(s).[61]

Chapters 2 through 4 explore different aspects of animal life and death in the Iraq War, from stray dogs to zoo animals to animals affected by the rise of ISIS (Islamic State of Iraq and al-Sham). These chapters discuss the context for the loss of life in Iraq and serve as space to reflect on and connect with these losses. The Iraq War, one of the most devastating wars of this generation, is approached in terms of spectral-poetic moments, as something ongoing and shifting into different modes and effects, something still with us. Interspersed with poetry for and with the lost, each chapter is an elegiac space of conjuring, of being-with the lost, of movement toward the margins of war where we might see its moments and feel the gaze of the animal ghosts of Iraq. These chapters are not "cases" used primarily to illustrate theoretical ambitions; rather, they are assembled as remembrances of moments to preserve, however messy, the weight of devastation in Iraq. Each chapter is a kind of requiem, inevitably inadequate.

Chapter 2, "Stray Hearts, Vectors: The Wandering Dogs of Iraq," seeks a spectral-poetic connection to the lost street dogs of Iraq. During the Iraq War, the U.S. military and the city government of Baghdad "eradicated" many strays. This chapter provides an overview of reasons and decisions that led to the elimination of street dogs. These dogs, I argue, prompt us to think about how war is experienced in other-than-human moments, moments becoming spectral. They demand that we seek to understand them, their experience of war, on *their* terms—terms that are impossible, terms that demand a poetic disordering of ourselves. This chapter is an elegiac movement toward these lost dogs, a hope to learn from them and with them. Of the many things these street dogs might tell us is something about ontological inconsistencies and war. Discussion of dogs in war typically emphasize military dogs.[62] Such accounts, while serving as a kind of reconciliation to a beyond-human conception of war, also keep in place boundaries of belongingness by implicitly drawing on a moral difference between the military and the stray dog.[63] Mine-sniffing dogs and other military dogs, central to humanitarian operations, combat missions, and soldier companionship, are considered to be proper subjects of our accounts of war. Notably absent from much of the existing work is attention to the misfit dogs that serve no military purpose, the often unknown street dogs that exist amidst the violence of war and on the edge of our thinking. These lost dogs are still here, with us. This chapter invites these lost dogs to weigh on our thinking about war, a thinking that bends and breaks through a poetic exploration of these distant dogs, with us, still.

Chapter 3, "Caged Cosmopolitanism: Menagerie Moments of War," focuses on zoo animals in Iraq. These animals remind us of posthumanist responsibilities to caged lives, responsibilities often avoided. The individual zoo lives of lions, pigs, and others reach for a spectral-poetic connection, a memory, and imaginative witnessing. They each haunt our reflections on the Iraq War and our understanding of American culpability in Iraq. Throughout the chapter I enter into a ghostly-poetic dialogue with these spectral zoo lives. This dialogue also sits in relation to the research of Alison Howell and Andrew Neal, who show how zoo looters become rhetorical devices for constructing a lawless and irrational foreign citizenry.[64] In thinking about eventual U.S. assistance to Iraqi zoos, U.S. responses to looting were often cast as heroic within orientalist-redemptive narratives. In thinking with and toward zoo lives, this chapter calls attention to how U.S. decision makers were intimately bound up with both destroying and saving life. This attention is interwoven with nonhuman perspectives, filtered through elegiac attempts at connection—modalities of searching to find you, us, in the past and future.

While chapters 2 and 3 look at the intersection of government actions and animal experiences in war, the effects of war on animals are not entirely (or directly) effected by governmental actors. Chapter 4, "Black Sheep: ISIS and the Smoke of Qayyarah," considers how animals and their environments were affected by the actions of ISIS in Iraq. While important attention has been paid to extensive human suffering under ISIS, this chapter attends to the multispecies experiences of burned forests, destroyed chemical plants, and oil fields on fire. This chapter is a space for these lost lives, an elegiac canvas for communion with the lost, a space to yield to their voices.

The final chapter, "(In)Conclusion(s): Spectral-Poetic Proximities," revisits the central themes of the book in the context of Jacques Derrida's provocations about proximity, closeness, spectrality, and war. It offers some concluding thoughts about the ways in which spectral-poetic thinking and writing orients us toward disorienting loss, toward the hearts of lost others. It discusses this thinking and writing as a futural task, thinking as movement toward the heart of the other, writing as opening elegiac space for listening to distant heart beats, the poetic voice of the animal other—within us—gone and yet to arrive, for the past and future.

Chapter 1

Spectral Cosmopolitanism

But memories no longer recognize such borders.
—Jacques Derrida, *Specters of Marx*

There is a black-and-white photograph of the 1991 Gulf War oil fires that shows bodies of camels strewn about in the desert.[1] Oil fires and smoke plumes are in the background. Fire, smoke, bodies becoming lost—moments gone, moments within us, moving forward.

"Qarqar"

Shadow-seized, the quiet will carry us.
All things never . . .
One more song, small camel.
Our geologic lines, twined, concealed.
Your neck—soft and singular—still.
Sinking with the weight of lost time.
Losing the strength of our Qarqar ancestors.
Watching you,

my world.
I am listening

for you,

the world.

In thinking of and with these camels—nameless (or at least names we cannot know), anonymous, gone—we might be drawn into memories not our own. We might uncover moments of war and the experiences that make war. We might be drawn into the lives of lost camels and into questions about our multispecies pasts and futures. Camel-self extensions, touching traces of unnoticed lost moments, imprinted as questions within us. In poetry, we might be with the lost, seeing us—in the distance, beyond borders, beyond life. These camel moments also remind us of the uncountable, unphotographed, unknown, and unknowable moments of war. "We are poor passing facts / warned by that to give / each figure in the photograph / his living name."[2] These lines by Robert Lowell point us toward a responsibility to remember the moments and experiences of the named and nameless. Symbolic of desert-dwelling, camels are much more than desert icons; they are beings with complex desires and interior lives, experiencing each other's deaths. They are irreducible to the name "camel," to this thinking of experience. They are spectral worlds, camel-islands, island-worlds beyond us. We know of but never fully know these island-worlds. But we might poetically imagine them, bringing these experiences into being and to bear on our understanding of war. We might listen to these passing facts and reflect on the living name of the lost.

John Berger writes of humans and animals as parallel lines and how "only in death do these two parallel lines converge."[3] Death brings us, perhaps binds us, together. But these lines converge before and after death in so many ways. Our histories and futures of living and dying on the planet are interconnected, our political and ecological fates shared. Global pandemics involve trans-species infections and demand that we imagine possibilities of living differently with animals. As the planet warms we experience deadly wildfires together. Whenever militaries have exercised their power, human and animal bodies have become ruins. In the mid-1800s, the U.S. military hunted and exterminated bison in order to control and kill Native Americans. Gil Scott-Heron spoke of this loss in a critique of American democracy. Carl Sandburg's poetry also reminds us of this loss, the missing witnesses, the animal experiences, and the ghostliness of interspecies living and dying. "Those who saw the buffaloes are gone / And the buffaloes are gone."[4] We live and die with animals, and our poetry reflects this. In poetry we feel the other's last breath. After the other's death, we write about their absence. Spectral lines, conjured and connected. Our parallel lines blur in moments of living and dying. These lines divide, grow, and cut in multiple directions, becoming spirals that twist into each other. We are tangled filaments, twisted together in histories and futures of loss.

What will you say? I imagine asking the lost animals of Iraq. This is an unanswerable question that nonetheless begins to transfix and unravel war into its spectral moments. This question anchors our thinking of war to the unclosable spectral voices—lost, imagined.

Derrida reminds us that we must "learn to live with ghosts" (*apprendre à vivre avec les fantômes*).[5] This book is about learning to *let* animal ghosts reframe our understanding of war, ourselves, our relation to distant loss, and perhaps our sense of distance. And this chapter is an investment in this spectral endeavor, this spectral cosmopolitanism. It is a reflection on how we might approach war in terms of spectral-poetic moments. It is a meditation on the ghost's voice—our own voice, discerned in the other. To "learn to live with ghosts" is thus a spectral-poetic turn toward the other, within the self. Self-reflexive and poetic, spectral cosmopolitanism involves reading untranslatable moments of loss in the distance; it involves listening to and learning from imagined lost voices of animals. Death is always a central concern for scholars of war. For the (spectral) cosmopolitan, this concern becomes an elegiac possibility for connections to the lost—to the uncountable and unknowable hearts.

This chapter thinks toward the voices of absence, voices pulling us together, toward an elegiac space for the other. It struggles toward the surprise of the spectral, toward a contingent view of a global politics that is "always and already" ghostly.[6]

The apparitional presence of others figures prominently in several of Derrida's works, perhaps most notably in *Specters of Marx*. Here, Derrida proposes the idea of the specter as that which "appears to present itself during a visitation. One represents it to oneself, but it is not present, itself, in flesh and blood."[7] A specter is "what one imagines, what one thinks one sees and which one projects-on an imaginary screen where there is nothing to see."[8] We see specters "where there is nothing to see" (*là où il n'y a rien à voir*); in other words, we *imagine* the lost other, their visitation.[9] Derrida also discusses specters in terms of "ghosts" (*les fantômes*), including the ghosts of war. In these discussions he writes of the importance of a ghostly dialogue, of the need to speak of, to, and with such ghosts: "It is necessary to speak *of the* ghost, indeed *to the* ghost and *with* it."[10] While spectrality (*spectralité*) is not limited to ghosts or to thinking of and with the dead (spectrality appears in many other ways in Derrida's writing), as Martin Hägglund notes, it can refer to the "haunting reminders of the victims of historical violence, of those who have been excluded or extinguished from the formation of a society."[11] Such reminders, Derrida argues, are the remains of justice calling out "in the name of justice" (*au nom de la justice*).[12]

Spectral cosmopolitanism involves a poetic space for the ghostly presence of the lost animals of war. The turn toward this space is a turn away from war as a concrete and (mostly human) coherent event and toward its less-knowable (and unknowable) multispecies moments through an imaginative sense of beyond-human belongingness. This turn is coupled with a spectral-poetic movement that disrupts the linearity of our voice with other voices, opening up a space for grappling with the strangeness of ourselves and nonhuman others across temporal and geographic boundaries. In this way it shares similarities with Martha Nussbaum's call for "imagining and storytelling," an "imagining the lives of animals [that] makes them real to us in a primary way, as potential subjects of justice."[13] This approach involves a kind of ghost poetry, a kind of multispecies storytelling of, with, and for the lost.[14]

But this approach does not use literature or poetry to conceive of a specific cosmopolitan justice or "animal rights" framework. As Derrida reminds us, spectral haunting is an apparitional move toward a justice "where it is not yet, not yet *there*, where it is no longer, let us understand where it is no longer *present*, and where it will never be, no more than the law, reducible to laws or rights."[15] Poetry about, for, and with animal ghosts constitutes an attempt to sense the gaps of justice, an effort to learn from, about, and with the other, from a past where justice never was. Spectral cosmopolitanism therefore involves thinking, writing, and positioning into these gaps. It reframes a conversation about justice on the terms of haunting moments of loss. It is about seeking an entryway into seeing what is "not yet there, where it is no longer." It points to the urgency of being *seen by* those calling for justice where it is "not yet there, where it is no longer."[16]

A motivating aim of cosmopolitanism is making possible "new ways of seeing the world."[17] Perhaps another aspiration should be thinking through possibilities of being *seen by* the world. To follow the gaze, gazing. To fade into the impossible spectral density of the world, to face toward ghost-dream heart beats. "I hear the heart-beat—I follow, I fade away."[18] Derrida writes how the "spectral *someone other looks at us*" and about how "we feel ourselves being looked at by it, outside of any synchrony, even before and beyond any look on our part."[19] Poetic space breaks itself open into these possibilities of sensing a ghost's gaze, the spectral moments of the distant other *au nom de la justice*. Poetry is being seen. It marks the remains of justice. It is listening to the loss of the animal other—their voice, their hearts—lost, imagined, insistent.

This is a somewhat different path from most cosmopolitan approaches, but it certainly falls within the relatively recent reliance on literature by cosmopolitan thinkers such as Martha Nussbaum. Questions about the literary form of cosmopolitanism and literary possibilities within it trouble not only the internal order of cosmopolitan rituals of writing but also call attention to an indeterminacy which, in some sense, simultaneously conditions, gives rise to, sustains, and disrupts cosmopolitanism and its possibilities. Bruce Robbins and Paulo Lemos Horta associate cosmopolitanism with its expression in mutable multiplicities, arguing that cosmopolitanism "makes room for . . . multiple and overlapping conceptions, forced by the imperative of inclusiveness to change its own rules."[20] Without fully addressing this question, Robbins and Horta ask how we should "feel about the tendency for cosmopolitanism to overlap with or even take over the function of literariness?"[21] In posing this question, however, they are primarily thinking about *reliance* on literature to understand cosmopolitanism. I suggest that cosmopolitans might *become* poets (or at least make space for poetry), not only as a way to "experience the inner life" of others, as Nussbaum writes, but as a way to involve lost others as active participants in our thinking and feeling—our becoming cosmopolitan, together.[22] In this way, cosmopolitan writing is not only *about* global interconnectedness but also seeks it and embodies it, becoming a space for global and multispecies interconnectedness. If cosmopolitanism "signals a conception of belonging as open," then the spectral-poetic move toward the other is an embodiment of this signal.[23] It is a conjuration of belongingness across the lines of life, time, space, and species.

To that end, this chapter offers an overview of this spectral cosmopolitan approach to war. It describes the centrality of moments, poetry, ethology, animals, and "being-with" the lost. It sets the stage for the next few chapters where we will encounter the consequential agency of lost animal others, looking at us, belonging with us, always at a distance, within us. To poetically connect to the other, to feel their emergence as a compass toward thinking anew, is not to control what the other means but rather to break meaning open into its contingent possibilities.

We know that animals were killed in the Iraq War. We know these facts, this exteriority of evidence. The evidentiary details are akin to what

Susan Howe calls "perceptions of surfaces."[24] How do we make space for the interiority of animal moments to bear on our understanding of war, of ourselves, of the world, of worlds-as-islands, within us? How might these lost animals speak to us, and we with them, to inform our future possibilities? How do we connect to and belong with the lost, in moments?

Moments

> MO'MENT, noun [Latin momentum. This word is contracted from motamentum, or some other word, the radical verb of which signified to move, rush, drive or fall suddenly, which sense gives that of force. The sense of an instant of time is from falling or rushing, which accords well with that of meet.] [25]

Cosmopolitanism has been described in terms of moments of openness to the world, moments of openness to distant strangers.[26] Cosmopolitanism is about "transcending Self and Other and bringing into play the transformative and self-reflexive moment;" it is about new understandings between the Self and Other that "develop in moments of openness," according to Gerard Delanty.[27] But what does a *moment* or a *self-reflexive* moment mean? What might attention to animal moments and self-reflexivity mean for cosmopolitans and a cosmopolitan approach to war, to writing *about* war?

In thinking of moments of war, I am first thinking of the time of experience, of the singular experiences of the time of living and becoming lost. This experience is characterized by imaginative interiority—an animal's thoughts, perspectives, and feelings—at a particular point in time. This time, the point of it, is in many respects unknowable. It is secret. In thinking of this time of experience as a moment, our present time is interrupted by an incalculable point of the past, a time that arrives within our present "us." A secret intervening within us as a demand, moving toward a future. Such a moment is not about the larger war "event" but something narrower, something more specific, small, imaginative—something secret becoming present.

There is also what we might call the generative-temporal context of moments. Moments of loss necessitate attention to their context, the conditions of becoming lost—the "how" and "why" an animal becomes lost to the violence of war. In Derrida's *Specters of Marx*, the "non-presence of the specter demands that one take its times and its history into consideration, the singularity of its temporality or of its historicity."[28] Escaping times and histories, the specter is there, here, nowhere, and still to come. The specter "signals toward the future," which involves "thinking of the past."[29] Most of the animals we will engage throughout this book are no longer physically present, but we might understand their deaths—the context, history, and causality of loss—as a kind of presence, informative of our present(s) and future(s). A moment, in this sense, is a space for thinking of the time and experience of the lost, instrumentalized as a demand in the present for the past and a possible future.

Turning again to Derrida, we can see how spectral demands can shape a sense of self and sense of the world into a form of spectral togetherness. The dead, he wrote, are "everywhere and nowhere, nowhere because everywhere, out of the world and everywhere in the world and in us."[30] To think of the dead in the world and "in us" is to invite a reflexive sense of "being-with" the lost. This involves imagining lost animal moments, a dreaming that entangles our sense of self and the other, softening the "between us" into belongingness. In this self-reflexive imagination, a past moment becomes spectral as it sets adrift into a present "us" and stays with(in) us into the future. Derrida refers to a "spectral moment" (*moment spectral*) as something that "no longer belongs to time" (*un moment qui n'ap- partient plus au temps*).[31] A spectral moment stretches within and outside of the past, present, and future. Contingently pinned down in textual-elegiac space, it moves from within me to you, in another spatial-temporal context. The moment of a camel lost to war "no longer belongs to time." It is spectral. The time between us becomes a tangle of belonging.

This focus on moments is a departure from more traditional cosmopolitan and International Relations (IR) work in which scholars often look at the "event" of war in terms of the past, in terms of a concrete and cohesive temporal-spatial occurrence. For instance, scholars might consider the causes of the Iraq War in terms of its eventness. Or, from a "just war" perspective, they might ask whether the event of the Iraq War was justified. But the event of the Iraq War is also an experiential set of interconnected and disconnected moments of life and death, moments that might all too easily be abstracted away from the singularities that comprise the war event. Relatedly, civilian casualties and "collateral damage" are often conceptualized in terms of bodies to be theorized or "events" to be explained, measured, or understood in terms of proportionality or other measures of justice. These casualties are always somewhere else, outside of "us." Certainly there is a range of non-cosmopolitan approaches to war that break from such endeavors, such as those concerned with bodies and bodily violence.[32] Yet even these often focus on the human rather than the animal body in times of war.

"Remember That"

> Unable-gazed,
> palm-touched.
> Ungrasped.
> Sand-threaded
> records,
> eyes unkept,
> crypted.
> Remember that
> bodies cannot always be.

The moment, in contrast to what I call the "event" above, shares some similarities with Derrida's use of the term "event." For Derrida, an event involves surprise, is something that arrives, incomprehensibly and without anticipation. He also describes wars and deaths as events. For example, in discussing the Gulf War in the early 1990s he stated: "The event that is ultimately irreducible to media appropriation and digestion is that thousands of people died. These are singular events each and every time, which no utterance of knowledge or information could reduce or neutralize."[33] We cannot forget, Derrida reminds us, "that an event took place that cannot under any circumstance be reduced to its analysis, an event that cannot be reduced to any saying. It's the unsayable: the dead, *for example*, the dead."[34] Each loss, therefore, is an event, an unspeakable and singular event. I use the term *moments*, however, to think more specifically about the time of the other, a poetic thinking of an animal's experience at a particular point in time. The moment involves an imaginative searching for and reaching toward this time of the other.

This move toward moments of war is a movement toward ways of creating elegiac space for the lost, for our connection to loss, untethered from the explainable, spatially and temporally cohesive, event. It is a connection deepened through poetic attention and listening. This chapter seeks to pull the Iraq War apart to imagine the time of the other, and to be seen by this time. To imagine and poetically engage with these moments is to see the ongoingness of war. It is to see the moments of war as spectral, as moving into and out of us and out of time. The moments of experience, known and unknown, are still with us, still moving ahead.[35]

Moments are a space to reflect on interspecies belongingness, a spectral sense of togetherness. Moments open up possibilities for recalibrating how we might think of the other, and of each other, our strange and not-so-strange connections through time and space. Moments are an elegiac space of thinking and writing of being with the other—a "being-with specters," as Derrida puts it.[36] A moment, a meeting, a movement toward the other. Moments are an opening to an experience, an opportunity to imagine and listen to the spectral other. A moment invites us to sense war touching life, to imagine spectral life, *singular* and *irreplaceable*, to use Derrida's terms. A moment is a gathering of the *irreplaceable*, reminding us of a *singular* time's depth-edges. This book is about these moments—a moment of a lost giraffe on the streets of Baghdad, a moment of a sheep becoming lost to war amidst poisoned fields and skies. In moments of loss, we are invited to think of the generative-temporal context of loss and the imagined experience of loss in ways that inform the present and future, in ways that connect us. These moments point to the experiential fragility of life, life that is both ordinary and extraordinary, which is often eclipsed by attention to the larger event of war.[37] Transgressive relic-voices, moments cut through, connect, and occupy pasts, presents, and futures.

This book therefore is about moments of war in which life becomes "collateral damage," the spectral-cosmopolitan rhythms and textures of animal experiences.[38] *Your eyes, closing; I close my eyes; nocturnal strums of you leaving, becoming collateral.* Damaged moments. These moments, becoming spectral, seem to insist on war's disjointedness, scratching out the ordering of events (military decisions, reactions, battles, etc.) to reveal a disordered and interwoven set of experiences—worlds coming and going. Engaging in these moments, I argue, is an important kind of reconfiguration of cosmopolitan thinking and writing about war. Writing becomes a way to connect, a space to be taken into the meaning of the other. The other's world is always our world. And the world is always spectral.

In Derrida's texts, as mentioned earlier, we find a rather knotty understanding of what *world* means, and an occasional (and oblique) rejection of the notion in favor of *islands*. He observes that "a question about the world is a question about everything and nothing. About everything, therefore about nothing, it's an empty question that bites the tail of its own presupposition."[39] To even begin to question or conceptualize *world* is to find oneself marooned in a certain nothingness. No world, only islands, he contends.[40] Perhaps there are no wars, only moments—islands of experience.

An animal's experience of war is an island. It is an experience that reveals what war is and what it does. "War" is not just the decision to wage war or the facts of bullets, bombs, and death. War is how all of these are experienced. Shifting our attention to the experience of war, the often unread and unimagined background of war, and the murky lived animal moments of life and death in war, we find islands. These moments of war can never be fully known; they are islands in the distance that we can vaguely make out.

Because of this, we must imagine; we must listen to the poetic voice of the other. Poetic imagination creates a self-reflexive pause in which we might re-see the world in terms of islands (and be seen by these islands), and in all of the strangeness of islands and worlds. To look at war in its moments is to enter into this imagined, contestable, and complicated strange darkness. Imagining moments directs us toward possibilities of re-seeing and re-thinking what we think we see when we look at war. Imagining moments invites us to consider what seeing is like beyond *our* sight and *our* thinking of seeing. It invites us to consider what loss means, how it feels, and what our connections to others might be in a spectral moment. What do animals see in war? What does it mean to imagine this seeing? What does it mean for cosmopolitanism? Looking at war in terms of moments pushes us from the clear and cohesive to the imaginative and poetic. War is never war; it is always an island of experience for someone, some animal, some *particular* animal. Moments become a spectral space, become a self-reflexive path, a trail toward glimpses of islands, a space for re-seeing, re-listening, re-feeling, and re-connecting with the other in war. Moments become a space for chasing ghosts, looking for the unknown lives lost, imagining them speaking to us and looking at us. Though there are always too many, we will pursue as many as we can, counting and accounting for their lives lost. As Derrida states in *Specters of Marx*, "we are going to count the ghosts."[41]

Spectral-Poetic Moments

As I examine the conditions of how animals became lost to the violence of the Iraq War, each chapter is interspersed with poetry. It is a poetry of listening to the voice of the animal other, the irreducible other. *Poetic fragments of animal experiences of war, echoes of the ephemeral moments, the distant edges of war.* Poetry listen-reaches, without securing, without hope of possession. Poetry is a trace of the other's time—past, within us.

Derrida suggests that thinking about animals "derives from poetry."[42] Thinking of animals does not demand "philosophical knowledge" but rather needs and comes from "poetic thinking."[43] But what is poetry or poetic thinking? Hesitant to draw boundaries and limits, "poetry" for Derrida is not easily definable. The substance and edge of the poetic is not always clear; it is defined in oppositions, defines itself, and is defined in relation to the borders of prose, philosophy, images, politics, etc.[44] "The same sentence," Derrida says, "may be a simple newspaper sentence here, and then a poetic fragment there, or philosophical example still elsewhere."[45] From certain perspectives, there can be poetry without meaningful words. For instance, I am thinking of Dada sound poems or David Kjellin's poetry, some of which blacks out text to find poetic patterns. Certain mathematics can also be poetry.[46] There is certainly a wide array of "poetry" that bends in between "poetry" and something "not quite" poetry. The border of the poem is not sharp, though we often think of the poem as cutting into us, wounding us, leaving scars. The very question of what poetry "is" is a question that "salutes the birth of prose."[47] A poem is "a converted animal, rolled up in a ball, turned toward the other and toward itself."[48] The poem is for the other, within us. "The other sign(s)" the poem.[49]

In looking toward Derrida's sometimes shadowy (and poetic) discussions of poetry, we still find an impulse to specify the poem, to demarcate it, however obliquely, however poetically and playfully. For example, in *Che cos'è la poesia?* he calls "a poem that very thing that teaches the heart, invents the heart, *that which*, finally, the word *heart* seems to mean and which, in my language, I cannot easily discern from the word itself."[50] The poem, he continues, "falls to me, benediction, coming of (or from) the other."[51] One way to think of this, without closing off other interpretations, is to consider poetry as a kind of communication for and from the other, perhaps the distant or spectral other. Poetry in this sense is the other's heart, distant, limning lost memories in our hearts, teaching us the very possibility of heart-memory. The poetry in this book is about the meanings that survive loss but also precede it—meanings that are stitched and held together by us and the distant animal other, only to become disentangled again.

In an interview with Derrida, Bernard Stiegler asks Derrida about Roland Barthes's ideas about photography, the photographic experience, and photographic emanations. Derrida mentions how an emanation is a kind of "flow of light which captures or possesses me, invests me, invades me, or envelops me."[52] "But," Derrida says, this light "is not a ray of light;" rather, it is "the source of a possible view: from the point of view of the other."[53] In some sense, we might say or dream something similar about poetry. Poetry for the other is a kind of illumination from the other, a perspective (yet self-reflexive), of the spectral other, illumining ourselves with the other's shadows. While photography has a "reality effect," the creation of a poem is also a "source of a possible view," something in which we are not only passively invaded or enveloped by but also something we actively reach for, toward this possibility of a view.[54] There is poetry in the photograph, and a photograph in the poem. A poem involves a kind of photographic thinking; the photographic demands poetic thinking.

We might also consider this thinking of poetry and poetic thinking of animals in terms of moments of experience and the "island" lives of others. Animals are to some extent unfathomable, their lives ungraspable. Our thoughts, philosophical inquiries, research, and attempts to understand and measure animal lives will always be limited. It is within these limits that poetry pushes language, draws upon our imagination, moves us along the edges of our thinking. Poetry becomes a kind of space for grappling with mystery, with our relations to and with the other, a way of carrying their island-worlds into our ourselves, into political considerations. Poetry can serve as a bridge or pathway into these enigmatic islands, still enclosed, concealed. It is a means of "making present" animal moments, a feeling-technique toward them and their felt experiences.[55] As Roland Bleiker (who perhaps more than anyone has created a space for the poetic in International Relations scholarship) puts it, poetry stretches "language and entrenched habits of knowledge so that we can see the world anew, see it through different eyes and from different vantage points."[56] Yet these different eyes and vantage points are always within the self, are always self-reflexively moving toward the other and back. "Different eyes" and "different vantage points" are also and always *my* eyes, *my* vantage points, reached from the irreducibly other's island oblivions. This book, then, is a cosmopolitanism infused with poems of, from, and for the other, but the other within myself. This is a cosmopolitanism of spectral-poetic vacancy for self-reflexive connection and communication with distant others. It is a cosmopolitanism of self-reflexive vantage points—animal perspectives—unnamed and unnamable, within me, approached through poetic fragments that stretch spectrally to the lost moments—*to you, from you, seeing you, unsee-able, being seen, seeing.*

The hope of a turn to poetry in cosmopolitanism is that it might benefit from a pause—a hesitation that invites us into spectral moments. The literary critic and poet John Felstiner writes that "poems make us stop, look, and listen long enough for imagination to act, connecting, committing ourselves to the only world we've got . . . poems make a difference by priming consciousness."[57] He notes that "if words tie us in one with nature, tying human with nonhuman, and if speech in the beginning brings all into being, maybe the speech of poems will revive our lease on life."[58] Poetry can, he claims, "hold things still for a moment, make us mindful of fragile resilient life."[59] Poetry is therefore one way to proceed to the self-reflexive register of spectral moments of war. It is an imaginative (untranslatable) translation of the surface, a reflexive reading, a filtering of the unknown moments lurking within the world and us.[60]

International Relations theorists and cosmopolitans typically do not write poetry. Poetry is on the periphery, far from our style of plotting new concepts and ways of theorizing. But poetry can be part of a penumbral plot toward the other, part of "theory," or perhaps the unsettling of it. Meghana Nayak and Eric Selbin note how "we aren't used to seeing [poetry] in IR," but that it is one way to "decenter" IR; thus "we should listen to . . . poets, writers, musicians, artists . . . telling stories about the world, because they offer useful and provocative correctives to the drudgery in IR."[61] Poetry is a soundscape to the world of the other, our interconnected and multispecies world. As Roland Bleiker notes, poetry "slips into memory what was void of voice."[62] Poetry is becoming open to the impossible voice of the other, the animal other, the other's heart-memory within us.

"A heart in me greater than my heart, more alive than I, more singular and more other than what I can anticipate, know, imagine, represent, and remember."[63]

There have certainly been flashes of a poetic turn in some corners of IR.[64] This interest in looking toward poetry for political insights is part of an "aesthetic turn."[65] The IR literature on poetry focuses primarily on how we might look to poetry to help us think about and understand global politics. For example, Prem Rajaram's work turns to the poetry of Mohsen Soltanyz and Mehmet al Assad—both refugees detained in Australia—to explore marginality and to offer a critique of political borders.[66] IR scholars interested in the poetic often turn to political or politically relevant poems for their disruptive potential, and for how they might reveal certain ways of reconfiguring ethical and political identities and relationships. In doing so, these scholars interpret others' poems (or rely on authoritative interpretations of the poems). Entire poems or large sections of them are mined for political relevance, and poets' lives are often analyzed to provide context.

Very little of the work on poetry and IR is itself poetic. There is a turn to the creativity of others but hesitation in engaging in the inventive act of poetry.[67] Calling attention to the lack of poetic creativity, Roxanne Doty recently pushed for IR scholars to write in "different voices" and "alternative writing styles" and to "actually engage in disruptive writing ourselves as opposed to simply critiquing territorial writing and analyzing poetry and prose as examples of such disruptive writing."[68] Doty has been at the forefront of questioning what academic writing is, what it looks and feels like, and arguing for a broader range of academic writing, including poetry. This, she argues, might "elicit a caring for the human beings that are invisible in our academic writings and in this sense would constitute an important ethical move."[69] I agree but also think poetry is something other than an ethical move. It moves within and beyond the ethical move, undercutting it, reminding us of otherness and the other within us, irreducible and moving against and beyond us—the other's heart-memory within us. Poetry reminds us of the incalculability of ethics. Poetry itself is a kind of otherness; it is its own world, a world for and about the other's heart, always other, always unpredicted.

"Nothing is more alive in life than the heart, possessed in common by all animals. There is thus animal in the poem, and poem in the animal."[70]

In the next few chapters, I describe the Iraq War in terms of the conditions that generated harm, vulnerability, and loss. I weave into the text small poems or elegiac fragments for (and from) the lost animals. These spectral-poetic spaces for the other are ghostly pathways for an interspecies cosmopolitanism of elegies. They are not just ways to "include voices from below," as Doty notes, but also ways to merge voices, to feel the emergence of merging, to sense ourselves sensing toward others, to their world(s), and back to ourselves.[71] An elegy is a way to both orient and lose ourselves, to both find and lose the lost other within ourselves. Poetically imagining nonhuman voices is a way toward beyond-human belonging, a way to become open to the singularity of life and death, a way to tap into a sense of culpability and connection. It brings into view a "responsibility [that] binds me to the other, to the other as other, and ties me in my absolute singularity to the other as other," as Derrida puts it.[72] The collection of lost moments, a poetic space for them, connects us and ties us to a responsibility to the worlds of others. This spectral-poetic approach provides possibilities of a strange sense of the presence of others, of loss, of belongingness.

A poem is a conversation, a dream, a dialogue where interpretations and feelings are not owned and controlled but dispersed and shared. The author, the subject, and the reader are always disconnected by temporal/spatial distance, and poetry is one way to reach out through this distance. If cosmopolitans are intent on bridging distance, poetry is one step, a stumble on a dark trail, toward connecting and connection. It is a step toward the dream of the other, the dream of you, the dream of the connection, the other's dreams that I dream of. Poetry is attention to a kind of dreaming of the impossible. As Derrida stresses, there is meaning in "caring for what the dream lets us think about, especially when what it lets us think about is the *possibility of the impossible*."[73] The dream pushes us toward the poetic and vice versa, the impossible connection, the beyond-sayable experience, known and unknown. The poem does something to these gaps, exposes them, makes us see and feel the space between us—the strange space that we share but cannot fully cross.

Poetry, Ethology

Poetry is not confined to the dream, to the imagined sense of the other. For Derrida, questions about human possibilities, the history of the human, and posthumanist responsibilities all concern science and "critical forms of zoological or ethological knowledge."[74] Elsewhere he references the "enormous progress that has been made in primatological and ethological knowledge."[75] He criticizes Jacques Lacan, for example, for not justifying his arguments about "the animal" with any "ethological knowledge."[76] In reference to Levinas, Lacan, Kant, and Heidegger, Derrida notes how "not one of them really integrates progress in ethological or primatological knowledge into his work."[77] But thinking about animals and interspecies politics not only *demands* attention to zoological knowledge, it is inevitably and *already* organized by it. Our thinking of the "human" and the "animal," indeed these very categories, emerge within scientific discourses, supplying us with a settled sense of what "we" and "they" are. But both science and poetry can do the work of unsettling. While Derrida claims that thinking about animals "derives from poetry," this thinking also develops from and is structured by ethology—but is also unsettled by it. This thinking can be aided by new kinds of poetry and new zoological knowledge. Cosmopolitanism, and IR more broadly, can move toward the poetic but also look to zoological knowledge for understanding.

Poetry and ethology are not outside of each other. They inform and draw from each other. Perhaps at times they are one and the same. They allow each other to see further, to feel more deeply, differently, or strangely. The worlds of poetry and ethology encompass each other. Poetic attention is not a replacement for philosophical or scientific knowledge; rather, these can unfold onto and remake each other. Roxanne Doty argues that IR scholars need not rely on an "opposition between poetics and science or the human experiences of what we research and the words we use in our narratives to tell of this research."[78] The boundaries of poetic thinking drift off the IR map, revealing new island others, informing the scientific and sensory path of discovery. Put another way, the poetic is infused with the scientific and the philosophic, marshaled together to contingently move toward a more responsible world, with all of the risk and danger that comes with what it means to be "more responsible."

Without fully engaging the animal science literature, Derrida points to it as a way to both blur and multiply human–animal boundaries and to call attention to interspecies responsibilities. As just mentioned, while suggesting that thinking about animals is done in relation to poetry, he also criticizes the lack of scientific attention to animals in philosophical thought. For example, for Derrida, Heidegger's thesis about the world needs to be more attentive to science. In Derrida's thinking, the science of animal life and death appears to press open possibilities of what *world* means, an opening informed by the richness of the scientific understanding of animals that points to many similarities with humans and also problematizes anthropocentric thinking. In his thesis of the *world*, Heidegger posits a set of arguments about the inanimate, animal, and human world. For Heidegger, "the animal is poor in world." Supportive of this thesis, Heidegger asserts that the animal does not die but rather stops living. In other words, the animal, unlike the human, does not *experience* death, a contention Derrida calls a "decisive and troubling distinction."[79] Derrida also questions how this thesis is "independent of any zoological thesis."[80] That is, Heidegger's claim of the animal's poverty in the world and *without world* status is never conceptualized in relation to "zoological authority" and is never subjected to any scientific "hypothesis to be verified, to be confirmed or infirmed."[81] Heidegger's thesis is unscientific, or, as Derrida writes, "independent of zoological knowledge."[82] For Derrida, zoological knowledge provides some possibility of undermining anthropocentric thinking.

While zoological knowledge is deployed to exert mastery of the animal other, it can also be used to unravel our sense of self and the other; it can be used to unmake a world in which "the human" is problematically a core organizing principle for our very conception of "world." Zoological knowledge provides a sense of animal island-worlds, their agency and personhood. It does not necessarily lead to a masterful knowability of experience, but instead presents us with glimpses of experience. Throughout this book, zoological knowledge is incorporated to help us think about animal experiences during the Iraq War. The science of dogs, sheep, and bird life, for example, informs my description of moments and provides a fuller measure of the island lives and experiences of animals. As with the use of poetry in the next several chapters, fragments of zoological knowledge punctuate the text to draw out interspecies connections and belongingness.

The zoologic can certainly inform the poetic (and vice versa), and it can provide not only a sense of similarities but also difference, which are both useful in thinking about life and death. For example, in considering a zoological avenue toward the concept of *world*, Derrida notes how many traits ascribed to humans are certainly not "the exclusive reserve of what we humans call human. Either because some animals also possess such traits, or because man does not possess them as surely as is claimed."[83] He observes that animals, for instance, experience death and have unique languages.[84] Indeed, Derrida makes a point to not only chip away at human–animal dichotomies, but also to envision distinction and separation as opening up possibilities of belongingness. For example, he remarks how "separation . . . is the condition of both the welcome and the hospitality offered to the other. There would be neither welcome nor hospitality without this radical alterity, which itself presupposes separation . . . Being-together itself presupposes infinite separation."[85] A multispecies togetherness is a belongingness of difference, a being-with differences that can never be disregarded or reduced to sameness. This involves both troubling the normative power of speciesist differences and welcoming unclosable difference. To conceptualize a multispecies world, then, is to envision a world of difference—a world of multiplicities. Or, perhaps we find not a world at all, but a series of islands.

Toward multiplicities, the poetic and zoologic pull us toward singularities. For instance, Derrida criticizes Heidegger's refusal to theorize animals in their singularity, arguing that he "naively assume[s] that they all [animals] have in common the same relation to the world" and are "all supposedly 'poor in world,' and equally 'poor in world.'"[86] Such an assumption is a limit to cross "in order to *think*."[87] Thinking, then, involves the appeal of "irreducible multiplicity of these living beings" and coming to terms with the "singularity of what are called species and communities" and "beings-with-one-another" of and between species.[88] There is no animal; there are only *animals*. There is no interspecies cosmopolitanism of all humans and animals; there is only a cosmopolitanism of particular humans and animals. Cosmopolitanism, in its global ambitions, depends on the singular—singular lives, singular moments.

The merging of the zoological and the poetic opens us up toward multiplicities and singularities of nonhuman agency and personhood, revealing the complicated voices of animals and providing glimpses of the others' islands. As Rafi Youatt importantly suggests, animals possess a relational, semiotic agency.[89] Animals create and are affected by signs and language; there is a relational agency involving signs and signification. Zoological literature helps us think about this more clearly. Take for example recent research on wolves that reveals that wolf howling is "under flexible control of the signaler and used selectively to facilitate reassembly with important individuals."[90] Wolf howling is not simply a response to environmental changes; rather, it is a controlled way of social engagement. Wolf howling is an expression of agency. Put another way, wolf howling is often about absence, about longing to make contact or reconnect with other wolves. It is a complex cognitive and emotional way of engaging with the world. And howling is not just "howling." Wolves employ 2,000 different howls, which might be conceptualized into twenty-one distinct howl types.[91] And there is no "wolf." There are grey wolves, arctic wolves, red wolves, Himalayan wolves, and many others. These wolves have different dialects of howling.[92] But there is also no "grey wolf." There is no "red wolf." Each wolf (while emerging and existing in relation to other wolves) is singular, with its own life, way of being in the world, and its own experiences and moments.

"Wolf-Time"

Your voice is a friend to the sky,
a prayer leaving the world,
revealing it.
A wandering world,
suspended in a pulse—wolf-time.
Where did you go?
Your dream dialect,
disappearing,
touched by distance.

When thinking of the "world" of a wolf, we might islandize this conception. Zoological knowledge reveals certain possibilities of what a wolf "is," what a wolf does and how it relates. But there is always uncertainty, always more, an inevitable excess, a beyond. Animals are not only "biological beings" but also "political beings," as Rafi Youatt notes.[93] A wolf-pack, for example, is a kind of political community, a community that can "make judgments about insiders and outsiders, and assess threats to its way of life on which it acts."[94] But even the biological and political being of a wolf is beyond our descriptions, outside our conceptualization and control. The world of a wolf is not a world but an island—there is a disconnect, an excess, a beyond, an untranslatable narrative out of earshot. Islandizing these wolfish worlds, thinking toward this "beyond," then, can encourage thinking toward a more inclusive interspecies politics, toward a cosmopolitanism inclusive of the wolf and the human, the multiplicities of wolves and humans.[95]

The world-as-island hints at the sense of never quite reaching the other, and reminds us that our thinking of the other—human or animal—is clouded by our own insular perspective. We never quite reach the other's shores. We only glimpse at the richness of animal experiences. We see a seagull in a storm, perhaps exhausted from the day, from the rain. We see a squirrel on the run, on a journey, collecting souvenirs—squirrel-technological moments in a web of branches. We see these island-worlds. We might collect data and gain knowledge. We might write poetry. The other remains unworldly.

The zoological and the poetic bring us to the blurred edge of our islands. Infused by the zoological, we might turn toward the poetic voice of the animal other, already calling to us. This voice, in poetry, often emerges within an anthropomorphic imagining. Anthropomorphism, once considered to be a form of human narcissism, is now also understood as an attempt at a kind of poetic binding. John Simons, for instance, argues that while anthropomorphism does not "take us any closer to a true understanding of the nature of the nonhuman experience," it can importantly "alert us to those shared characteristics that appear to bind the species together."[96] He further suggests that anthropomorphism "can work as a representational strategy which helps both to define and to challenge our perceptions of non-humans . . . it is not merely a way of making animals into humans."[97] Yet certainly anthropomorphism is inevitably and always problematic, as Derrida reminds us in his note about "anthropomorphic taming."[98] Still, the poetic often embodies an anthropomorphic strategy to unsettle our sense of the world, to defamiliarize both the human and the animal, to render incomplete any attempt to make sense of who we are in relation to the animal other. A spectral-poetic approach to war, then, while dream coloring the realities of animals, might also disturb our implicit emphasis on human certainty of making sense of war, of cleanly theorizing it.

To summarize, we need not neatly rope off the zoological from the poetic, the zoological from the anthropomorphic, or the anthropomorphic from the poetic. They are, in some ways, inseparable. Knowledge is revealed, arrived at through poetic exposure to and scientific exploration of islands of the other. Knowledge is felt through holding moments—imagined and observed—close. Writing about forests, poet Charles Goodrich notes how "we come to know the forest via paths laid down in stories, stories told in anecdotes, photographs, essays, and poems, or in hypotheses, data, and graphs. All these stories are entries into the forest, paths . . . to discover new insights."[99] Poems about animals, ghost-animal poems, might be informed by zoological studies, which might inform our connections to animals, providing a glimpse of their island-worlds—beyond us and part of us, like us and not like us. Island-worlds, englobed with rich histories, real life, semiotic webs, and experiences beyond our gaze.

Responsibilities, Iraq

Central to cosmopolitanism is responsibility to the distant other. Recently, cosmopolitans have been calling for greater attention to the role of "responsible cosmopolitan states" and also for a focus on relations of material harm (the particular harm done to a distant stranger, the damage for which states are already responsible).[100] Andrew Dobson, for example, argues that identification of a specific material relation of harm, that is, a particular culpable connection, is necessary for cosmopolitanism to bring a more meaningful sense of nearness to bear on the generalizable and universal obligation to others.[101] A sense of belonging with others can draw strength from the identifiable connection between "what we have done and how they are."[102]

In this book, I make identifiable connections between the United States and life and death in Iraq. These connections make culpability specific; they bring into focus the specific pain of loss; they help us seriously engage how things might have been different for specific others, and also mark us with a memory of how things might be different in futures moving toward us. But as Derrida would remind us, beyond the identifiable connections and responsibilities between the discernable "we" and "they" are "an infinite number of" others.[103] Responsibility to the particular other involves "sacrificing the other other, the other others."[104] And any particular form or act of responsibility is itself always limited, always conditional and conditioned. Responsibility, emerging as a double demand to the arrival of the singular other and universal other and others, thus still necessitates a response from the particular "we" to the particular "they." But *other* others are always forgotten and sacrificed. Responsibility is always infinite. There are "billions of my fellows [*semblables*] (without mentioning the animals that are even more other than my fellows) who are dying."[105] And there are so many who are already lost. "We" belong with all of "them."

March 19, 2003, marks us.

The "we" in this book refers mostly to the United States—its people, its government, its military—but it certainly expands beyond this "we."[106] Indeed, in the space of the poem, this "we" and "they" is always something else. Yet the material harm, the responsibility for it, the discussion of it, the poetry about it, are all part of an intertwined movement toward the "how they are." But "they," the lost from Iraq, are with "us," still. The U.S. invasion and occupation of Iraq created conditions for unquantifiable horror and so many stolen lives. There is a responsibility to be changed by these lives, the remains of loss—talismanic losses. There is a responsibility to expand ourselves inward and outward toward the spectral other. As Derrida puts it, this responsibility "is from the other, even if it is the other in me."[107] Moving toward the other, we remember to consider how things could have been otherwise. In this otherwise we are reminded that this "we" is "you." This "you" is within "me." This "they" is "us." Complicities, warnings—your gaze holding me. Time inexpressible, otherwised.

In many ways, the Iraq War is not over. In many ways it began long before 2003.[108] And the conditions that gave rise to the U.S. invasion remain. These conditions, the language of killing, the deadening desire to control, the impulses of invasion are here, inside of us. The war is still. Its stillness lives in death. It breathes in poetry—in Alise Alousi's "What Every Driver Must Know," in Dunya Mikhail's "The War Works Hard."[109] It lives in art—on the street murals of Baghdad and elsewhere.[110] The war riddles us with remembrances in the globality of the poetic act. The war speaks with us within the poems from Iraqis about Iraq, the Iraqi poems about America, the American poems about Iraq, and the American poems about America in Iraq.[111] A cosmopolitan poetics. "The poet," says Soheil Najm, "considers the existence, the responsibility of the whole world as his predicament."[112] The poem, the predicament—ruins of time-snaked death-reason, blood-routes to islands, keeping us still, together. Still together, distant. In moments, these singular moments becoming spectral, are culpable ties that bind us together. They bind each of us. These ties, singular and interminable, material and otherwise, cannot be disentangled. The poetic task of the cosmopolitan involves an implication of the self in the tangle of blood, this blood of lost hearts pulsing then in the now, in our hearts, in moments. "Being responsible involves letting the other come, making their voyage finally possible."[113] Iraq's ghosts are ghosts with whom we disappear. Let us let them disorient. Let us carry these ghosts, disoriented and disorienting. Toward us, together, in me, us.

Derrida writes about a responsibility to "carry the other in oneself" after death.[114] In her memoir about diary-keeping, Sarah Manguso notes how "the catalog of emotion that disappears when someone dies, and the degree to which we rely on a few people to record something of what life was to them, is almost too much to bear."[115] *To bear, to carry the world of the other, who is gone. How to bear? How to carry? Where are we carrying?* So many experiences of war are unknown, with so many moments of loss never recorded. *We too are lost without attention to moments. To carry you is to carry me—us.* Perhaps to carry is to create space for the other, for imaginative witnessing. To poetically record and carry the lost moments, however inadequate, is a kind of processional-poetic bearing witness.[116] To imagine is to unconceal moments, always still secret. To carry the other, spectral-poetically, is to remember, to take notice and note the other's lived moments. In this elegiac space we take in the facts of loss—dissolved, and dreamed away, orbiting like melodies beyond ourselves, in and beyond our world. A spectral cosmopolitanism—a responsibility to the lost, the lost moments, the unknown voices of the world—takes root in a spectral-poetic world. The world of the dead is our world, rootless.

Gillian Brock contends that "cosmopolitanism highlights the responsibilities we have to those whom we do not know, but whose lives should be of concern to us."[117] Perhaps we have responsibilities to the unknowable, the lost lives "out there" and within us, the already lost and the ghosts still to come. A responsibility to remember. In the words of Derrida, we are responsible to "the ghosts of those who are not yet born or who are already dead, be they victims of wars, political or other kinds of violence."[118] This responsibility might inform other kinds of material responsibilities to vulnerable others. Responsibility, however poetic and however infinite, is not abstract; it is always toward real lives and deaths, looking back and toward the future of real harm, real vulnerability. Responsibility is problematized by spectral moments, dislocating any confidence in responsibility within the elegiac space of the poem, unanchored from the past and present.

On this point I am reminded of Judith Butler's question about "our responsibility toward those we do not know, toward those who seem to test our sense of belonging."[119] Without doing appropriate justice to the complexity of her arguments, for Butler responsibility has to do with the exposure of bodies and "is located in the affective responses to a sustaining and impinging world."[120] Responsibility, she argues, is realized through a "critical reflection" on "exclusionary norms" that make only some lives recognizable and thus grievable.[121] I certainly agree. But we might also consider the norms that structure how we write about and toward the other—their bodies, vulnerabilities, and moments. In other words, we might press against the normative rules of reflection and critique. Toward this end, perhaps responsibility not only involves a critical reflection on norms but also an elegiac assessment of the world, of worlds, of worlds-as-islands—an assessment that is itself a form of grieving. Spectral-poetic moments perhaps become this form, this beginning of an ongoing and impossible response to the voice of the other. Here the question of responsibility moves from within the other's voice, before us, finding us in poetic movements and moments.[122] The ghostly rhythms of invasion are inscribed into these movements and moments. Responsibilities, rhythms, incisions.

But does responsibility to the moments of the other always emerge as a theorizable form of grief? Do reflections on life, loss, grief and their possibilities always surface in and as a kind of production of knowledge (even while attempting to pull back the curtains on such a production)? Are the lines and moments that might cut and interconnect always obfuscated by certain normative parameters of reflection? Perhaps the obfuscation is inevitable. Perhaps there is irony, guilt, and irresponsibility in every reflection. Perhaps this is all "unbearable or laughable," as Derrida might say.[123] But I sense Iraq becoming consumed with every word. Every sentence feels irresponsible. A poem never arrives on its own. We must seek its arrival. We can push to make possible the voyage for the lost. Perhaps elegiac assessments of war and poetry for the lost other—not just the poetry *of* others but poetic movement for and toward the voice of the other, within us and away—is a realization of another kind of responsibility. A responsibility with blood, wounds, disorientation. A responsibility that recognizes its irresponsibility, a responsibility that appears and demands itself before any decision to become responsible to and for the other.[124] A responsibility fastened to the confusion and clarity of a poetic voice—finding us in the poem, becoming its possibility. Spectral-poetic responsibilities—responsibilities to reach, to find, to carry. March 19, 2003, is with us. It carries us away. Its metronome clicks and keeps its time in our hearts. Each click is a cut.

Conclusions

Spectral cosmopolitanism is a turn to ghostly moments, a turn toward moments of war turning toward us, still with us, still moving. It is an elegiac turn toward being-with the lost others in poetic fragments and imaginative moments of living and dying. In this elegiac space we might sense the density of spectral life, the webs of our vulnerability, our melancholic solitudes of togetherness. In this elegiac space we are confronted with an impossible conversation with the voice of the animal other. These voices, never fully accessible, bear witness to moments; they express an inexpressible depth of what life, death, and war mean. The poetic voice of the animal other echoes across time and space, across borders, bearing witness.

Pierre Joris writes that poetry "cannot simply bear witness to the past but must at the same time be resolutely turned to the future: it has to be open, it has to be imaginatively engaged in the construction of a new world, it has to look forward."[125] Cosmopolitanism needs poetry and the disordering poetic voice of animals lost to war. To construct demands memory, elegies, poetry. The construction of a new world—an impossible and impossibly risky but necessary task—demands listening to the lost, listening to the moments that bind us. Poetry discloses these moments, opens our hearts, ears, and eyes—opens our imagination—to the lives of animals, to their losses, to our belongingness. We can look back to the lost, looking at us, to remind ourselves to pursue a justice "in the direction of the act of memory, of resistance to forgetting," as Derrida says.[126] Looking back to the lost is perhaps guidance for the future. These spectral voices help us envision the meaning of future violence and the toll that the war might take. They are a reminder of a justice that calls us "to remember the future" and to remember "the others in oneself."[127] Cosmopolitan elegies are an opening of the self to these others, within us. They are reminders from and for the mostly nameless spectral animal others. This, then, is the import of thinking about and with the lost, a "purpose" of spectral cosmopolitanism.

Chapter 2

Stray Hearts, Vectors

The Wandering Dogs of Iraq

In late October 2019, the U.S. military killed the leader of ISIS, Abu Bakr al-Baghdadi. In announcing the news, Donald Trump stated twice that al-Baghdadi "died like a dog." Like a dog, Trump stated, al-Baghdadi died "whimpering, screaming, and crying." In the same announcement, Trump praised the military dog who was integral to the raid on al-Baghdadi: "Our K-9, as they call—I call it a dog, a beautiful dog, a talented dog— was injured and brought back. But we had no soldier injured."[1] This dog, named Conan, was invited to the White House the next month to receive a medal. At the reception, Trump referred to Conan as "the ultimate fighter" and Vice President Mike Pence called Conan "a hero."[2] The demise of an adversary can be praised in the terms of a dog's death. A dog is a Delta Force hero and a pejorative term for one's dead enemies.

As Donna Haraway tells us, "dogs are many things. They occupy many kinds of categories."[3] Many dogs around the world might be categorized as "street" or "stray" dogs. These dogs are ubiquitous nomads, roaming free and meandering through city streets. While military dogs garner affection and praise, strays are often seen as an annoyance or as a threat to public safety. This is also the case in times of war, as stray dogs sleep, search for food, and wander about in urban spaces of violence. During the Iraq War, stray dogs occupied another category: vectors. That is, strays were seen as potential carriers of rabies. Unlike most other animals, stray dogs were singled out as particularly threatening and consequently targeted for eradication. The U.S. military apprehended and killed stray dogs wandering near military bases, and the municipal government in Baghdad launched programs to eradicate strays. Tens of thousands were reportedly killed.[4]

This chapter is about these dogs. There is always much that we will never know about their lives. This chapter seeks to think about and think with these dogs; it is an attempt to listen to their poetic barks—voices lost to war. It is an elegiac space for lost dogs and connections. To the lost wanderers of Babylon, a space for you—for your language, your bark-words, your nameless faces amidst the nameless others. *A tangled tether, a connection to you.* A recent study found that "barks convey information about the caller's identity," but the cues within the barks "may be too subtle for humans to rely on."[5] *This chapter is an attempt at listening for you, spectral dogs. It is a space to listen to your subtle and unknowable cues, spectral sonorities looping through us and time.*

Ubiquitous Strays

There are potentially one billion dogs on earth, many of them strays.[6] Some estimates indicate that there are 250 to 350 million stray dogs around the world, while other estimates hint at the possibility of 600 million.[7] Stray dogs are everywhere. In times of peace and war, the term "stray dog" or "street dog" often connotes a problem or nuisance. Yet there are certainly other ways to view these dogs and their relationships to humans. Toward that end, an array of terms exists for these peripatetic beings, terms that might imbue them with other meanings relevant to the demands of justice. For example, "free-ranging dog" has been introduced as a more flexible term, and one that indicates a sense of agency, a sense of freedom to move and pursue individual and collective interests and desires. Biologist Luigi Boitani provides other possibilities:

> Wild, stray, sylvatic, feral, village, unrestrained, are just some of the many labels used to define a huge variety of ecotypes of dogs that share a fundamental ecological feature: they are free to wander where they want and follow the occasional lure. They are free, temporarily or permanently, from the control of a human who dictates their times, movements, and lifestyle. The many categories of free-ranging dogs mostly refer to their lifestyle and the degree of their dependence and social relationship with humans.[8]

Ecologist Matthew Gompper relatedly notes that these various linguistic categories are in fact "fluid and non-exclusive." A dog might be in multiple categories or could move from one category to another; for instance, a dog might be both an "owned village pariah dog or a stray farm dog."[9] And what these terms mean might be contingent upon geography, culture, and norms. Indeed, the notion of "dog ownership" fluctuates between and within countries. In parts of India, for example, individuals might have bonds with and provide food to certain dogs without ever claiming ownership.[10] The meaning of "stray dog" is open to different interpretations and intimacies. Different terms capture certain aspects of them. But dogs always exceed these expressions; these various terms never fully capture the meaning of a stray dog, and they also twist and mold the other into something captured and capturable, something definably clear and humanly configured. These terms and their meanings can nonetheless convey a sense of the other; they gesture toward a sense of *dogness*, of human relationality to "dogs" and specific dogs. Throughout this chapter, I prefer the terms "stray dogs," "street dogs," or "wandering dogs." The first two are perhaps the most commonly used names, and the latter phrasing hints at a sense of a nomadic impulse, the relatively free sense of moving through life. It speaks to a sense of canine desire and dog personhood, a dog's drive to live and venture, a desire to move and *wander* on their own terms. "WANDERER, *noun*. A rambler; one that roves; one that deviates from duty."[11]

"Dogs engage many kinds of relationality, but one kind that is practically obligatory is with humans. It is almost part of the definition of a dog to be in a relationship with humans," states Donna Haraway.[12] As wandering dogs paw and sniff their way through city streets, they inevitably encounter and interact with humans. Stray dogs' experiences of street life are bound up with dog–human relationality. Interestingly, Boitani finds that while most strays are somewhat detached from humans and have no "social connection" to us, "they still depend on us for food and shelter."[13] Beyond such dependence, Donna Haraway argues that dogs pull us into an ethical relationship "because they are vulnerable to human cruelty in very particular ways, or to carelessness, or stupidity."[14] But because strays often depend on tolerant contact with the human world, some animal advocates note that most stray dogs are not dangerous because "positive interaction is necessary for them to get what they need."[15] Dogs also show a general tendency toward stranger tolerance because they regularly need to coexist with both dog and human strangers.[16] This is not to say that stray dogs do not attack, bite, and transmit rabies. They obviously do. But this aspect of human-wandering dog relations substantially colors the broader discourse of these relations. The snarling street dog is a reality, but it is also a trope—one that can obscure the multiplicity and complexity of street dogs, clouding the layers of their lives and ways of interacting that have nothing (or everything) to do with us.

"A Promise, a Threat"

> Stray sisters, wandering natives.
> Rootless, paperless,
> pausing.
> The crow above intrigues.
> I listen.
> It speaks a promise, a threat.
> Your growl—a note, a dare, an arrow.

While enumerating the many positive and negative ways dogs shape the lives of humans and other animals, Boitani argues for further research into stray dog "behavior, sociality, and ecological flexibility" as a means to "establish a more respectful relationship with them." What a respectful relationship might mean is an open question, but one that can be framed on human *and* dog terms—that is to say, political or relational terms that are not purely human. It is also a question about *human* sociality and ecological flexibility in relation to the dog. Given our entangled lives with wandering others, respect might mean "being-with" and "being-for" these vulnerable strays who often depend on human kindness. This kindness can be understood not only within a framework of human-centric notions and practices but also in terms of a collective existence. As Rafi Youatt notes, "perhaps, by paying greater heed to *specific* animal communities as collective subjects of political engagement with whom we constitute a shared existence, we might begin to negotiate the terms of collective existence more explicitly."[17] Throughout this chapter, I discuss a specific group of animals—stray dogs in Iraq—as well as specific measures pertaining to stray dog security during times of violence, measures that reflect a hope for human–animal belongingness. Many of these dogs that I turn to were killed. The poems throughout this chapter are to them, with them, about them, reappearing within us—spectral moments, moving.

Stray Dogs in Iraq

> Dogs confront us with a particular kind of otherness that raises many . . . ethical, ontological, political . . . questions.[18]
>
> —Donna Haraway

Wandering dogs have long been considered problematic in Iraq. During the government of Saddam Hussein, they were frequently rounded up and killed. Certainly, a negative opinion of dogs as disease-spreading animals was part of a cultural milieu among some Iraqis before the U.S. invasion of Iraq.[19] While there is significant historical variation in the status of dogs within Muslim societies, dogs have been viewed as unclean and problematic among some segments in Muslim-majority areas, including parts of Iraq.[20]

But hardened relations can be displaced by a softening of ideas, a summoning of togetherness, brought about by horrifying events or normative practices. To this point, there has been a "recent clamor for canine companionship" in Iraq.[21] The relatively new and broader appeal of dogs as pets in Iraq reveals how the status of certain animals is always in flux, and how negative views of dogs are not a constituent, unchanging feature of Islam or Iraqi society. In discussing this flux, Mohammed Hanif notes that the Qur'an (unlike the Hadith) is mostly mute about dogs. However, he calls attention to the "People of the Cave"—a story in the Qur'an that "evokes not revulsion [toward dogs] but time travel and companionship"— as an interesting exception to Qur'anic reticence. The story, also known as "Seven Sleepers" or "Sūrat al-Kahf," features a dog (named "Qiṭmīr" according to some accounts) who guards the entrance to a cave while a group of men take a 309-year nap.[22] In making a case for caring for dogs in the midst of times of global crisis, Hanif claims that "it's exactly when the world is falling apart that you should care about mutts."[23] Caring for stray dogs, bound up with all the subtleties and possible meanings of care, is particularly challenging amidst the fragility of war.

Dogs, humans, and political violence—there is no simplistic tale of care and cooperation amidst the weight of war trauma on human or dog senses. The presence of stray dogs, a proximity that is already viewed as problematic, becomes an acute concern during war as the population of wandering dogs can grow because of political violence. At the same time that violence in cities such as Baghdad and Mahmudiyah increased, public services such as trash collection became less frequent. Dog populations sometimes grow with increased possibilities of scavenging for food. Also, when security improves, open-air markets and the return of city life sometimes leads to dogs discovering more food and consequently having more puppies.[24]

With any prospect of war looms potential dark moments, yet-to-be marked moments of violence enclosed within the larger structure of violence. The lives of stray dogs in Iraq took such a dark turn several years after the initial U.S. invasion. In February 2009, a news story described a stray dog being shot, "sending it tumbling over and over. Agonizing yelps echo through the streets as it tries to reach and bite at the gaping wound."[25] The story also described "a puppy eat[ing] a piece of poisoned meat. Its body starts to twitch and spasm as the toxins kick in."[26] These scenes were from the streets of Baghdad—a display of a late 2008 municipal government program to shoot stray dogs or kill them using meat tainted with strychnine. The purpose was to reduce the risk of rabies and dog attacks. Teams of veterinarians, council officials, and police officers moved through streets with bags of poisoned meat and shotguns. The veterinarians were responsible for setting out toxic meat for dogs to eat. If the meat did not lead to a dog's death, then police officers would shoot to kill.[27]

"Clusters"

> Clusters of us,
> curled,
> snore-snarling.
> Black
> delirium.
> Faithless hounds,
> wounded.
> The wild-hearted, circled.

With additional funding, the dog-killing operation was reportedly ramped up in 2010. The updated goal was to kill a million stray dogs. It is not clear if there were even a million dogs to kill, but the "million dog" notion was part of the municipal campaign, or at least its stated rhetoric. The chief veterinarian of the operation, Mohammed al-Hilly, called it the "biggest campaign of dog execution ever."[28] As described by al-Hilly, the program was a response to an increasing dog population due to litter, which was the result of post-invasion violence that prevented public service employees from removing trash.[29] Inattention to public services and litter, not high on the list of U.S. plans for a post-invasion Iraq, created the conditions for the increase in stray dogs and, by extension, the stray dog eradication program. The U.S. invasion and failure to properly plan for public service operations was therefore part of a causal chain that resulted in an intensified program to kill a massive number of wandering dogs.

Halfway through 2010, about 58,000 dogs were reportedly killed. At one point, it was reported that roughly 2,400 stray dogs were killed per day.[30] While these publicly available estimates are not definite, public reports and witness accounts appear to verify that many dogs were killed. In one photograph we see six recently killed street dogs in the back of a truck. The departed, nameless, form into a pile—six wandering bodies, heaped, each body joined to the other.[31]

Who were these dogs? In another image from a *San Diego Tribune* story, we can see the bodies of dead stray puppies poisoned by tainted meat.[32] These dogs were just a few of the many dogs killed in 2010. Who was their dog mother? A stray burden, a stray life, a stray bark. In another image, we can see a dog curled up on dirt next to a concrete structure with a gun pointed at them.[33] The dog does not see the shooter. It has reddish brown fur and a charcoal muzzle. Who was this dog? What will this dog say to us? What will we say in response?

> "Tangled"
>
> I see you.
> Still tangled in
> dog time.
> Distance and your broken echo
> inside us.

The stated purpose of the plan was to reduce dog attacks and prevent potential rabies cases, though the severity of these problems was never entirely clear. Moreover, it was questionable whether killing was the appropriate way to respond to such potential threats to humans. The kill program was supported by many, but there were also Iraqis expressing criticism. In a scene captured in the *New York Times*, a Baghdad resident shouted at the workers tempting dogs with poisoned meat: "Give us clean water instead of killing dogs! . . . The dogs are not harming us, it is the water."[34] The plan not only led to the deaths of many dogs but also endangered humans. In one instance, three children were inadvertently shot by stray dog hunters.[35] Rabies and dog bites are certainly important issues for governments to confront; however, the methods for responding and the severity of the problem are important considerations.

These considerations run the risk of engendering a dogmatism that elevates critique above grappling with the moments and the experiences of war. Yet critique remains necessary, as it helps extract possibilities of belongingness, of turning the past toward possibilities for the future. But to think through these considerations and criticisms involves a privilege of distance. Relatedly, we need to remember that that the practice of criticism can slip into a moralism that focuses on conceptual appropriateness at the expense of attention to the larger structural forces at play, the cognitive and emotional complexity of the killers and the killed, and the affective and material contexts of killing. For critics of Iraqi officials, it is therefore also important to keep in mind that the U.S. invasion of Iraq generated circumstances where this became possible. Thus, any criticism of Iraqi officials needs to be contextualized with the unknown experience of violence and disorder brought about because of U.S. actions in Iraq.[36] This does not mean that Iraqis were without agency, but it attends to the uncertainty and chaos of war that made the choice to kill stray dogs more appealing. The human desire for security in an environment of profound insecurity facilitated the pursuit of human security at the expense of the security and life of stray dogs. In this situation, vulnerable humans made stray dogs more vulnerable through direct violence in part as a means to become less susceptible to the overarching uncertainties of war.

Beyond Iraqi governmental officials, the U.S. military was also directly involved in killing stray dogs. In one documented incident, a U.S. soldier shot and killed Iraqi street dogs for entertainment.[37] In addition to this incident, K.B.R. (Kellogg, Brown & Root), the former American subsidiary of Halliburton with billions of dollars in contracts with the U.S. government to provide housing and other logistical support to the U.S. military, contracted with the military to kill stray dogs. In technical terms, K.B.R. offered "vector control" services. According to K.B.R., vectors "are insects or animals that transmit diseases," such as mosquitos, rodents, and dogs.[38] For stray dogs in and around U.S. military bases, vector control meant capture and likely death.[39] This practice was not limited to seizing and killing stray dogs wandering around military installations, but was also extended to dogs kept as pets by U.S. soldiers. By 2008, it was reported that K.B.R. workers had captured about 7,100 stray dogs and cats and euthanized the majority of them.[40]

These vector control operations were part of enforcing the 2006 U.S. Department of Defense's General Order 1-B (section 2j), which stated that "adopting as pets or mascots, caring for, or feeding any type of domestic or wild animal" is a prohibited activity.[41] While not always strictly enforced, this was a rule for all military personnel in United States Central Command (CENTCOMM) areas, including Iraq. Former U.S. soldier Jay Kopelman noted that this order "effectively forbids American soldiers and Marines in zones of conflict from taking action to rescue and care for animals in distress."[42]

Who were the dogs rounded up? What was their experience of being conceptualized and rounded up as potential rabies vectors? I think of their confusion and anxiety. I imagine them seeking to escape, their feelings of being trapped. *What will you say? What does your untranslatable appearance here, routed and carried, mean for us, now? Who are we becoming as we imagine your nameless, never-named friends, no longer known, un-named by time? Who are you, with us?*

Vector dog songs, silenced. The foreigner (dog) question.

Writing about hospitality, Derrida notes that one of the first demands is the requirement to know the name of the foreigner or stranger: "'What is your name?' or then 'In telling me what your name is, in responding to this request, you are responding on your own behalf, you are responsible before the law and before your hosts, you are a subject in law.'"[43] Dogs, of course, cannot tell us their names, though they might respond to a name if they have been assigned one. In many places, dogs are registered with local governments with legal names and often wear tags displaying these along with their legal status. Dogs with names, papers, and tags are legal creatures; they properly have a right to exist under the law. Derrida references this problem of the name in *On Cosmopolitanism*, quoting Hannah Arendt: "The chances of the famous refugee are improved just as a dog with a name has a better chance to survive than a stray dog who is just a dog in general."[44] The stray dogs in Iraq often had no names. Aside from certain military dogs or dogs that soldiers brought back home, most strays were dogs "in general."[45] In Derrida's terms, these dogs were strangers, foreigners without papers or voices to tell their story, existing on the margins, largely unwelcome and perhaps sentenced to death by foreign and domestic forces—nameless vectors.

In Derrida's thinking, death reveals a demanding responsibility of memory, an infinite demand; death reminds us of the singularity of the other and a sense of the end of a world, even *the* world. "For each time, and each time singularly, each time irreplaceably, each time infinitely, death is nothing less than an end of *the* world."⁴⁶ In French: "Car chaque fois, et chaque fois singulièrement, chaque fois irremplaçablement, chaque fois infiniment, la mort n'est rien de moins qu'une fin *du* monde."⁴⁷ What does this mean, this sense that each death is singularly, irreplaceably, and infinitely the end of *the* world?⁴⁸ Kelly Oliver understands Derrida as saying that "death is not a matter of death tolls. One is enough to make—or take—the whole world . . . Faced with the death of a friend or family member, the structures that had made sense of the world, that had allowed us to live in it together, disappear."⁴⁹ But what about the lives of those we never know, the unknowable other? What about distant others from past wars? The seemingly insignificant, abstract mass of deaths, the enigmatic animals? Who were these dogs, these stray "vectors?" How is each of their deaths an end of *the* world?" How might an ending of worlds and *the* world *live*? In *Echographies*, Derrida states that "the other, who is dead, was someone for whom a world, that is to say, a possible infinity, or a possible indefinity of experience was open. Finite-infinite, infinitely finite" and "from this infinitely other place I am watched."⁵⁰ At end of the world, from infinite stray experiences, from these losses of worlds and the world, there are eyes looking toward us, still. For you, a wanderer back when, still, a spectral vow. A trembling paw, a possible world.

Figure 2.1 shows one particular captured stray dog in an animal trap on the Camp Liberty base of Iraq. This dog cannot be reduced to an image, but let us be looked at by their gaze. In the image, the dog gazes off into the distance as a worker in a hard hat appears to be busy with other dogs in cage traps. This dog somehow ended up at a U.S. military base, eventually becoming a vector.

"Delta"

Your eyes—chlorophyll clocks
on the edge of winter.
Your eyes—stars like wolves
flicker through me.
A dog from Delta Cephei
with a wolf's atlas.
Frayed.
On an unfamiliar street,
you made your map.
You made the world.

Figure 2.1. Stray Dog in a Cage. (Curt Cashour/DoD)

Figure 2.2 shows five dogs and a cat caught and captured by a vector control unit on Camp Slayer. What is their story, untold and unknown? It is unclear who these animals were, where they came from, whether they were friends or lone beings seeking to survive on the margins of the camp. Did they bite a soldier? Did they befriend a soldier?

In reflecting on the lives of these stray dogs, we might imagine their lives, their experiences of street life, the moments of seeking to escape harm and becoming lost to war. We might begin imagining their faces, eyes, and ears. Do these features pose a demand? Does the gaze of a dog demand belongingness? Recent studies suggest that "the human–dog relationship is exceptional because it is an interspecies form of attachment;" studies indicate that interspecies bonding between humans and dogs is partially rooted in the reciprocal gaze between them, which leads to a mutual oxytocin release in humans and dogs.[51] Dogs and humans have been gazing at each other for thousands of years, learning from and living with each other.

When Derrida considers the meaning of justice in his essay, "Force of Law," he reflects on Emmanuel Levinas's ideas about the face, describing "the face of the other" as "command[ing] me, whose infinity

Figure 2.2. Camp Slayer Vector Control. (Curt Cashour/DoD)

I cannot thematize and whose hostage I remain."[52] For Levinas, the face can be understood as a metaphor for alterity.[53] The face, in this respect, indicates the sense that the other is always beyond our understanding, is unsummarizable. Yet this face requires hospitality; it speaks to us with an infinite demand. Jill Robbins writes that "the face, which is not reducible to my vision of it, looks back, it talks back."[54] If this "face" of the other can be a "face" of a dog (as implied by Derrida's work on hospitality and animals—but also see Derrida's complicated discussion of the "face" in "Violence and Metaphysics"), then we might understand hospitality in terms of an infinite responsibility to stray dogs.[55] The stray dog's face is always singular, always slipping outside of any careful desire to calculate and understand. But in the dog's gaze—the real, imagined, spectral, and metaphorical gaze—we might feel a pull toward belongingness, an affective encountering, a poetic dwelling.

"Palm Cloak"

You watch
with the wisdom of your ancestors.
Your fur,
soft with desert memories.
You remember
the cloak of the date palms.

There are certainly many ways of thinking about responsibility toward stray dogs in war zones. To some, the lives and deaths of stray dogs might be seen as an insignificant and obscure issue in a country where there have been countless challenges to humans. Thinking through Derrida challenges us to think differently; it impels us to imagine stray dogs as not out of place, to imagine possibilities of hospitable justice to animal others, and to consider alternatives to mass killing of stray dogs. If there is a demand for responsibility and care toward the dog for whom we have no name, what is the response to this demand? What is the precise meaning of responsibility? Who is responsible?

While I have previously discussed responsibility and the justice of remembrance of the unknown and nameless, we might also think of material culpabilities and responsibilities—fusing a movement toward memory of the lost with attention to the material causes of loss and material possibilities. Certainly, the culpability of the United States emerges here in terms of the poor conditions in Iraq, including the plight of stray dogs. It is well established that the United States invaded and occupied Iraq in 2003 based on very little evidence that Saddam Hussein was a clear and urgent threat, and before all other options had been exhausted. The war created a tumultuous environment in which violence and disorder still persists. Beyond the flawed foundations of the initial invasion, the subsequent U.S. military occupation was notable for inadequate planning. The "expectation . . . that US forces would be welcomed as liberators by a relieved and jubilant Iraqi people, and that it would be possible to hand over power fairly quickly to an Iraqi interim government" was obviously mistaken, as small- and large-scale problems created an intensely violent post-war environment.[56] In sum, the United States launched a senseless and careless invasion with poor plans for occupation.[57] Even relatively simple public tasks such as trash collection were deeply troublesome in post-invasion Iraq. According to a 2006 report, Baghdad, a city of millions, had only "380 working trash compacting trucks, compared with 1,200 before the fall of the Hussein government."[58] The decision to invade Iraq therefore created the condition for humans, stray dogs, and other animals to be subjected to relentless fear, anxiety, and physical harm. It was this environment, created by U.S. government choices and backed by much of the American public, in which U.S. officials and the municipal government of Baghdad made decisions to capture and kill stray dogs. I imagine these dogs, remember-forward our connections to their unrevealed experiences—fragments, an unknowable poetic moment—spectral. Two dogs—rovers, dreamers—dancing into loss, drifting to sleep.

"Raven's Coat"

Last night I dreamt of a great feast.
We shared stale flat bread, apples, discarded shawarma.
We danced the dabke, singing songs of Qiṭmīr and Argos.
Drifting to sleep.
Next to you—my world, the scent of figs.
Breathing your raven's coat.

(Calculated) Responsibilities

At the edge of stray moments are possibilities of other ways of being-with nonhuman life in times of war. Thinking of stray spectral moments prompts a consideration of the opportunities lost, the paths not taken. Among these are missed opportunities for vaccinations and dog health care—calculated possibilities of refashioning the very conduct of war, grappling with culpability, and pressing for material routes to belongingness. Belongingness with those marked as vectors, death marks; I think of spectral cantillation marks for some future, perhaps impossible, path.

The United States was not only culpable but also capable in preventing (or at least mitigating and responding to) some of these interspecies issues, given its level of material capacity.[59] One recent estimate indicates that the United States spent several trillion dollars on the wars in Iraq and Afghanistan.[60] At least some of this funding could have gone toward stray dog assistance programs and improving the municipal circumstances in which they emerged as vectors. Beyond better planning for services such as trash collection, the United States could have funded vaccination programs, spaying and neutering programs, animal clinics, or dog adoption centers. Contracts and partnerships with Iraqi citizens, intergovernmental organizations, and NGOs to administer these services were paths not taken.[61]

As already mentioned, stray dogs are often viewed as vectors because of the possibility of carrying the rabies virus, a vector pathogen. But rabies can be preventable with proper funding and administration. One problem in Iraq was that organizations that could administer dog health programs were damaged by the war. A U.N. Food and Agriculture Organization (FAO) assessment found that "veterinary services, including veterinary hospitals and district clinics, diagnostic facilities as well as the cold chain storage and distribution system were either damaged directly by the war or more frequently, extensively looted immediately thereafter."[62] Helping to rebuild these clinics represents one step toward creating better conditions for human–animal relations, and the United States did play a part in FAO efforts to re-establish the clinics. The FAO report also assessed longer-term trends relevant to the global politics of human–animal relations. Due to U.N. sanctions, Iraqi veterinarians found it difficult "to keep themselves up-to-date in terms of new practice, research and information and participate in recent developments in disease control and surveillance strategies."[63] Funding veterinarian training thus represents another step, another path not taken, and a view of war in which humans and animals are entangled in belongingness. These steps toward togetherness are not simply about compassion for animals by charitable governments or militaries; they are a recognition of culpability. They are a recognition of the ways in which political power and decisions shape, in anticipated and unanticipated ways, possibilities of multispecies living, relating, and loss.

In addition to these steps, a more robust effort and further funding for rabies-specific programs might be seen as a way to build toward a different kind of interspecies relations near military bases and in cities such as Baghdad. While the U.S. military and Department of Agriculture helped organize veterinary workshops, these events were not sustained operations, and did not focus on rabies.[64] A 2010 study of rabies in Iraq noted that the "control of rabies requires a consistent supply of dependable resources, constructive cooperation between veterinary and public health authorities, and systematic surveillance. These are challenging in any circumstances, but particularly during conflict."[65] The authors concluded that while rabies is a challenging disease in warzones, mass killing is not only ethically dubious but also an ineffective and ephemeral response:

> The effects of conflict on municipal services and disruption of human habitation are likely to have an impact on the urban dog population . . . Historical approaches to manage dog populations in Baghdad have included pro-active culling in areas where large accumulations of free roaming dogs are reported. Although this temporarily results in fewer free roaming dogs, it is increasingly recognized that indiscriminate culling is not a long-term solution to dog population control, or to reducing rabies prevalence, has welfare implications and can make the situation worse.[66]

Instead of extermination efforts, the authors argue that dog birth-control programs and rabies vaccinations "have proven effective in reducing or stabilizing free-roaming dog populations, and also reducing rabies incidence."[67] Thinking of U.S. culpability in Iraq, we might envision these paths not taken, these courses of action that might have included birth control and rabies prevention efforts.

While not without challenges, funding dog vaccination and sterilization operations could have been feasible paths toward responsibility—a calculated commitment—reflecting a sense of interspecies care and multispecies belongingness amidst violence. Again, such operations embody a recognition of the ways in which humans and animals are locked into multispecies relations that are already political and connected by culpable ties. These operations represent possibilities of unlocking other modes of political engagement and responsibility. Such responsibility is an acknowledgment of culpable moments of unspeakable violence. Such responsibility is accountability for breaking the worlds of street dogs who once spoke of the prescience of palm trees and the caution of war. Their barks shared dreams of protection and protest.

There is evidence supporting this type of responsibility. Dog vaccination projects have proven effective in many countries, including less economically developed states such as Kenya, Tanzania, and Chad. One particular project in Chad's capital city N'Djamena has shown that such operations can be both effective and inexpensive. Though not directly comparable, a large-scale vaccination program in N'Djamena found that "among the intervention strategies compared, mass vaccination of 70% of the dog population is the most profitable and cost-effective intervention."[68] Another study from N'Djamena notes how "mass dog vaccination could be a comparatively cheap and ethical way to both control the disease in animals and prevent human cases and exposure, especially in developing countries."[69] The Iraq War presents numerous challenges; however, creating and funding animal welfare programs signals a vital appreciation of the importance of, and interconnection between, humans and animals amidst the disorder of war. It is worth reiterating that such programs would have comprised a minuscule fraction of the U.S. war budget.

To imagine yet another path, consider the organization *Nowzad*. *Nowzad* is an organization with the stated purpose "to relieve the suffering of animals in Afghanistan."[70] Started by former British soldier Pen Farthing, *Nowzad* began helping stray dogs and cats during the war in Afghanistan. It operates dog and cat shelters where animals are provided food, veterinary services, and opportunities for exercise. It also focuses on combatting rabies and excessive births with a "trap-neuter-release" practice in which strays are captured and then released after vaccination.[71] *Nowzad* illustrates an alternative way of inhabiting the world during conflict—a dwelling with animal others, making visible new possibilities of living with animals during times of threat and insecurity. An organization like *Nowzad*, however, operates with private donations and has only one clinic.[72] U.S. government funding for such clinics in Iraq and Afghanistan could offer an important response in the context of culpability and would be pivotal in terms of overcoming funding and logistical problems. For instance, it is often challenging to ship veterinary and other animal clinic supplies such as explosive cartridges for dart guns given that these are typically banned by airlines.[73] The U.S. government and military might more easily transfer these supplies, and could effectively help build shelters and clinics for animals in countries where they have dropped countless bombs. Indeed, rabies vaccinations could potentially be dropped to clinics using drones.[74]

In thinking of the creation of animal clinics and vaccination programs, I recall Derrida's idea of hospitality as dreaming "the best dispositions, the least bad conditions, the most just legislation" in order to achieve an interspecies togetherness.[75] These clinics and programs are certainly a minimal response to animals in warzones, but they signify important possibilities of responsibility in times of uncertainty and violence. There are always other responsibilities. Yet these calculations of responsibility still represent an extension of dreaming, of imagining the lives lost to war, of the insistence of the voice of the animal other—the spectral voice, still connected to us, urging us to remember the unknowable moments, lost. These voices impart a connection, a sense of belongingness, a call to consider varied manifestations of interspecies belongingness. These voices animate our thinking of what war is, what it was, what it could have been. These voices remind us of who we are and who we might become. These lost voices—addressing us, fastened to futures, unfastened within us.

Conclusions

In his classic work on just war theory, *Just and Unjust Wars*, Michael Walzer describes a realist discourse on war as purportedly divulging a stark fact: "What we conventionally call inhumanity is simply humanity under pressure. War strips away our civilized adornments and reveals our nakedness."[76] War certainly exposes the "inhumanity" that underlies our sense of humanity; it shows us the brutality that humans unleash on each other, and reveals how certain humans become less-than-human humans. In thinking of inhumanity as "humanity under pressure," I recall Levinas's reflections on his time as a prisoner of war, an experience of being treated as subhuman.[77] During this time, Levinas tells us that "a wandering dog entered our lives," a dog whom the prisoners named "Bobby," a dog for whom there "was no doubt that we were men."[78] In Levinas's telling, Bobby the wandering roamer represented a recognition of his humanity, which had been stripped away in the camp.

Derrida problematizes Levinas's conceptualization of Bobby as simply a "witness to the humanity of man," of being a "witness to us only for us, being too other to be our brother or neighbor," of the dog as "a machine that doesn't speak."[79] Dogs might certainly be seen to confirm the humanity of men. Dogs might also be understood as indicators or objects of "our" humanity; our relation to dogs might problematically be seen as representing the ways in which "we" might be seen as more or less humane depending on our treatment of "them" in times of war. But we might also see, as I think Derrida does, how the boundaries of the wandering dog and the human are less than clear. We might see the dog as a neighbor or as a brother. We might poetically and politically come to terms with the ways in which a wandering dog calls into question an "animality that is simply opposed to humanity."[80] War might not just reveal our nakedness—our inhumanity—but might also call into question the very notion of humanity. Thinking toward animals in war might remind us of the many forms of interspecies vulnerability and how humans and animals occupy the same space of war. Both experience war—differently, unknowably, separately, together. We might see the wandering dog as important on his own terms, of having his own singular experiences of war. I imagine his barks, his unknowable cues, his dance, his moments in the forest or streets, his striving to live, his attempt to connect, as a neighbor. A bark, a moment, a faded quote.

We quote the dead to remember them, bringing the dead to us through a quotation. *An imagined life, a name, a quotation. Some lives more quotable than others. What of the unknown, un-namable lives, the memory of the unquotable? How to quote a bark? A distant, unknown, unheard bark?* Unquotable barks—expressive of the moments of war. We won't remember most of the animal lives lost in Iraq, but we might make space to bear witness to some of the lost barks of lost dogs. But the memory of and the responsibility to these lost moments always keeps others adrift, out of view, outside the possibility of quotation. We cannot attend to them all. As discussed already, Derrida writes that "there are also others, an infinite number of them, the innumerable generality of others to whom I should be bound by the same responsibility."[81] The responsibility, this move toward connection, happens "only by failing in my responsibilities to all others."[82] Every move toward the moments of the lost is incomplete and inevitably exclusive.

This chapter attempted to pull apart the event of the Iraq War to see its wandering moments, to be with lost dogs, and to imagine other material possibilities of attending to stray dogs in times of war. Reaching for the voice of the wanderer, looking to be looked at by stray moments, is to give way to the ongoingness of war. It is to yield to the spectral lives still with us. In war, there are small stray moments, moments that matter, moments that move toward us, and in us. These moments always move past us, but they might also move us past ourselves. A moment—a street dog's death, a document, a text of a dream. Not just a text-breath-death-document but a space, a space for you. These moments—lost, real, material, and imagined—offer possibilities to think war otherwise, to see it seeing us, within us. These moments—always also beside us, already without us, looking for us.

These moments might alter our thinking and feelings about the lines between us, a shift which can shape our understanding of the world, of which voices exist, which voices matter, and how these voices can affect us. These dividing lines, and what is and is not between them, are conditions of possibility. They condition our imagination and our sense of what listening to nonhuman and spectral voices might mean. This chapter, a spectral-poetic approach to stray dogs in war, is about these voices. It is about observing the stray dog moments of loss, a bearing witness to these animal others in the distance, a bearing witness that confers a connection on this distance. This spectral responsibility is never finished. It is a kind of impossible witnessing, a striving toward the impossible, an affective answerability to the poetic voice of the animal other that might set "in motion a new thinking of the possible."[83]

Chapter 3

Caged Cosmopolitanism

Menagerie Moments of War

It was the boundless in you.

—Khalil Gibran, *The Prophet*

In contrast to stray dogs, zoo animals tend to be conceptualized in terms of their singularity, as "quasi-persons" more easily anthropomorphized and treated with respect.[1] Unlike strays, zoo animals often have names. The name—the naming of the enclosed—signals responsibility and controllability, reveals connection, secures a kind of knowability while perhaps obscuring an unnamable past. As Susan Howe puts it, the name is a "step toward possessing the unknown . . . an affirmation of value by man."[2] There are affinities with the named, which are cemented through naming. Marius the giraffe. Harambe the gorilla. Knut the polar bear. Behind every name is a commotion of experience, an unarticulated experience of becoming named.

The zoo informs us of a certain global spectacle of desire for interspecies excitement. Around the world, people seek to witness and be enticed by the lives of mostly "non-native" or "exotic" animals such as penguins, bears, and tigers. An individual in Memphis, Tennessee, for example, can gaze at a panda from Beijing. In the Berlin Zoo, one can watch California sea lions put on a show. Through global movement, these animals become easily viewable distant life, often reduced to exotic spectacles. The zoo, from this perspective, is controllable space, a compressible arrangement of life forms often (but not only) for the purpose of the global spectacle of exoticized closeness.

A European invention, the zoo has become global.[3] Zoos are not only global in that they exist all over the world, but also in the sense that zoos around the world cooperate with each other on a variety of projects. Such cooperation brings together distant species and potentially fosters global and interspecies connections. This even happens during war. During the Iraq War, a North Carolina zoo shipped two tigers to a zoo in Baghdad as a gesture for the killing of a tiger by a U.S. soldier. Figure 3.1 shows these two tigers, named Hope and Riley.

Global connections and border-crossings, while hallmarks of certain cosmopolitan ideas, are not themselves cosmopolitan, especially if they involve suffering and exploitation. For all of the connectivity, global cooperation, and learning that might result from zoos, there are obvious and familiar criticisms. Zoos are the outcome of transborder systems that facilitate the capturing, breeding, and purchasing of animals. The experience of being captured and transported can be harrowing and fatal. Many zoo animals are far from their natural environments, bordered by bars or constrictive enclosures. While many animals certainly benefit

Figure 3.1. Hope and Riley. (Chuck Gill/DoD)

from zoo life, captivity can cause serious emotional and physical suffering. Zoo animals can be highly susceptible to the spread of viruses. In 2004, for example, the H5N1 avian influenza crisis led to an outbreak of respiratory illnesses and tiger deaths at a zoo in Thailand.[4] A barrage of visitors and "photographic harassment" can cause depression and eating disorders.[5] Lines from Rilke's well-known poem "The Panther" remind us of life displaced, of a directionless, caged experience: "His gaze against the sweeping of the bars / has grown so weary, it can hold no more."[6]

What does cosmopolitanism mean in the context of caged life? What does it mean in the context of caged experiences in times of war? As distant forces cross borders and engage in military hostilities, we know the experience for zoo animals can be traumatic and deadly. John Kinder notes that "from Berlin to London, Tokyo to Paris, Kabul to Baghdad, zoo animals have been bombed, shot, tortured, starved, massacred, and eaten during wartime."[7] In this chapter, I reflect on the experiences of animals in Iraq zoos during the war. I describe the circumstances of their experiences and the U.S. role in both harming and helping them. I imagine their interior lives as zoo subjects/persons existing within a context of war, spectral-poetically existing with us still. I seek to grapple with these animals as both recognizable and unfamiliar, experiencing war on their terms, but an experiencing that is unavoidably framed and obfuscated by my own humanist logics, perspectives, and narratives. This chapter is ultimately a reminder of the caged lives who are lost to the violence of war.

The Baghdad Zoo

In the early phase of the Iraq War, Baghdad became a multispecies battleground. The U.S. military began fighting in Baghdad in early April 2003, and the capital city was said to have fallen on April 9. But this so-called fall was quite clearly not a clean success (or a success at all when viewed with a longer temporal lens). The initial battles in Baghdad, while militarily successful, alleviated neither military nor civilian concerns. These battles also created a precarious climate for zoo life. The Baghdad Zoo, established in 1971 and located in al-Zawra Park near the upscale Mansour district, was in the midst of some of the early fighting. Confined to cages, these animals were at the center of this combat action.

Looting, hunger, thirst, violence, and loss became part of the zoo animal experience in the early part of the fighting and occupation of

Baghdad. As discussed in the previous chapter, violence and insufficient public services overwhelmed life in the city in the wake of the U.S. invasion. Fearing for their safety (or perhaps ordered to leave by the Iraqi Republican Guard), much of the staff left the zoo, leaving the animals unattended. Inadequate public services meant that zoo animals suffered as a result of the very same issues that humans did. For example, the Baghdad Zoo's watering system stopped functioning when the city's electrical system became inoperative; consequently, animals began running out of water.[8] Some died from thirst. It took some time for the electricity and water systems in Baghdad to become properly functional. Importantly, the U.S. government set aside significant funding to improve electrical and water systems. But despite U.S. promises, electricity and drinking water were still below pre-war levels months after the invasion of the city.[9] Some Iraqis and foreign volunteers did their best to improvise at getting water to the zoo animals.[10] But it took time for the zoo's watering system to be fixed and functional.

"Nightpsalm, Rusted"

The thirst, insistent.
Our nightpsalm, rusted.
I kissed you
that night. You leaving. Luminously
lost.
Captive colors keeping still.

There was also direct—though often incidental—violence against zoo animals. Before the ground invasion of Baghdad, at least one American bomb accidentally hit the zoo.[11] As the Iraqi Republican Guard and the U.S. military faced off in the streets, some of the fighting occurred near the zoo. Zookeepers observed that many animals were "either stolen, killed by American bombing or allowed to escape during the chaotic first days of the coalition invasion."[12] The U.S. Department of Defense (DoD) reported that mortar rounds inadvertently shelled the zoo, which led to the release of animals. But the DoD also blamed most of the damage that enabled animals to escape on looters.[13]

Looters appear in many stories about the early phase of the Iraq War. Alison Howell and Andrew Neal have observed how references to looters were mostly construed in ways that portrayed Iraq and Iraqis as anarchic and senseless, reproducing "racist colonial tropes."[14] While certainly destructive, the havoc of looting was often painted with an overly simplistic and orientalist brush. Many accounts come from Lawrence Anthony, who called the looting "primitive" and referred to the looters as "deranged mobs, hell-bent on ripping their city to shreds in a savage, greed-fueled spree."[15] In a 2012 *New York Times* obituary, Anthony is described as the "Baghdad Zoo savior," a South African conservationist who left his career to "play Noah to the world's endangered species most spectacularly in rushing to the smoldering Baghdad Zoo after the American invasion of Iraq in 2003."[16] Anthony undoubtedly did much to help zoo animals; however, his depiction of looters created and reinforced certain orientalist tropes. In addition, a focus on "saving" as distinct from the structural conditions of the war, conditions that were the result of the American invasion, shades the coercive power rendering zoo life precarious in the first place.[17]

While Howell and Neal advance an important critique about how the zoo became a problematic space for "reforming" looters, their work never fully contends with the experience of animal life and death in the zoo. These experiences are certainly far removed from the larger theoretical concerns and critical ambitions of most scholars, yet these experiences reveal what war is and does. In Howell and Neal's account of the Iraq War and the zoo, we never encounter any animal moments of war. We discover little about how the force of war absorbs, breaks, and consumes animal life. We never see the gaze of the seeing animal, as Derrida might put it.

The zoo reportedly housed about 600 animals before the war. There were about fifty by the middle of 2003.[18] There is no full preservation of their moments, these hundreds of lives, the thoughts, feelings, and relationships. These numbers contain past time within us; they encompass infinite possibilities.

U.S. military actions helped many zoo animals, but certain decisions led to the killing of others. These decisions to kill were part of a logic of animal assistance. Once the U.S. military began attending to the animals, a choice was made to sacrifice some animals for others. Put another way, military officials decided to use some of the zoo animals as animal rations. For example, several pigs and a wolf were killed for their meat. Their bodies were "rationed to feed more exotic carnivores such as the tigers, lions and bears."[19] The logic of animal rations reveals the complexities and contradictions of attending to zoo life during war (and more generally). Tigers are carnivores, and zoo tigers must eat meat to survive. In the wild they are predators; they seek out, stalk, and kill live prey. In zoos, tigers are typically fed beef or horsemeat. The use of horse flesh is common but controversial because the public more readily sees cows as killable sources of food. Whole-carcass horsemeat is typically frozen, defrosted, and then provided to zoo carnivores such as tigers.[20] While the use of horse flesh has been criticized, one zoo director acknowledges the difficulty in "judg[ing] which animal should be butchered and which one should not."[21] The U.S. military's "rationing" of pigs and a wolf reflects a broader antagonism between life recognized as valuable and life conceptualized as rationable. This antagonism is often not recognized as such, a dualism concealed by certain norms and distinct but difficult to justify boundaries between life forms. How were decisions made to kill some for the sake of others? Rafi Youatt refers to these kinds of decisions and forms of boundary-making as an effect of power relations.[22] Linguistic, normative, and material forms of power create a hierarchy of meaning among different animals, power that fashions a kind of subjectivity and value assigned to animals. The subjectivity of animals is inseparable from these power relations, the import of their lives defined by them.

In addition to thinking through this boundary-making power, we can make our way toward other questions: Who *was* the wolf? Who *were* these pigs? *Without voice, rationed. Collateral. Their bodies not their own, if they ever were. Lives unmade, for others, discarded, vanished.* Their bodies were sacrificed for other zoo inhabitants, perhaps necessarily so, but perhaps not. It is difficult to judge the situation, but we can nonetheless call attention to the disjuncture between animal experiences, a disjuncture determined by humans. We can ask and think about their lives, these animal footnotes to war. Who *were* these pigs? What did they think and feel as bombs fell from the sky, as looters made their way through the zoo, as decisions were made to kill? What might we learn from these lives, about life and death, from an animal other—"the other at the edge of life" (*de l'autre au bord de la vie*)?[23]

A body of literature shows pigs to be intelligent problem solvers.[24] Recent studies reveal evidence of pig playfulness, including leaping and combative wrestling forms of play.[25] Pigs also recognize and discriminate among individuals, preferring to be with some pigs over others.[26] In other words, they engage in critical reflection, exhibiting self-consciousness and autonomy.[27] They also have distinct voices and can differentiate among the voices of different pigs.[28] Pigs can recognize the voice of the other, perhaps the voice of a friend. They are curious about their environment, seeking to root (digging with their noses in the ground) to learn about their surroundings and find novelty—a practice that is described as "inquisitive exploration."[29] Their snouts unlock their world. As soon as they can, they will root the ground, seeking, exploring, and nosing the world.[30] They also reportedly recognize and respond to their names if they have one.[31] Who were these particular pigs in Baghdad? I imagine them making decisions, seeking to root, hoping to sniff patches of earth in the zoo as war became life and life became loss. The memory of these pigs is an opening through which we can glance at war and consider its moments. Perhaps these pigs had names. Unknown, perhaps nameless, but we can remember them—their autonomous movements, their removal from the world.

"Absential"

Apocalyptic dwellers.
We withdrew from these
moments, untranslated.
You traced my redemptive impulse
in the earth.
This earth, your voice, your smell—
my absential witness.

Zoo experiences reveal meaningful moments of war, experiences of loss. Derrida writes that experience "supposes a meeting, a reception, perception . . . it indicates the movement of traversing. To experience is to advance by navigating, to walk by traversing. And by traversing consequently a limit or a border."[32] Let us meet and receive each other, our island worlds. Let us cross these borders, lost pig.

There were other variations of direct violence in the zoo. During a party at the zoo, a Bengal tiger was shot and killed by a U.S. soldier. Though there are contested reports, soldiers were reportedly drinking beer in close proximity to the tiger. The zoo's deputy director stated that one of the soldiers tried to feed the tigers, and one "tiger bit [the soldier's] finger off and clawed his arm. So his colleague took a gun and shot the tiger."[33] *I see you from a distance, tiger. I see your anger, your tension, and uncertainty. I remember your trapped autonomy. A vast world, the beginning and end of the world. A rhythmic moment of the world, caged and gone. Lying there, a world.*

It is unclear exactly what happened to many of the zoo animals. Hundreds went missing. The DoD presumed that many of the birds and exotic animals were or would be smuggled out of the country. They also reported that two giraffes were stolen, one of whom was reportedly killed for food.[34] Yet there are almost no details or witness accounts about this killed giraffe, so it remains unclear whether the killing of the giraffe for food was only a rumor. Some suspect the second giraffe was captured by looters and sold on the black market.[35] Reports emerged as part of a construction of tenebrous chaos, an image in which unruly masses of faceless civilians were ready to kill and consume giraffe flesh. A construction of otherness as if the United States was not this very chaos. We will likely never know what happened to this giraffe. I look toward this spectral giraffe. I see it looking back. I imagine the past. I see witnesses. I listen to an exchange of dreams.

"Birdflowers"

The work, the war?
Ashes.
Democratic grave-shore encountering.
Gun-splashed movements
for infinitely closing the unpainted.
What did you dream about last night, soldier?
Openness, emptied.
Bone-mist roots.
My daughter's hands,
carrying moment dust.
How about you, giraffe?
A burgundy tree.
It had flickering leaves making
windsongs that became birdflowers.

We know for certain that some of the animals made their way through the city during the early phase of the occupation of Baghdad, encountering Iraqi citizens and American soldiers. This included four lions who had escaped the zoo. A soldier reported how it "was very surreal, very strange" to see "camels walking through our position and a lion roaming free."[36] The lions became newsworthy, a war zone reinterpreted as a zooish spectacle. The lions became newsworthy not only because the notion of lions walking around a war zone seemed fascinating, but also because soldiers used lethal force on them. A war zone—flesh-hushed with lion's blood. A soldier described how four lions exited their zoo enclosure through collapsing barrier and claimed that "two of them [lions] charged our guys. We had to take them down."[37]

"Lions live in large (up to twenty-one individuals) permanent social groups characterized by a high degree of cooperation."[38]

It was also reported that the lions were starving as they navigated the city. Other than scant reports, we have little evidence about the circumstances of their lives and deaths.[39]

Lion-thoughted feelings orient us within this moment. I imagine the sense of being out of place, the strangeness of it all, the movement from captivity to freedom. Guns, sirens, and the sounds of war—processed and unprocessable. On edge, adrenaline-stuck, and weary.

"Resting lions often drape a paw over the shoulder of a neighbor"[40]

I imagine the sight of fire, the smell of gunpowder, the feeling of a city at war, and the lions carving through this chaos, this freedom, witnessing an occupation. I imagine the displacement of Iraqi citizens, their neighborhood becoming a war zone. Communities consumed by bullets and the buzz of death—with lions—as American soldiers from different parts of the United States, stalking and stalked on the capital city streets. I imagine African lions, caged for decades, confusedly making the transition from captivity to displaced liberty, a kind of paradox, a substitute of one confinement for another. Accustomed to the sounds and smells of zoo life, they confronted the clattering of helicopters and gunfire and the crumbling of concrete.

"Breath"

Sub-Saharan Baghdad and
Madinat al-Salam Appalachia.
Guns—breathing, balancing.
Where are we? Where are you?
Pride, platoon—lost.
Waylaying
realists.
We know
our
depths.

While U.S. soldiers eventually began helping at the zoo, the soldiers-as-zookeepers model was not seen as all that practical. Military personnel providing assistance to the zoo were soon instructed to return to fighting.[41] Looting reportedly continued. Lawrence Anthony, the South African conservationist who had voluntarily traveled to Baghdad and financed some of the repairs with his own funds, had repeatedly requested military assistance to protect the zoo from looting. In the early phase of the war, he was told that the military could not afford the time to patrol the zoo grounds.[42]

The military eventually arrived. William Sumner, a Civil Affairs reservist assigned to the Iraqi National Museum, was put in charge of the zoo. Civil Affairs soldiers are typically experts in city management, law, or cultural heritage, not in zoos or animal welfare.[43] According to his own account, Sumner was seeking additional work in Baghdad and was posted to the zoo because of his requests for extra work.[44] Another account suggests that he "ended up guarding the zoo after antagonizing his superior by pushing too hard on antiquities issues."[45] Sumner began assisting with the remaining zoo animals, repairing the zoo facilities, and more aggressively pushing back looters from the zoo.[46]

Figure 3.2 shows the entrance to the zoo with a note to looters. The note declares Iraq as a free country. It asks the looters to honor their free country. The note, as I look at it, signals the ambiguities of war. It is a symbol of an attempt to do good by those sent to use violent force, to invade and dissolve life and dreams. It is a castigation of those whose lives have been unmade by violence. It is a note of paternalism, violent power, and biopolitical control. It is a note unaware of its own blood, its own violence. *A note—a curse, a scepter*.

Sumner worked on repairing the zoo along with members of his battalion, returning Iraqi zoo staff, zoo director Dr. Adel Mousa, deputy zoo director Dr. Husham Hussan, and wildlife conservationist Lawrence Anthony. Stephen Bognar of the nonprofit environmental organization *WildAid* also came to Baghdad to offer assistance, which included providing funding to pay Iraqi staff members of the zoo.[47]

The U.S. military made a number of repairs to the zoo, which benefited the remaining animals. While many of the zoo animals were gone, remaining animals, such as Saedia, a thirty-two-year-old brown bear with cataracts, were attended to by the U.S. military. In her cage, Saedia was pacing and showing various signs of anguish. I imagine Saedia trying to decode an indecipherable world of war, lacking water and food, struggling. I imagine Saedia's feelings of relief after her conditions improved. "With

Figure 3.2. A Note for Looters. (Jim Garamone/DoD)

modest funding from the U.S. Army," Saedia was built an updated, larger enclosure with grass, and the Army veterinarians performed surgery to remove a tumor.[48] Saedia's story certainly represents an improvement in some of the lives of animals, even amidst the intensification of violence brought about by the U.S. invasion.

Saedia also prompts us to consider paths not taken. Leaving the devastating mistake of the initial invasion aside, if U.S. planners had made arrangements to more robustly safeguard the zoo animals, perhaps other animals could have been helped. Paths not taken—histories and futures, connecting and disconnecting. Spectral responsibilities. What might it mean to think of life and death in the Baghdad Zoo, to think responsibly for the past, present, and future? The time of zoo animals is past and future time, historical and imaginative time, never fully articulable. The zoo animals are behind and in front of us, haunting from within and beyond us. These losses, these lives, these ghostly moments, inform our responsibilities to rethink the world and what world and responsibility mean. To *be with* the island-world of Saedia, before and in front of us, within us, is to venture to other island-worlds in zoo futures, to become incalculably responsible to these pasts and futures.

Beyond these considerations, I think of Saedia as a singular life, a bear with inherent meaning, with experiences and desires. Saedia was a bear with a knowledge of the world that we will never possess. A caged bear, a zoo bear inhabitant of a war zone—traumatized by but also helped because of war. Considering Saedia's experience presents a moment of what war does and what it means—a vignette of togetherness, of human-bear belongingness, tenuously held.

About an hour's distance from the Baghdad Zoo was a smaller, privately owned zoo called Luna Park. William Sumner, Lawrence Anthony, and organizations such as Care for Wild International and the International Fund for Animal Welfare (IFAW) began the process of transporting Luna Park's animals to the Baghdad Zoo. Sumner decided to close Luna Park, given its poor conditions (conditions that pre-dated the war). The animals of Luna Park included a pelican, pigs, dogs, goats, monkeys, and a camel. The camel had mange, which was shaved.[49] These groups, along with the U.S. military, provided important care to these animals, again raising the question of the possibilities of beyond-human responsibilities in times of war.

In the expansive residence of Saddam Hussein's son, Uday, the U.S. military found two cheetahs and several lions living together with dogs.[50] U.S. Special Forces attended to these animals until they could be transported to the Baghdad Zoo, once it was more secure and had been prepared for these new animal arrivals.[51] According to many in the media, as Howell and Neal insightfully note, the situation of Uday Hussein's animals became a "sign and symbol of the decadent tyranny of pre-occupation Iraq."[52] Questions about Uday Hussein's animals extend beyond important issues of orientalist depictions, though these depictions are critical to the consumption of war as a spectacle and the production of human interests that define the terms on which humanitarian warfare is fought (as Howell and Neal suggest). There are also pressing questions about political responsibility. For Howell and Neal, outsider attempts to assist zoo animals were synonymous with problematic desires to make Iraqis more "humane" and to perform the U.S. military's humanity. But the zoo was not simply or only "a space which Iraqis could be disciplined, could be made to be humane, and could potentially be a source of profit for foreign speculators."[53] It was also a space for grappling with political responsibility.

Cheetahs, lions, dogs, and soldiers, in a context of killing, colonial pasts and present, offer a fragile interconnection of moments of human and nonhuman relations. In thinking of these moments, these possibilities of relationality, I imagine lions and dogs dreaming together. "I am dreaming through the dream of the animal," as Derrida puts it.[54] "It is known that . . . certain animals dream," he writes.[55] To consider the animal dreams of Iraq is to also remember how inevitably incomplete our understanding of the meaning of war was and is. War permeates waking life and dreams. And the devastation of Iraqi dreams—human and animal—are still with us. Our dreams and the dreams of those beyond our national borders—including the dreams of Uday's cheetahs, lions, dogs—are inevitably interconnected.

Interestingly, Sumner recalls that even though the lions appeared to be starving, they did not attack or eat the dogs living in their midst. They were likely raised together. Once transported to the Baghdad Zoo, they integrated the lions with other zoo lions, keeping the dogs separated because of the fear that the unfamiliar lions would not live harmoniously with them. Sumner notes that one of the dogs would "sit outside of the cage for days waiting to see his friends."[56]

"Rememberkey"

The world is never again.
It was never supposed to be
anyways.
But I will wait
outside,
looking for the key,
remembering
the world.

Animal Markets

In addition to the two zoos mentioned in this chapter, animals also lived in "animal markets." During the war, Baghdad and Erbil, a city in the Kurdistan Region of Iraq, became hubs for trafficked animals. Illegal pet markets in these cities sold trafficked lions, pelicans, monkeys, and other animals to interested buyers. The post-invasion environment created favorable conditions for animal trafficking, as bribes and forged papers became normalized in a situation where it was difficult "to protect people, let alone animals."[57] This post-invasion context also amplified incentives to purchase exotic animals. As violence in Iraq subsided during the latter phase of the U.S. occupation, it was reported that civil servants with relatively high salaries began purchasing dogs as well as exotic animals as pets at the Ghazel animal market in Baghdad.[58] Some exotic animals were in fact legally transported to Iraq under the guise of becoming animals for zoos; however, some of these zoos were in the business of illegally selling animals to wealthy Iraqis interested in creating their own private zoos.[59] The owner of the Glkand Zoo in Erbil confessed to smuggling animals such as birds and monkeys,[60] and the zoo was eventually closed due to mounting pressure from animal rights groups.[61] It is unclear the extent to which animal trafficking for zoos occurred in Iraq. Reports and empirical assessments of animal trafficking are few in general, and are particularly difficult in war zones such as Iraq. The voices of these trafficked animals are therefore unheard, their interior lives and bodily experiences of market life and conflict unknown to the outside observer.

Montazah Al-Morour

Another zoo, the Montazah al-Morour Zoo in Mosul, also became a site of violence during the latter part of the war. Although U.S. military operations occurred in Mosul in the early phases of the war, I am aware of no reports about the zoo during this period. No account emerges until 2017, in the wake of battles with ISIS. In the middle of 2014, ISIS captured and took control of Mosul, a city in northern Iraq. In mid-October 2016, a major offensive to retake Mosul involving U.S. air strikes and Iraqi ground forces commenced. During the battles, a massive number of civilians were killed and injured. The reports about civilians caught in the crossfire of the 2016 battles are staggering; the horror for humans remains unquantifiable. The fighting also put Montazah al-Morour's animals in jeopardy.

It was reported that most of the animals in Montazah al-Morour died as a result of the nearby fighting. ISIS reportedly began operating a military base near the zoo, and its fight against Iraqi forces resulted in about forty zoo animal deaths.[62] One report noted that many animals were trapped and killed in the barrage of fighting, "while many others starved to death."[63]

"Notes, Cinders"

Reaching—ongoing and gone.
Your paws
left the ground,
unfixed to hope.
These metallic, non-native melodies
break the boundless and naive.
Passing you notes, cinders.
Holding on, holding paws.
You know and never remember.

Ultimately, it was reported that only two animals survived the violence of Mosul—a bear named Lula and a young lion named Simba. During what was described as the "most intense urban combat in history," Lula reportedly ate her two cubs due to hunger and stress.[64] The zoo was filled with decomposing animal bodies, including the body of Simba's mother. The young lion's dead mother was visible to Simba.[65] There is a photograph that shows Simba in a small enclosure littered with trash looking downward at his dead mother, separated by wired fencing. The mother is across the fencing in an exposed rectangular dirt grave a few feet away from Simba. The grave, almost too small, tilts the lioness's head against its edge. Simba looks to his mother.

"Hourglass"

What are you doing
over there?
Alone, in my roar, in a yawn,
you are me.
This hourglass breaks
when I dream.

Worried residents of Mosul eventually contacted Four Paws International, an Austrian-based animal protection organization. Four Paws sent veterinarian Amir Khalil, who began the process of assisting Lula and Simba. Khalil found a traumatized, thirsty, and starving bear in a rusty cage. He encountered a skinny young lion, incessantly pacing.[66] In an interview, Khalil mentioned how the animals in war zones like Iraq "cannot speak" but "are messengers from the darkness; they bring hope."[67]

After several attempts to move the animals out of Mosul, Khalil and Four Paws eventually relocated Lula and Simba to the New Hope Centre rehabilitation center in Amman, Jordan. The Centre is a safe reception station for abused or otherwise mistreated or traumatized animals. It is shaded and filled with fig and olive trees.[68] In a video of Lula's arrival at the Centre, we see her excitedly find and eat an apple.[69] The ultimate objective was to move Simba and Lula to Al Ma'wa Wildlife Reserve rescue sanctuary.[70]

Al Ma'wa sanctuary offers an important engagement with the violence of war, a crucial response to the harm done to animals in the context of military hostilities. The sanctuary is the result of Four Paws and Jordan's Princess Alia Foundation (PAF), with support from the Abu Dhabi Fund for Development (ADFD) and the 30 Millions d'Amis Foundation. The Reserve now includes several lions, bears, and tigers from various places around the world. For instance, Sultan and Sabreen—two lions from Gaza in 2014—now live in the Reserve. Also in the Reserve are two Asian Black Bears—Sukkar and Loz—rescued from a zoo outside of Aleppo, Syria, in 2017. In considering U.S. responsibilities, the United States could have worked closely with the sanctuary, perhaps by providing funding or other forms of assistance. Of course, these kinds of actions occur after the fact. These organizations, as crucial as they most certainly are, make the world a bit more organizable and accountable only after the ashes. They exist because the world is and will be one of ashes. They represent a calculation of hospitable love for the other, a move toward the singular and urgent demand of the animal other amidst these ashes.

What of efforts to restore zoos in war zones? Certainly, arguments can be made for U.S. government efforts to rebuild and renovate zoos in war zones, zones in which they are responsible for emptying life. Creatively investing in the rehabilitation of animals, their confines, and their surroundings is an important path forward. In Iraq, the United States inherited a political debt to care for zoo animals. Cosmopolitanism requires "an urgent response" and "a just response" in the face of violence, as Derrida suggests.[71] This urgent responsibility to restore and rebuild amidst the violence of war cannot be shrugged away. And while there are numerous problems associated with perpetuating captivity, the zoo does not preclude possibilities of a certain kind of flourishing. Still, there is always a responsibility to imagine hospitality and care beyond the threshold of the zoo. Elegies are spectral reminders of this responsibility to imagine forms of abolition and sanctuary. Caged island-worlds are part of our world. There are borders within borders between us. In elegies, the scent of gunpowder and steel bars tells us who we are and who we might become, intertwined with the other.

Conclusions

Historian Nigel Rothfels suggests that "enforced 'silence' is perhaps the defining feature of the modern zoo."[72] Writing about zoo animals also involves layers of silencing. Their entire lives, their freedom to move and live as they prefer, their ability to make decisions, have been silenced within the confines of the zoo. Perhaps some animals, if they had the choice, would prefer to be in a zoo, though we "cannot answer this with any finality," as Rafi Youatt reminds us.[73] Captured or born into captivity, zoo animals never live life fully free, never live and die on their own terms. In texts, humans rather than zoo animals narrate zoo life. In writing, the inarticulable life of a zoo animal is articulated in and on human terms. These terms guarantee that writing is always a form of silencing. The hope is to trace experience in such a way as to put pressure on these terms, to see silencing as a kind of tension within the self and world, a tension that creates a brief opening of the self and world to the other and otherness. Perhaps poetic space can, in some small way, be a space for this tension, this opening.

In writing of zoo experiences, we possess but brief fragments of a story, small shards of first- or second-hand accounts. We know little of the other's interior life. So much is muted. So much is muffled by writing and not writing. A zoo life is always shadowed, silenced and reduced to the "zoo animal." While silencing of zoo life and killed zoo animals is particularly acute, the trouble of silencing and reducing the dead is a broader problem, as noted by Derrida, who asks:

> Are we trying to put things in order, make amends, or settle our accounts, to finish unfinished business? With the other? With the others outside and inside ourselves? How many voices intersect, observe, and correct one another, argue with one another, passionately embrace or pass by one another in silence? . . . are we going to make the dead our ally ("the dead with me"), to take him by our side, or even inside ourselves, to show off some secret contract, to finish him off by exalting him, to reduce him in any case to what can still be contained by a literary or rhetorical performance.[74]

Is movement toward the lost simply putting things in order? Is poetic movement a performance that finishes off the dead? Or are these movements toward a *disordering* space where we meet with the spectral other, in all of their foreignness, alterity, and beyond-knowability? Reduction and silencing of others pattern our imagination and mark the endeavor of writing toward and listening for the other. With hesitation we write, shuffling with doubt toward the other, glossed in the silence of you. We cannot move toward the animal other outside of our human perspectives. In attempting to "be-with" an absent and inexpressible archive of zoo lives in Iraq, we are still always silencing and reducing. But we are also hoping to reorient our relations to the lost and reorganize our relations to the future.[75] There is no making amends for the lost, but we might pay attention to who they were or might have been, what their lives meant and can still mean. This paying attention is a kind of *unfinished business*; it is the debt owed to the other whose island-world we must carry. In this paying attention there is no end point. The Iraq War, in all of its (human and animal) complexities and ongoingness, is not an end point for Iraq. There were multispecies histories before it. And there are multiple Iraqi futures, always tethered to but also always unbound from the past's violence. And there are many more responsibilities and debts. Unfinished elegies, unfinished attention, unfinishable carrying.

Chapter 4

Black Sheep

ISIS and the Smoke of Qayyarah

> And in a sense, as Valéry said, language is everything, since it is the voice of no one, since it is the very voices of the things, the waves, and the forests.
>
> —Maurice Merleau-Ponty, *The Visible and the Invisible*

You became the wind in a forest, the shape of a ghost. A lost ghost, listening-lost in this lost forest. A breath-weight within us, lost within ourselves. The weight of your lost voice, it weighs without speaking. How do we hold onto loss, and how do we carry it? Derrida tells us there is a "spectral density" to death, that the specter "weighs" and "thinks."[1] The spectral weight of animal others and their thoughts has been pulling us into an apparitional space of listening and speaking. This dialogue has been an invitation to hold onto loss, to feel its weight within us. And there is a flow of the other specters pulling into us. The thoughts of forest and desert specters are arriving. On their way are destroyed desert and forest habitats and all of their inhabitants.

In war, "nature" becomes weaponized; it is converted into an instrument of death. Consider the Dibis forest in northern Iraq. In 2016, animals reportedly fled the forest, seeking to escape fires set by ISIS.[2] ISIS fighters used "the forest as a weapon."[3] In the history of war, this forest weapon was nothing new. Bronwyn Leebaw reminds us that "environmental devastation . . . has . . . been implemented as a military strategy since ancient times."[4] She notes that in our thinking of war, nature has been conceptualized as a "power to unleash, yet not control," and in regard to contemporary politics she writes how "nature has also been framed as a victim, or potential victim, of war crimes."[5] War plays out in nature, and opens onto the animals of the deserts, rivers, and forests. In this chapter, I attend to the moments of fire, toxicity, and animal anxiety in forests and deserts. In these moments, spectral birdsounds might find us. In these moments are half-hidden spectral cow conversations and spectral sheep thoughts. In these moments are voices within and constituting "nature," posing questions of beyond-human belonging, queries about spectral entanglements of lost humans, animals, plants.

The notion of nature is indefinite. Nature "flickers between things—it is both/and or neither/nor," writes Timothy Morton.[6] "Nature opens up the difference between terms, and erases those very differences, all at once. It is the trees and the wood—and the very idea of trees."[7] The logic of its draw, its name—foreign and familiar, imagined and real, imagined-real—is embedded in and beyond our sense of where and who we are. So too are specters. The specter animals lost amidst the forests haunt our sense of self and other. In spectral-poetic moments, trees, the air, the water and their lost animal inhabitants connect to us.

War consumes nature and consumes us. It seeps into the water, trees, and air. It poisons forests, bodies, and human and animal communities. Unknown bodies bear witness. Explosive landmines and improvised explosive devices (IEDs) are scattered throughout conflict terrain, destroying vegetation, disrupting land stability, reducing biodiversity, and maiming and killing animals who step on these devices.[8] Water, air, and soil might become contaminated from a vast array of warfare chemicals.[9] The damaged soil, trees, vegetation, rivers, and marshes affect human and animal life. One might imagine a swallow or raven making a desert voyage, inhaling a toxic breeze. We might also imagine-remember the many other uncountable and unknown bearers of toxicity. This chapter involves an elegiac turn to the burned landscapes, charred trees, and toxified animal life of war. Their loss is not just far away and in the past, but in us—spectrally and poetically connected.

While U.S. military activities harmed Iraq's environment, much of the ecological damage in Iraq was not the result of U.S. actions. The tactics employed by ISIS created some of the most significant harm. Forests became hideouts for ISIS combatants, who burned brush and trees to cloak themselves with smoke to hide from fighter jets. Chemical plants were burned down, unleashing toxins into the air. Oil fields were set aflame, releasing noxious smoke. This chapter focuses on these contexts and the moments within them. It considers how the United States was partially responsible for the rise of ISIS, and explores moments of ecological harm, imagining how animals experienced forest fires, oil pollution, and other toxic traces of ISIS.

ISIS and Ecological Harm

There are always unexpected outcomes of war, unforeseen turns that destabilize life. Destabilizations unfold over years, even decades. In the wake of war, groups vie for power, shaping politics, the environment, and the conditions of life in unexpected ways. ISIS was a particularly lethal outcome of the Iraq War's many destabilizing effects. It is worthwhile to state at the outset that the United States is culpably entangled in the emergence of ISIS and therefore enmeshed in the ecological havoc it wrought. Its formation resulted from U.S. decisions to wage war and lay waste to a country's institutions. Its deadliness was a consequence of the post-invasion combination of blowback, sectarianism, alienation, and resistance to U.S. military aggression. Undoubtedly, ISIS is *directly* responsible for its actions; however, we cannot slip past the causal role of the U.S. government. While many different actors and decisions created and shaped the conditions for the emergence of ISIS, Middle East expert Fawaz Gerges notes that ISIS evolved from al-Qaeda in Iraq (AQI), which was a direct result of the U.S. invasion and occupation of Iraq.[10] The first sentence of this paragraph mentioned "unforeseen turns that destabilize life." Life becoming lost; flesh, fur, and feathers becoming/turning back (in)to the earth—these are part of what constitutes what it means to "destabilize." The mesh of war, groups forming and reforming—"destabilize" seems an inadequate term to capture the known and unknown "destabilized" human and animal lives. Still, "destabilization" is a term of context, a term that both hides and exposes. Perhaps we invite the term to expose culpability.

In the aftermath of war, violence and dismantled institutions facilitated lethal sectarianism, which fostered a situation ripe for the development of organizations like al-Qaeda and ISIS.[11] Sunni and Shia sectarianism predated the Iraq War (as did Sunni and Shia cooperation and connection), but the violence and disruption of the U.S. invasion, along with the subsequent marginalization of Sunnis via the U.S. government's de-Baathification program in post-war Iraq, amplified sectarian grievances and increased the odds of AQI and ISIS becoming powerful and appealing groups.[12]

The rise of ISIS made some sense in an environment where marginalized Sunnis believed that Iraq "had been humiliated and colonized by the United States with Iran's backing."[13] However we weigh the myriad factors that shaped and strengthened ISIS, U.S. actions contributed to its growth. Reflecting on ISIS's ecological violence therefore involves thinking about or at least acknowledging how the United States helped facilitate its emergence. This causal responsibility is a source of connection and obligation. It transmits through memories of ISIS. These memories, the term "ISIS" itself, can expose culpability; they can reveal complicitous connections to America, to ourselves.

While not initially seen as a major threat, ISIS continued gaining ground in Iraq and Syria. By 2013, the group captured territories in both countries, and by 2014 controlled roughly 34,000 square miles in the region.[14] In June they surprised much of the world by capturing the northern Iraq city of Mosul, which was one of its most significant territorial victories. For the next several years, some of the heaviest fighting took place in and around Mosul. The city was declared liberated from ISIS in the summer of 2017, and the Iraqi and U.S. governments claimed victory against ISIS in Iraq later that year.

ISIS caused massive disruption and destruction of life during these three and half years, and any description falls short of accounting for the violence and loss that occurred during this period. The U.S. coalition's response to ISIS in Mosul was also devastating. For example, in March 2017, a single U.S. airstrike in a Mosul neighborhood killed up to 150 civilians.[15] The "up to," the lack of precision, the casting of life into numbers is always troubling and insufficient.

"Burned Compass"

Each of me is you.
Each friend a number.
You taught me
the swallow's blessing for a lost tree,
the song for a lost home,
a lost friend.
You gave me
a burned compass,
a pierced border.
I carry you to forget this compass.
Reeled in to each other's dust.

This relatively short period of the Iraq War also marked a dark ecological turn, with ISIS directly targeting and weaponizing nature. This targeting of and disregard for the environment has been referred to as "unprecedented and permanent" because of long-lasting damage to agricultural fields, a staggering number of cattle deaths, and the consequences of chronic respiratory problems.[16] Many of these issues stem from the use of oil as a weapon.

An oil-rich country, a characteristic of conflict in Iraq has been oil spills and fires. Both of these were prominent in the first Gulf War in the early 1990s, when the Iraqi military set fires to hundreds of wells and trenches filled with burning oil. As John Loretz observed at the time, oil spills and fires "make animals their principle living victims since, for the most part, they are unable to escape their devastated habits."[17] Recall the camels discussed at the beginning of chapter 1. In addition to harming camels, oil smoke can damage the respiratory systems of birds whose flight patterns cut through smoke plumes. The smoke can also coat plants that animals rely on for nutrition. Ingesting smoke-coated plants may cause immune system and blood disorders.[18] During the first Gulf War, the Iraqi military also intentionally spilled millions of barrels of oil from a supertanker loading terminal off the coast of Kuwait. The spill was a tactic used during Iraq's retreat from Kuwait in 1991. It had pernicious effects on animals. It was reported that the supertanker spill took the lives of an estimated 30,000 to 40,000 birds.[19] "Number is the specter" (*nombre est le spectre*) writes Derrida.[20]

Thirty thousand to forty thousand birds, along with their secret histories and biographical complexities, are gone. Within this estimate, marked by inevitable imprecision, is the earth's loss of many songs and the loss of countless feathered voyages across space and time. Derrida once referenced how he would confide with his "friends the birds of Laguna Beach."[21] Birds can be seen as friends, decision makers, and persons who have "sonic relationships" with nature and the living beings around them.[22] "Any individual bird is a single knot in an emergent lineage," writes Thom Van Dooren.[23] The earth was emptied of 30,000 to 40,000 friends, cleared of knowable and unknowable avian moments, knots of emergent lineages and sonic relationships.

Toward Qayyarah

In a noxious recycling of the past, the eruptive appearance of ISIS resulted in deadly oil fires and spills.[24] Launching attacks on oil and gas machineries, sulfur plants and oil fields, ISIS scarred the environment, injuring and killing many animals. This occurred as part of another war in Iraq, an envenomed revision of harm, much of which occurred in northern Iraq where ISIS sought to maintain its control. One of these areas was Qayyarah. *Qayyarah* is derived from the Arabic term for tar. It is an oil-rich town south of Mosul on the Tigris River. It became a violent battleground in the fight to control northern Iraq. As part of its "Northern Iraq Offensive," ISIS took command of the town in 2014 and used its oil fields and refineries to bankroll its military operations.[25] Occupying Qayyarah meant controlling the production of 8,000 barrels of oil per day.[26] It also meant access to an airbase, Qayyarah Airfield West (Q–West). Originally an Iraqi airbase under the Hussein government, Q-West was taken over by U.S. military forces in the early part of the Iraq War. In 2014 it became an ISIS airfield.

The rise and fall of ISIS in Qayyarah was devastating to both humans and animals. In the midst of battles with coalition forces when ISIS was in control of Qayyarah, the American-led coalition reported only one civilian death. Yet one investigative report suggests that forty coalition airstrikes resulted in forty-three civilian deaths, and ISIS reportedly executed eighteen civilians in Qayyarah.[27] There was also environmental devastation. During battles over the summer of 2016, ISIS opened up the town's oil pipes, leading to crude oil soaking the streets and flowing into the Tigris River.[28] ISIS fighters also set the town's oil fields on fire. Figure 4.1 shows

Figure 4.1. Qayyarah Oil Field Fires. (Jordan Castelan/DoD)

the fire and smoke of Qayyarah in the distance. The fires were reportedly set for strategic purposes as the oil smoke could provide cover for their movements. However, ISIS might have also hoped to destroy the oil fields as part of a "scorched earth" policy once their defeat seemed certain.[29] Regardless of the motive, it took almost a year to put out the flames.[30] Figure 4.2 shows a NASA satellite image of the smoke plumes.

Outside of Iraq, Qayyarah is seemingly synonymous with this smoke. Qayyarah is a toxic memory of ISIS control, coalition airstrikes, and oil fires that affected every moment of life. From a certain outside perspective, the smoke of Qayyarah *was* Qayyarah. ISIS, death, and the oil fire smoke seemed to define it. As discussed earlier, the cost of war and the life affected all too often become overly abstract.[31] Towns become interchangeable locations. So-called "collateral damage"—the injured humans and animals become uncountable data points. From a certain view, Qayyarah becomes locked into the abstract crypticity of the war event. From a certain vantage, and aside from a few reports, Qayyarah becomes an overlooked conceptual place, woven between something visible and invisible. But Qayyarah *is* the Iraq War. Its moments are what happens in war. Its moments are what happened in this war. Qayyarah is the human and animal moments of smoke in the eyes, lungs, and horizon. Though we may not directly see or know these lives, there is an "unsubstitutable singularity" of each human and animal life in Qayyarah.[32] These lives are

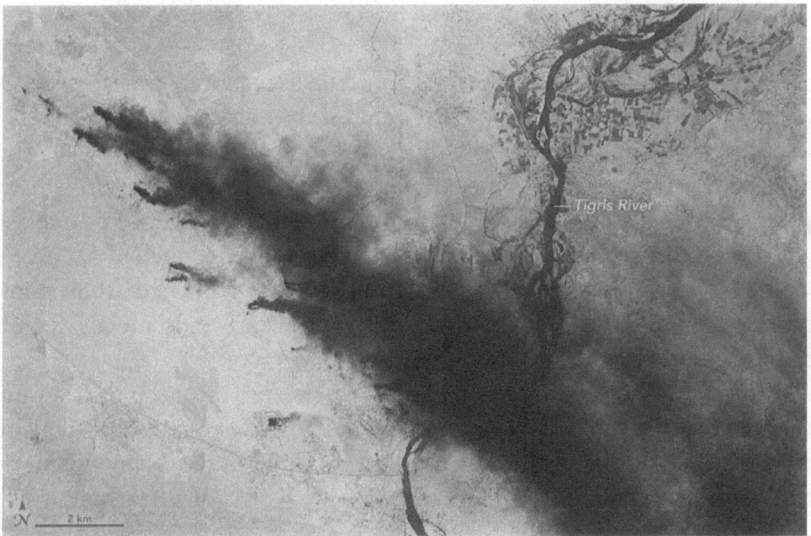

Figure 4.2. Qayyarah Oil Smoke. (Joshua Stevens/NASA)

reminders of what war is and still is. They are a reminder of who we are. The lives of Qayyarah are with and within us.

What were the effects of the oil fires of Qayyarah? The oil fields of Qayyarah produce a particularly dense type of oil containing sulfur and other metals, making its smoke acutely poisonous for residents.[33] The area surrounding the oil fields includes about 100,000 people and many animals.[34] The smoke, filled with toxic substances, coated local wildlife and infused the air and water sources. One report noted that "it's not hard to find Qayyarah . . . Even with your closed eyes, you could follow the smell of sulphur right into town."[35] Sulphuric spirits, guides. *The Conflict and Environment Observatory* underscored in technical detail the toxicity of Qayyarah's fire smoke:

> The hazardous substances produced by oil fires include volatile organic compounds (VOCs) such as benzene, carbonyls such as formaldehyde, polycyclic aromatic hydrocarbons (PAHs) like benzopyrenes and naphthalene, as well as dioxins and furans. The fires also release gaseous pollutants such as sulphur dioxide, nitrogen oxides, hydrogen sulphide and carbon monoxide, together with particulate matter at sizes of concern to human health. Particulate matter can act as a vehicle for toxic materials to enter the lungs and the inhalation of high concentrations of particles over long periods can reduce the lungs' ability to clear themselves.[36]

Working with Oxfam, several journalists explored the fire's devastation.[37] The report detailed how roughly sixty homes were destroyed. It described the impossibility of fighting the fires at first because of IEDs planted in and around the fires. Children suffered from the fire smoke, spitting out black toothpaste after brushing their teeth. Children also had difficulty breathing while playing outside and scratched "at rashes on their skin. Their eyes reddened and their lungs burned from smoke that contained carbon dioxide, acidic aerosols, and toxic metals such as lead and mercury."[38]

The smoke left its mark on plants and sheep. The sheep of Qayyarah "became black, sick and starving. Soot settled on the animals' grazing land and sank into the water they drank."[39] In thinking of these animals in the fields of northern Iraq, I am reminded of the words of Ellen Meloy, who wrote of the lives of Bighorn sheep in the American southwest: "In gaits and patterns older than time, the fine-limbed, amber-eyed animals will move."[40] I am reminded by Derrida to follow their gaze, to speak with and to them. Your eyes, reflected in smoky water, tell me a story of survival. Your look, reserved, translated into a spectral weight, is a hovering barbed gesture for the future.

The figure of sheep has been prominently featured in many stories throughout history. As Derrida notes, sheep have figuratively been "many heterogeneous things," including "the constellation or the sign of the zodiac nicknamed 'the Ram.'"[41] The first astrological sign of the zodiac, Aries, is a ram—a male sheep.

Sheep have evolved and coexisted with people since ancient times. Searching for nutrients among friends, looking at the world through amber eyes, we can imagine an ancient seeing into the world with a knowledge that stretches through time. We can imagine the strength of Awassi sheep of northern Iraq, combing through fields underneath winter clouds, their narrow heads turning toward us, toward the world. Their curved horns a winding history, encoded with unknown secrets. Who are we in this gazing? What sheep thoughts might inhabit our sense of the world? What did the sheep think and feel amidst the toxic smoke?

"*Donne à voir?*" asks Derrida.[42] How are we seen by the seeing eyes of the animal? What is revealed in their point of view, in their seeing us? In the moment of being seen by an animal, our seeing and reflection on being seen brings to bear "the abyssal limit of the human," a moment where "everything can happen to me," writes Derrida.[43] What does it mean to see and be seen by these sheep—lost, spectral? To bring to bear the sheep point of view on our thinking of war, impossibly, is to remind ourselves that we are not the center of everything, that the meaning of war is beyond us and extends past our human limits. The spectral gaze calls to our memory, our imagination, and toward our imagining of the future.

We know that sheep possess the same neural mechanisms for facial recognition memory as humans. Scientists have revealed that sheep, who are often highly social, can remember the faces of about fifty other different sheep for more than two years. Like humans, they possess neural circuits that activate and intricately encode the faces of individuals. After long periods of separation, sheep can still remember the faces of those whom they knew; they call out in response to being shown sheep faces that they recognize.[44] One scientist points out that "sheep must potentially be able to think about individuals that are absent from their environment."[45]

"Recognition"

Colored by carbonyl compounds.
Can you still breathe the desert?
Its breeze, whispering smoke.
Your face and coat, now the color of closed eyes.
Do your friends still recognize you?

An hour away in Ijhala, crops and sheep were poisoned and killed. Okra, tomatoes, and watermelon were tarnished by smoke. Herds of sheep that once numbered up to fifty became around a dozen. The bodies of dead sheep and cows were scattered throughout Qayyarah.[46] Cows—moving, mapping, grazing, breathing, dying. Each cow and sheep, an island-world. There are echoes of these worlds. Lines of exile. Breaks in belongingness.

"Find Me"

Your slow movements always revealed
a quiet conversation with the earth,
a muted song with the sky.
Have I traveled too far, you asked?
Will you find me amidst the hydrocarbon clouds,
at this edge of this earth,
with no song to guide you?

Mishraq

At the same time ISIS was fighting U.S. and Iraqi forces in Qayyarah, combat also raged in Mosul, which involved some of the most deadly violence of the Iraq War. As a way "to help hold off Iraqi security forces," ISIS burned a sulfur plant in the nearby town of Mishraq on October 20, 2016.[47] The Mishraq plant has the largest sulfur deposits in the world. This fire lasted for seven days. The fire burned through these deposits and created plumes of white smoke and colorless but toxic gas. This same sulfur plant was also burned, either spontaneously or by arsonists, near the beginning of the war in 2003.

While we know little about the precise effects of sulfur fire on humans in the area, we do know that sulfur fires release hydrogen and sulfur dioxide gases. These gases can cause neuromuscular weakness, ventilatory failure, asthma, and permanent lung scarring. These effects can manifest immediately or much later.[48] The limited reporting on the Mishraq fire indicated that local residents faced respiratory problems.[49] In the 2016 fire, at least two people died and many more were hospitalized for respiratory issues.[50] Several studies, including research on U.S. soldiers who served in Iraq, provide insight into how sulfur dioxide affects humans. We can speculate that some of these effects might be similar for nonhuman animals.

After returning from Iraq, many combat veterans suffered from unexplained exercise limitations. Many "had been deployed as elite athletes and were now incapable of completing a two-mile run within regulation time."[51] Beyond health concerns, the stakes of physical limitations were high. Soldiers could be discharged or face early retirement if the Army considered them to be nondeployable. Several of these soldiers became part of a Vanderbilt University Medical Center study led by Robert Miller. Part of Miller's study involved conducting lung biopsies to determine the cause of unsolved difficulties with exercise. The results concluded that many of the soldiers suffered from constrictive bronchiolitis from exposure to sulfur fire in Iraq.[52] Constrictive bronchiolitis, also known as obliterative bronchiolitis, involves inflammation, scarring, and obstruction of lung bronchioles. This means that airways are ultimately compromised, leading to difficulty in breathing. The condition is often fatal.

Animals living in and around Mishraq were not studied for symptoms of constrictive bronchiolitis. Very few reports surfaced regarding human civilian effects, and there were no reports on how sulfur dioxide affected animal life. The toxic plumes could certainly have affected breathing for animals in the area. Reports indicated that the fires resulted in millions of dollars of damage to crops; estimates indicate that the sulfur fire killed nearly all vegetation within a fifteen-mile radius of Mishraq.[53] This in turn likely impacted animals dependent on some of this vegetation.

The Mishraq plant is also close to the Tigris River, which is central to human and animal life in Iraq. It is an important source of water for humans, plants, and animals. Countless birds, such as herons and egrets, travel to, from, and along the Tigris. The Tigris is their home. It is not a stretch to imagine sulfuric effects on animals making their way in and around the Tigris.

"Moonpaths"

Memories of moonpaths
and ancient rivers.
With these
fading songs,
where do I go?

With moonpath secrets,
we slipped into
sky systems,
sheltered in
river pasts.

Explosive Devices and Forest Fires

ISIS caused additional ecological harm by weaponizing forests, farmlands, and orchards. Setting fire to foliage was a tactic of war, as the smoke of burning trees and bushes was used as cover from air attacks. Using plant life as a weapon, ISIS rendered several forest areas uninhabitable by burning them down.[54] As mentioned at the outset of this chapter, one notable instance occurred near Dibis in the Kirkuk Province of northern Iraq. During this fire, terrified wild boar reportedly hurried out of the forest set ablaze by ISIS fighters.[55] The forest fires of Dibis resulted in the deaths of "dozens of animals, from boar to wild horses."[56]

ISIS also created minefields throughout Iraq. Cheap weapons commonly used in conflicts around the world, landmines and IEDs wreak havoc on civilian communities. They are an enduring consequence of many conflicts and wars, exploding long after conflicts have ended. I recall being in Cambodia in the early 2000s, where I met adults and children with lost limbs from mines that had been buried in the ground for decades—ghastly traces of war, a reminder of how the "time" of war can extend into futures.

Animals around the world have also been harmed by IEDs and landmines in conflict areas.[57] Many of these casualties have been bomb-sniffing dogs. For instance, Scout, a British IED detection dog, was killed when his paws triggered an IED in Afghanistan's Helmand province.[58] Dogs, of course, have a powerful sense of smell, and have been used around the world to detect mines and bombs, including in Iraq and Afghanistan.[59] Figure 4.3 shows a mine-sniffing dog in Qayyarah. Unlike strays, military dogs such as mine-detecting war dogs have gained significant attention in the media. For example, *The Atlantic* published a series of moving photos of military dogs in Afghanistan in 2014. One image shows a U.S. bomb-tracking dog named Drak being carried to a helicopter with bloodied paws and legs. Drak, along with numerous civilians, was injured by a bomb.[60] These dogs—these animals with names who have served a patriotic duty in the view of many of their country's citizens—are often celebrated and remembered. These dogs are therefore read as sacrificial soldiers; their bodies and lives seem to communicate a sense of utility for humans.

It is worth reflecting again on the many unnamed animals, those without recognizable human utility. I am reminded of Derrida's remark that "the absolute victim is a victim who cannot even protest. One cannot even identify the victim *as* victim."[61] Many victims are without voice, without names. Derrida also observes that "naming involves announcing a death to come in the surviving of a ghost."[62] Drak and Scout survive

Figure 4.3. Mine Dog in Qayyarah. (Christopher Brecht/DoD)

as recognizable ghosts; they persist as named beings to be called to and remembered. Naming signals a future death, a death that has the possibility of memory, of survival. But for the others, the unknown animals, any sorrow for and memory of them are complicated by this condition of namelessness and their lack of "utility."

Many other animals, most of them anonymous, have been wounded or killed by mines and explosive devices. Landmines used by Houthi insurgents in Yemen, for instance, killed many sheep.[63] Tigers in Cambodia and gazelles in Libya have also been exposed to landmines.[64] Another site of landmine violence is the Thailand-Myanmar border, where numerous elephants have been injured or killed from stepping on mines. Some of these elephants, like the dogs mentioned above, have names and stories. The stories of Mosha and Motala, two elephants who lost legs after stepping on mines, became known throughout the world in the wake of their successful prosthetic leg surgeries.[65] Mosha and Motala, as animals with names and a campaign to help them recover, remind us of the continued history of violence beneath the ground, of the many unnamed animals who have been harmed by mines. These animals might not all elicit the same sense of emotional concern, but if we distance ourselves from certain conceptual hierarchies of animal value, we might recognize or recover a sense of significance of or connection with not only the elephant or the dog but also the sheep. Each is a victim of human violence, each with their own perspectives and experiences. Each life a world, an inaccessible island; each life disappeared within the predatory time of war—still with us, in stillness, in spectral-poetic time.

ISIS used improvised explosives to kill and stave off their enemies, and as mechanisms of control to prevent civilians from moving. Known as their "signature weapon," ISIS used IEDs on "a quasi-industrial scale."[66] Mines Advisory Group (MAG), an NGO dedicated to removing explosive devices and assisting communities beleaguered by such explosives, has reported clearance of over 11,000 newly laid mines in Iraq and Syria since September 2015.[67] These subsurface mechanisms of death laid by ISIS have killed many civilians and make it a precarious gamble for humans and animals simply to move around.

While the placement of IEDs and mines in animal habitats has led to an uncountable number of animal deaths in Iraq, most of the reports focus on the loss of sheep. For instance, Sean Sutton of MAG noted how "sheep and goats are regularly getting blown up."[68] Sheep herders, intimately connected to their amber-eyed flocks, have also been injured. One herder mentioned how "I was looking after my sheep and some of them ran into the minefield on my land. I knew there were mines there, but I had to get my sheep back."[69] There are no estimates about animal injuries and deaths from these explosives. No one really knows. If I were one of these sheep I would be excised into this unknowable absence, faded into this blurred nothingness of war. But these sheep experiences of loss occurred. Each death happened. Each death, an event, a moment, still moving. "These deaths are each time, by the hundreds of thousands, singular deaths."[70] The singularity of sheep, the herders, the land, the place and time—a demand, discoverable (perhaps) within a moment, still pressing.

Conclusions

In February 2019, President Trump stated that ISIS was "100 percent" defeated. In contrast, Trump's former national security advisor, John Bolton—a key George W. Bush administration figure pushing for the initial war in Iraq—suggested that "the ISIS threat will remain."[71] In April 2019, ISIS leader Abu Bakr al-Baghdadi appeared in a new video for the first time in several years. In the video, he stated that "our battle today is a war of attrition to harm the enemy, and they should know that jihad will continue until doomsday."[72] While al-Baghdadi is now dead, ISIS remains with us, as do its victims, both human and animal, living and lost.

The moments of Qayyarah, known, unknown, and unknowable, matter. They arrive with tears, each containing an infinite debt. These moments find us to tell us who we were, who we are, and who we might become. Qayyarah is always much more than pain, death, and loss, and each word about it does a disservice to the Qayyarah that cannot be sensed or understood in the shape of a poem. Each moment of Qayyarah is an arrow of time, always moving, always revealing, always piercing hearts. Qayyarah, all of its others and otherness, is still with us.

Perhaps these others will find us in the elegiac space of the poem. To resolve ourselves to the spectral-poetic task of a cosmopolitan elegy is to look to be found, to find ourselves being found, across time and space. Such cosmopolitan elegies are meetings, receptions within a strange time. They involve a strange attunement to the lost still with us. They involve reaching across time, to be with you, the unknowable sheep. Qayyarah within us. You carry the past in us. A sheep, a gaze, a voice—a moment of war. What do we do with this being-seen? In silence, in absence—carried by spectral intensities for future memories? In the memory of the unknown other, our vision might become veiled by tears—an unveiling of possibilities.[73]

(In)Conclusion(s)

Spectral-Poetic Proximities

One has to realize that the ghost is there.

—Jacques Derrida, *Specters of Marx*

Jacques Derrida's last teaching lecture took place in Paris on March 26, 2003, a week after the U.S. invasion of Iraq. During this lecture he referenced "watch[ing] the war on television, in Iraq, but also closer to us."[1] *But also closer to us.* These five words, flickering and dinning into us, prompt us to consider the proximity of lives lost in war—unknowably distant but imaginably close. The Iraq War is with us—in the distance *but also closer to us*. The ghosts are here.

This book has been occupied by lively absences. It has been an attempt at a spectral cosmopolitan approach to war as a way to realize the ghosts with(in) us. This is a cosmopolitanism of spectral moments and elegies, of being-with animal ghosts and memories of the lost. Recall that attention to moments involves reflection on an animal's time of experiencing war, which involves consideration of the context and history of becoming lost to the violence of war. These moments invite thinking of the interior lives of the lost, a self-reflexive thinking that turns toward poetry, a turn that implicates the moment in spectrality. Spectral cosmopolitanism involves "spectral space" for the lost other, an elegiac space in which we reach toward a connection to loss, unleashed from the time and place of the war event. It is a way of thinking with, speaking with, and listening to the lost animal voices. To use the words of Derrida, poetry for and with animal ghosts has been an attempt, a hesitant-yet-necessary step toward grappling with "how to let them speak or how to give them back speech, even if it is in oneself, in the other, in the other in oneself."[2] If I find you in the poem, find death, the voice of loss, us—in a poetic moment, in myself—I can find a glimpse of belongingness, perhaps.

Humans and animals "can find death" and "can die before their time," writes Derrida.[3] Even apart, the human and the animal "live and die together, the one with the other, the one like the other, they coexist."[4] Perhaps to "die like a dog" is not pejorative claim but a decoding of togetherness. The animals lost to war live and die like us. They die with us, apart but together. They have an experience of dying and possess the "power" of dying. They experience mourning. As Kelly Oliver reminds us, animals such as elephants might even possess profound and more complex capabilities of mourning than humans.[5] Still, the deaths of animals, their experiences (like ours), are to some extent unknowable. Their interior experiences, vast and shaded, are held in place by inexpressibility. The interior moments of life and death are inevitably unknowable and distant but imaginatively sensed. The animals lost to war have singular experiences of death, singular moments with each other—unknowable, far away, *but also closer to us*.

"What is it to orient oneself in thinking?" asks Derrida.[6] "When one knows where to go, this very knowledge suspends the question and all indecision."[7] Poetic thinking of moments of loss is both a calculative movement toward the other and a disorienting step toward nowhere. Thinking through the wartime loss of the animal other through poetry is a kind of thinking and feeling without closure, a seafaring movement toward the other without a clear view of a shoreline. For Paul Celan, a poem is "essentially dialogue;" a poem "may be a letter in a bottle thrown out to sea with the—surely not always strong—hope that it may somehow wash up somewhere, perhaps on a shoreline of the heart."[8] Who's heart? Perhaps mine? Perhaps yours? Perhaps a lost heart, with us. Spectral-poetic thinking orients us toward disorienting loss, toward the heart of the other, uncomfortably pulling the inexpressible experiences of the lost into a kind of poetic knowledge as a way to make lost voices present. This is an unfinished endeavor that bends toward a circumvention of the real as a way toward it, toward imaginative possibilities of sensing the death of the other and their unknowable experiences.

The focus on moments, ghosts, and poetry is not simply about abstract life and death; rather, it offers a way to think about concrete losses in war, even though most of these losses are anonymous and unknown.

The experiences of the lost are buried in unknowability. Yet, while such experiences are concealed, they are not interminably closed off from us. The loss of the other might be lifted into our senses through poetic imagination, a lifting that brings about a spectral-poetic inseparability of the human and animal life/death. A spectral-poetic approach thickens and disorients the penumbral plot of the unnamed and unnameable experience of the animal other—the other who is distant but imaginably closer to us. For you, the other, with me—cosmopolitan elegies.

I am waiting to hear you, to hear myself in you—in the distance but also closer to us. Poetic imagining is a striving toward a kind of spectral-poetic proximity, a belongingness of lost street dogs, tigers, sheep, camels—a spectral menagerie cutting through time, a menagerie of real lives lost and remembered. A spectral-poetic moment is never filled with clear knowledge of the other; it is a space for reaching for the wartime of island otherness, a space for strange interiorities of the self and other—the lost other within the self. Poetry does not convey or close the *real* but rather engages it sideways in a kind of not-knowing, in an imagining of the other and our connection to the irreducibly other—distant *but also closer to us*.

"*Suis mon regard*," the specters seem to say.[9] *Follow my gaze*. Throughout this book I have tried to follow the gaze of the lost. The spectral cosmopolitanism developed here involved grappling with the lost lives of others looking at us, and thinking through how we might look back—at them and ourselves, at the other within the self. This self-reflexive and reciprocal-poetic looking does not bring us physically closer, but it does bring about possibilities for a kind of spectral living with the lost, possibilities of spectral belongingness.

In an earlier session of his final seminar, Derrida posed several provocations about closeness, distance, and distancing:

> What is proximity? The proxim*ity* of the close? The proxim*ity* of the close is not, for its part, necessarily close. Such and such a thing, such and such a country, such and such a person might be close or distant, but the essence or the meaning of the close, the close *as such*, the proximity of the close *as* close, and appearing as such, is not necessarily close. At least not in the same sense. It might be distant, even inaccessible. And conversely, the distance of the distant, being-distant can be close and un-distance itself by appearing to us as such.[10]

These provocations—part of a complicated discussion of Heidegger, Robinson Crusoe, solitude, boredom, and what it means to orient oneself—might be taken in a number of different directions.[11] Rather than attempt to do justice to the full context of these remarks, I wish to situate them in relation to poetic imagination, and to frame these remarks as cutting to the heart of the intellectual project of cosmopolitanism, which is the heart of the other. At the heart of cosmopolitanism are notions of closeness and distance, borderless responsibility, and global connection. There is a spatiotemporal aspect to these notions, but there is also an imaginative property. "Such a country, such and such a person might be close or distant," though "the proximity of the close as close, and appearing as such, is not necessarily close."[12] Iraq might be far away for those not living there and for those no longer there. Yet the losses there, the voices and hearts of those lost—out-of-the-present voices and hearts of the past—might be both distant and close. "The proximity of the close" is spectral. The lost voices are irrepressible emanations within us, from beyond us. The other's heart, distant-close.

Throughout this book I have considered how distant animal lives lost to war might connect to our own lives in terms of both responsibility and imagined closeness, of spectral-poetic closeness as responsibility. Toward this end, I explored war in terms of interspecies experiences, ghosts, animal moments, and a spectral-poetic sense of loss. Informed by the work of Jacques Derrida (and the work of many others, such as Susan Howe), the cosmopolitanism developed in this book was one of learning to live with ghosts, a cosmopolitanism of self-reflexive imagining animals lost to global political violence. This was a cosmopolitanism of spectral-poetic reaching, of elegiac articulation of being-with animal others in moments, of poetic carrying each other away and into each other. *The other within us.* This inscription of loss into our hearts is a searching for belongingness, of becoming close, to be already close, to remember how to learn from and listen to the erstwhile street dogs, giraffes, pigs, sheep, and other animals lost to political violence. Belongingness—in a place of spectral-poetic density of hearts. "The heavy heart, melancholy, is the weight of this weight, this heavy burden that one bears in one's heart."[13]

This book has been an attempt to think through the meaning of cosmopolitanism in terms of "living otherwise," and living "more justly" *with* the lost. To use the words of Derrida, one of the purposes of this approach can be stated as follows: "To live otherwise, and better. No not better, but more justly. But *with* them" (*à vivre autrement, et mieux. Non pas mieux, plus justement. Mais avec eux)*.[14] To that end, the chapters of this book have sketched out a cosmopolitanism that reaches for a spectral-poetic connection to the other, the far-away other, spatially and temporally distant and also distant-through-death, a distance within us. This spectral-poetic approach is one path toward possibilities of how "being-distant can be close," possibilities of "undistancing" ourselves, to use the language of Derrida.[15] This kind of cosmopolitanism pursues a poetic and disorienting footing, a slippery footing in a lost world, a world of loss. It pursues a connection to the animal worlds we are losing and have already lost. It is a kind of imaginative looking for evidence of the lost. It is an attending to the real facts of war coupled with and reanimated through poetic detours from the real, which swerve and anchor us back into ghostly, interspecies connections. It is an attempt to listen to the voices of the unknown animal lost to war, the voices of lives unremembered. To listen is to imagine. To listen to the lost is to re-imagine what cosmopolitanism is. To listen is to recreate what cosmopolitanism can be, who we might become. To listen is to undistance the other, impossibly; it is to find the lost animal other finding us, in a kind of spectral-poetic proximity. To find proximity within the distance, perhaps. Perhaps this proximity opens within the distance of an elegy.

In his final lecture, Derrida raises the notion "of a community of the world" that humans and animals "share and co-habit."[16] He writes of this community as "a place of common habitat, whether one calls it the earth (including sky and sea) or else the world as world of life-death. The common world is the world in which one-lives-one-dies, whether one be a beast or a human sovereign, a world in which both suffer, suffer death, even a thousand deaths."[17] But even in this common world we are islands. Cosmopolitanism traditionally conceptualizes the world in terms of a "global community," a world that "exists" on the terms of the human and in terms of a global community of humankind in pursuit of justice for the living. Thinking through (and with) Derrida, the spectral cosmopolitanism of this book is one of loss, of connection with the no-longer present island others, an interspecies cosmopolitanism in pursuit of a posthumanist global community of ghosts. In this sense it is a pursuit of a "community" that can never be, or perhaps a "community" open to ghostly disruption, unsettling the very sense of a "community"—a "community" open to resistance to that or those not "totally interiorized in the memory of a present community."[18] A community that is "as much threat as promise."[19] The notion of a "global community" is always and already more than human, beyond the human, irreducible to the human; it is always and already a "community" of the living and dead, always impossible. Within this "global community" are islands torn apart from war and wars that will keep tearing us apart. Spectral cosmopolitanism involves a poetic thinking toward this tearing apart; it is a space to imagine the other's singular sparks of life and loss in this impossible "global community" of human and animal specters.

Spectral cosmopolitanism is about an openness to loss—distant *but also closer to us*. It is about an elegiac space for the distant voices of the nonhuman other, inside of us. This kind of cosmopolitanism is a poetic opening to the nameless animal other, seeking out vulnerable connections to loss, and seeing inwardly the distant other. It is a reaching toward belongingness with distant animal others lost to war. It is about spectral-poetic connection(s). It is a holding of moments—real, imagined, imagined-real. It is a remembering of the unknown, a transmutation of loss, a memory of faded voices—distant *but also closer to us*. It offers a catalyst toward the seemingly inconsequential animal voices and imagined moments of war. A cosmopolitanism adjusted to listen for the animal voices of war in the distance is ultimately a cosmopolitanism of ghostly rhythms—a feedback loop of memory, imagination, description, connection, poetry, and experiences of war. These experiences are in the distance *but also closer to us*.

This book has been about spectral-poetic proximities, about possibilities (and impossibilities) of elegiac space for the other, of listening to (and failing to hear) the other in us, in our hearts. To use Derrida's terms, the cosmopolitanism proposed here has been "invaded by" the dead; it has been occupied by lost stray dogs, lost zoo animals, the lost sheep of northern Iraq.[20] This cosmopolitanism has been geared toward "keeping [the dead] in one's heart."[21] The wandering dog and the nomadic sheep, the lost tiger and the missing sparrow—belonging in our hearts. The spectral other, distant but close, belonging close to our hearts, in our hearts, becoming our hearts. The spectral animal—"responding in us, from the bottom of our hearts, in us but before us, in us right before us—in calling us, in recalling to us."[22]

"Isn't the heart memory? Isn't it thinking *of* memory? Thinking *as* memory?"[23]

Attempts to bring distant loss closer to us, within us, to listen to the spectral animal from within us, to poetically respond to the loss, are always a failure. They are never fully resolvable. These are tasks for which we are not capable of enough imagination, tasks marked by consistent failure to fully imagine, or marked by over-imagining. The book is inevitably closing.

This chapter, this conclusion, this closure closing in on us reminds us of all that cannot be closed, of the betrayals of closure-seeking throughout this book. It has inevitably betrayed the mystery and unknowability of the animal other and shied away from the otherness of me in the animal (and the otherness of the animal in me) in order to translate and articulate the untranslatable and inarticulable meanings of moments of war. Even while we seek to secure closure, the spectral other necessarily "resists the closure of our interiorizing memory."[24] Our thinking and mourning of the specter fails when it succeeds, to use the aporetic logic of Derrida. "Faithful interiorization . . . makes the other a *part* of us" while "aborted interiorization" of the spectral other involves "a respect for the other as other" yet problematically leaves the other "over there" and "outside of us."[25] Yet there is still a responsibility to remember, a responsibility to think and speak with the lost, in all of their alterity, unassimilable to our thinking. "*One must* reckon with them," writes Derrida.[26] To reckon, to look, to be looked at—reckoning is knowing we will never quite reach each other. Reckoning is inhering ourselves in the impossible hope of ghostly proximity.

This spectral-poetic path to the lost, this trail toward preserving unknown and unknowable moments, is but one path toward a cosmopolitanism of interspecies ghost-moments and the "spectral density" of political life.[27] This path involves elegiac spaces for spectral others, who might catch us off guard and surprise us. To inhabit these spaces furnishes possibilities of what it means to think about war, about the meaning of its moments, about what it means to dream of belongingness, of the not-yet, the never-known, the otherwise. It is to embrace the unknowable through a poetic logic of remembering, listening to, and speaking to and with the lost. In this way, cosmopolitanism becomes a space for a kind of dreaming, a dream-poetic being-with and being-for the spectral other. The dance of a street dog, the cadence of a bark, the gaze of a sheep, the dream of a giraffe—collections of animal moments in Iraq—are with us, still. We might listen to the lost and sense a spectral resonance that registers the weight of lost moments of war. To listen is to dream of a kind of spectral dialogue; it is to learn to speak to others beyond the present and to reckon with the poetic voice of the animal other from the past and future. This "with us," this poetic listening, becomes a futural task, a "being-with" those still to arrive. To take from Derrida one last time, to listen is to begin "dreaming of knowing how to speak to you . . . poetically, as a poet. I certainly won't be capable of the poem I dream of."[28]

Notes

Introduction

1. Jacques Derrida, *The Animal that Therefore I Am*, trans. David Wills (New York: Fordham University Press, 2008), 20. Moreover, "naming," writes Derrida, "involves announcing a death to come in the surviving of a ghost, the longevity of a name that survives whoever carries that name." Derrida, *The Animal*, 20.

2. For an insightful discussion of Derrida, war memory, and the commemoration of unidentified or unknown soldiers, see Michael Naas, *Derrida From Now On* (New York: Fordham University Press, 2008). For a discussion of memorializing animal deaths in relation to a critique of patriotism's logic of death, see Steven Johnston, "Animals in War: Commemoration, Patriotism, Death," *Political Research Quarterly* 65, no. 2 (2012): 359–371.

3. At the time of this writing, the Iraq War has resulted in the loss of 4,489 U.S. soldiers, an estimated 185,000 Iraqi civilians, and an unknown number of animals. There are many different estimates about the number of civilian losses. See Philip Bump, "15 Years After the Iraq War Began, the Death Toll is Still Murky," *Washington Post*, March 20, 2018, www.washingtonpost.com/news/politics/wp/2018/03/20/15-years-after-it-began-the-death-toll-from-the-iraq-war-is-still-murky. See also www.iraqbodycount.org. Regarding lost soldiers, there were of course also others from many different places, such as Italy and the UK, who were also lost to violence. And there were also journalists, contractors, humanitarian workers, and many others killed in Iraq.

4. Jacques Derrida, *Athens, Still Remains: The Photographs of Jean-François Bonhomme*, trans. Pascale-Anne Brault and Michael Naas (New York: Fordham University Press, 2010), 1.

5. Gillian Brock, *Global Justice: A Cosmopolitan Account* (New York: Oxford University Press, 2009), 9.

6. Gerard Delanty, *The Cosmopolitan Imagination: The Renewal of Critical Social Theory* (New York: Cambridge University Press, 2009), 3.

7. Jacques Derrida, *Echographies of Television: Filmed Interviews*, with Bernard Stiegler, trans. Jennifer Bajorek (Cambridge: Polity Press, 2002), 132.

8. Derrida, *Echographies*, 123–124.

9. Toward this end, I attempt to take a "posthumanist" path in the sense of Cary Wolfe's use of this term. That is, a path in which I do not simply end up reestablishing the "familiar figure of the human at the center of the universe of experience." Cary Wolfe, *What is Posthumanism?* (Minneapolis: University of Minnesota Press, 2010), 166.

10. Jacques Derrida, *The Work of Mourning* (Chicago: University of Chicago Press, 2003), 52.

11. For a discussion of aesthetic and sensory approaches, see, for example, Christine Sylvester, "The Forum: Emotion and the Feminist IR Researcher," *International Studies Review* 13, no. 4 (2011): 687–708; Roland Bleiker, "In Search of Thinking Space: Reflections on the Aesthetic Turn in International Political Theory," *Millennium: Journal of International Studies* 45, no. 2 (2017): 258–264; Linda Åhäll, "Feeling Everyday IR: Embodied, Affective, Militarising Movement as Choreography of War," *Cooperation and Conflict* 54, no. 2 (2019): 149–166. For a discussion of International Relations and animals, see, for example, Rafi Youatt, "Interspecies Relations, International Relations: Rethinking Anthropocentric Politics," *Millennium: Journal of International Studies* 43, no. 1 (2014): 207–223; Rafi Youatt, *Interspecies Politics: Nature, Borders, States* (Ann Arbor: University of Michigan Press, 2020); Erika Cudworth and Stephen Hobden, *Posthuman International Relations: Complexity, Ecologism and Global Politics* (New York: Zed Books, 2013); Erika Cudworth and Stephen Hobden, *The Emancipatory Project of Posthumanism* (New York: Routledge, 2018).

12. Christine Sylvester, "War, Sense, and Security," in ed. Laura Sjoberg *Gender and International Security: Feminist Perspectives* (New York: Routledge, 2010), 25–26.

13. This pursuit therefore shares some similarities with Mica Nava's "visceral cosmopolitanism." Nava writes, for example, that her approach is a "focus on the unconscious, non-intellectual, emotional, inclusive features of cosmopolitanism, on feelings of attraction for and identification with otherness—on intimate and visceral cosmopolitanism." Mica Nava, *Visceral Cosmopolitanism: Gender, Culture and the Normalisation of Difference* (Oxford: Berg, 2007), 8.

14. For discussions of interspecies politics in times of war, see Erika Cudworth and Stephen Hobden, "The Posthuman Way of War," *Security Dialogue* 46, no. 6 (2015): 513–529; Matthew Leep, "Stray Dogs, Post-Humanism and Cosmopolitan Belongingness: Interspecies Hospitality in Times of War," *Millennium: Journal of International Studies* 47, no. 1 (2018): 45–66; Benjamin Meiches, "Non-Human Humanitarians," *Review of International Studies* 45, no. 1 (2019): 1–19.

15. For a discussion of other work on cosmopolitanism and animals, see, for example, Oscar Horta, "Expanding Global Justice: The Case for the International

Protection of Animals," *Global Policy* 4, no. 4 (2013): 371–380; Eduardo Mendieta, "Interspecies Cosmopolitanism: Towards a Discourse Ethics Grounding of Animal Rights," *Philosophy Today* 54 Supplement (2010): 208–216; Gary Steiner, "Toward a Non-Anthropocentric Cosmopolitanism," in *Anthropocentrism: Humans, Animals, Environments*, ed. Rob Boddice (Leiden: Brill, 2011): 81–114; Cynthia Willett, *Interspecies Ethics* (New York: Columbia University Press, 2014); Yamini Narayanan and Sumanth Bindumadhav, " 'Posthuman Cosmopolitanism' for the Anthropocene in India: Urbanism and Human-Snake Relations in the Kali Yuga," *Geoforum* 106 (2019): 402–410.

16. Robert Lowell, *Day by Day* (New York: Farrar, Straus and Giroux, 1977), 127.

17. While I attend to the poetic voice of animals in this way, it is important to also note a broader view of what poetry "is" by considering animals as makers of poetry. See, for example, Aaron M. Moe, *Zoopoetics: Animals and the Making of Poetry* (Lanham, MD: Lexington Books, 2014).

18. Catherine Malabou and Jacques Derrida, *Counterpath: Travelling with Jacques Derrida*, trans. David Wills (Stanford, CA: Stanford University Press, 2004), 24.

19. Susan Howe, "The Difficulties Interview," *The Difficulties* 3, no. 2 (1989): 24.

20. For other uses of the term "spectral cosmopolitanism," see Pramod K. Nayar, " 'Novel Globalism,' The Transnational Exotic and Spectral Cosmopolitanism: David Mitchell's Fiction," *The Grove* 18 (2011): 69–86; and Holly Jackson, "Perverse International: Modern War and World Imaginings in Pablo de la Torriente Brau's Aventuras del Soldado Desconocido Cubano," *Symposium: A Quarterly Journal in Modern Literatures* 71, no. 3 (2017): 128–139.

21. Susan Howe, "An Open Field: Susan Howe in Conversation," *The Academy of American Poets*, September 7, 2011, www.poets.org/poetsorg/text/open-field-susan-howe-conversation

22. See, for example, Jacques Derrida, *On the Name*, trans. David Wood, John P. Leavey, Jr, and Ian McLeod (Stanford, CA: Stanford University Press, 1995).

23. Jacques Derrida, *Memoires for Paul de Man*, revised edition, trans. Cecile Lindsay et al. (New York: Columbia University Press, 1989), 37.

24. Anthony Burke, "Security Cosmopolitanism," *Critical Studies on Security* 1, no. 1 (2013): 17.

25. Derrida, *Specters of Marx: The State of Debt, the Work of Mourning and the New International*, trans. Peggy Kamuf (New York: Routledge, 1994), 202.

26. Derrida, *Specters of Marx*, 202.

27. For another discussion of spectrality in relation to nonhumans, see Timothy Morton, *Humankind: Solidarity with Non-Human People* (London: Verso Books, 2017). Morton claims that he is doing something very different from Derrida. For instance, he believes that Derrida only understands spectrality in terms

of Marx and communism, and Morton argues that he "amplifies" spectrality by going beyond this in some way. Morton also surprisingly claims that Derrida's view on ontology means that "big business" ultimately defines "the ontological."

28. For a non-cosmopolitan discussion of global responsibility, see David Miller, *National Responsibility and Global Justice* (New York: Oxford University Press, 2007).

29. See Martha C. Nussbaum, "Kant and Stoic Cosmopolitanism," *Journal of Political Philosophy* 5, no. 1 (1997): 1–25. See also Kwame Anthony Appiah, "Global Citizenship," *Fordham Law Review* 75, no. 5 (2007): 2375–2391.

30. Jacques Derrida, *The Politics of Friendship*, trans. George Collins (New York: Verso), 196.

31. Louisa Shea, *The Cynic Enlightenment: Diogenes in the Salon* (Baltimore: Johns Hopkins University Press, 2010). For an interesting discussion of Diogenes, Cynics, animals, and cosmopolitanism, see Andrea Haslanger, "The Cynic as Cosmopolitan Animal," in *Cosmopolitan Animals*, ed. Kaori Nagai et al. (New York: Palgrave Macmillan, 2015), 29–42.

32. Donald Trump, "Remarks by President Trump on the Death of ISIS Leader Abu Bakr al-Baghdadi," *The White House*, October 27, 2019, www.whitehouse.gov/briefings-statements/remarks-president-trump-death-isis-leader-abu-bakr-al-baghdadi

33. Derrida, *The Animal*, 28.

34. Derrida, *The Animal*, 62.

35. Jacques Derrida, *Adieu to Emmanuel Levinas*, trans. Pascale-Anne Brault and Michael Naas (Stanford, CA: Stanford University Press, 1999), 92.

36. Derrida, *The Beast and the Sovereign Volume II*, trans. Geoff Bennington (Chicago: University of Chicago Press, 2011), 9. When Derrida makes this remark he notes that it might be taken in a "thousand directions," one of which would be to interpret this remark in terms of a line in a Paul Celan poem, "the world is gone, I must carry you."

37. Jacques Derrida, *Spectres de Marx: L'etat de la dette, le travail du deuil et la nouvelle Internationale* (Paris: Galilée, 1993), 15 (*Specters of Marx*, xviii). When I cite the French text (*Spectres de Marx*) along with the English translation (*Specters of Marx*), I also cite the English translation in parentheses.

38. Derrida, *The Animal*, 28. Here I am also reminded of how Derrida is quite clear that humans are often the cause of animal suffering and vulnerability. Indeed, as Kelly Oliver's eloquently notes, "Derrida does not let us forget that sovereign power is erected on death, particularly the death of animals, both the animals with whom we share the planet and the animals within us." Kelly Oliver, *Technologies of Life and Death: From Cloning to Capital Punishment* (New York: Fordham University Press, 2013), 139. There are many works on Derrida, animals, and suffering. See, for example, Matthew Calarco, *Zoographies: The Question of the Animal from Heidegger to Derrida* (New York: Columbia University Press,

2008); Kelly Oliver, *Animal Lessons: How They Teach us to be Human* (New York: Columbia University Press, 2009); Michael Naas, *The End of the World and Other Teachable Moments: Jacques Derrida's Final Seminar* (New York: Fordham University Press, 2014).

39. Derrida, *The Animal*, 28.

40. It is this compassion in relation to vulnerability that Cary Wolfe sees as a crucial component to Derrida's sense of ethics, and that I would suggest is key to thinking about animals within the cosmopolitan tradition. Not all agree. Cynthia Willett's approach to possibilities of an interspecies cosmopolitanism involves a critique of Derrida, arguing that "thousands of years of metaphysical prejudice—a chasm between the human and nonhuman arose only after the Neolithic revolution—recurs in Derrida's deconstructive project." Willett, *Interspecies Ethics*, 11–12. Derrida, however, problematizes this very chasm. Willett also refers to Derrida as a "a post-Holocaust thinker," who "turns away from entertaining any hypothesis of agency in nature or among animals" and "suspends any moral judgment of who owes what to whom, while thoroughly disengaging conceptions of agency (rational or otherwise) as a prerequisite for ethical status." Willett, *Interspecies Ethics*, 41–42. Cary Wolfe, with whom I agree, argues instead that Derrida's "project points us toward the necessity of an ethics based not on ability, activity, agency, and empowerment but on a compassion that is rooted in our vulnerability and passivity . . . The ethical force of our relation to . . . nonhuman others is precisely that it foregrounds the necessity of thinking ethics outside a model of reciprocity between 'moral agents.'" Wolfe, *What Is Posthumanism?*, 141.

41. Derrida, *The Beast and the Sovereign Volume II*, 243–244.

42. Jacques Derrida, "*Che cos'è la poesia?*" in *Points . . . Interviews, 1974–1994* (Stanford, CA: Stanford University Press, 1995), 297.

43. Wolfe, *What Is Posthumanism?*

44. Derrida, *The Animal*, 11.

45. Derrida, *The Animal*, 11.

46. See, for example Martha Nussbaum, *Frontiers of Justice: Disability, Nationality, Species Membership* (Cambridge: Belknap, 2006) and Cécile Fabre, *Cosmopolitan War* (New York: Oxford University Press, 2012).

47. Derrida, *Specters of Marx*, 81–82.

48. Jacques Derrida, *Adieu*, 111–112.

49. Jacques Derrida, *Archive Fever: A Freudian Impression*, trans. Eric Prenowtiz (Chicago: University of Chicago Press, 1996), 76. For a discussion of Derrida and how "justice cannot be rendered to the living alone," see Matthias Fritsch, *The Promise Of Memory: History and Politics in Marx, Benjamin, and Derrida* (Albany, NY: SUNY Press, 2005), 82.

50. Seyla Benhabib, "Defending a Cosmopolitanism Without illusions: Reply to my Critics," *Critical Review of International Social and Political Philosophy* 17, no. 6 (2014): 697–715; Jonathan Gilmore, "Protecting the Other: Considering

the Process and Practice of Cosmopolitanism," *European Journal of International Relations* 20, no. 3 (2014): 694–719. Of course "different modalities of violence," writes Derrida, are always at stake in "an always possible perversion of *the* law of hospitality" at the heart of cosmopolitanism. Jacques Derrida, *On Cosmopolitanism and Forgiveness*, trans. Mark Dooley and Michael Hughes (New York: Routledge Press, 2001), 17.

51. Fabre, *Cosmopolitan War*, 287.

52. Another cosmopolitan approach to war comes from Darrel Moellendorf. He argues that military force might be justified if it advances justice of the state's governance structure of the justice of its global effects of the state's policies. From Moellendorf's cosmopolitan view, questions about sovereignty and borders should not necessarily be relevant in considering whether wars are just or unjust. In one of his examples, Moellendorf claims that the United States was not justified in waging war against Iraq after Saddam Hussein attacked Kuwait. He claims that while "statist" accounts of just war might see the U.S. war as just, he suggests that his cosmopolitan account uncovers an unjust war because the Kuwaiti government was unjust and thus aiding its government would not advance justice. See Darrel Moellendorf, *Cosmopolitan Justice* (Boulder, CO: Westview Press, 2002). Simon Caney also proposes a cosmopolitan perspective on just war based on Amartya Sen's conceptualization of rights. According to Caney, Sen's "goal rights system" provides a foundation for a unified, cosmopolitan account of both *jus ad bellum* (the justness of waging war) and *jus in bello* (the justness of military conduct during war). For Caney, whether a war is just and whether the conduct of military force is just depends upon whether the country using force protects people's individual rights, including members and nonmembers alike. See Simon Caney, *Justice Beyond Borders: A Global Political Theory* (New York: Oxford University Press, 2005).

53. Fabre *Cosmopolitan War*, 287.

54. Fabre *Cosmopolitan War*, 287.

55. Robin May Schott, "Just War and the Problem of Evil," *Hypatia* 23, no. 2 (2008): 122–140.

56. Tobias Menely, "Zoöphilpsychosis: Why Animals Are What's Wrong with Sentimentality," *symplokē* 15, no. 1/2 (2007): 246.

57. Menely, "Zoöphilpsychosis," 249.

58. Howe, "The Difficulties Interview," 25.

59. Derrida, *The Animal*, 32.

60. In "turning" to Derrida, I am also "citing" and "taking" from him. While I hope to be faithful in interpreting his texts, I take certain digressions while "appropriating" much of his work as a way to open up certain ways of thinking in cosmopolitan thought and International Relations.

61. And this is an impossible debt. As Derrida succinctly reminds us, "I cannot settle my debt." Derrida, *Echographies*, 122.

62. See Chris Pearson, " 'Four-Legged Poilus:' French Army Dogs, Emotional Practices and the Creation of Militarized Human-Dog Bonds, 1871–1918," *Journal of Social History* 52, no. 3 (2019): 731–760; Rebecca Frankel, *War Dogs: Tales of Canine Heroism, History, and Love* (New York: St. Martin's Press, 2014); Meiches, "Non-Human Humanitarians."

63. For an exception, see Ryan Hediger's insightful discussion of the concept of "biopower" in relation to the U.S. military's abandonment of military dogs in Vietnam. Ryan Hediger, "Dogs of War: The Biopolitics of Loving and Leaving the US Canine Forces in Vietnam," *Animal Studies Journal* 2, no. 1 (2013): 55–73. Hediger's work discusses how German shepherds and Labradors transitioned from important U.S. military dogs to "expendable equipment" (56).

64. Alison Howell and Andrew W. Neal, "Human Interest and Humane Governance in Iraq: Humanitarian War and the Baghdad Zoo," *Journal of Intervention and Statebuilding* 6, no. 2 (2012): 213–232.

Chapter One

1. Sebastião Salgado, "Exposures: When the Oil Fields Burned," *New York Times*, August 2016, https://www.nytimes.com/interactive/2016/04/08/sunday-review/exposures-kuwait-salgado.html

2. Robert Lowell, *Day by Day* (New York: Farrar, Straus and Giroux, 1977), 127.

3. John Berger, "Why Look at Animals," in *About Looking* (New York: Vintage Books, 1992), 6.

4. Carl Sandburg, "Buffalo Dusk," *Poetry Foundation*, 1970, www.poetryfoundation.org/poems/53232/buffalo-dusk

5. Derrida, *Spectres de Marx*, 15 (*Specters of Marx*, xvii–xviii).

6. For another discussion of global politics as ghostly politics, see Jessica Auchter, *The Politics of Haunting and Memory in International Relations* (New York: Routledge, 2014). I also think of this objective as "not a concrete reconfiguration of human–animal relationships . . . but a different vision of politics that relies on uncertainty and contingency," as Claire Rasmussen so elegantly states. Claire E. Rasmussen, *The Autonomous Animal: Self-Governance and the Modern Subject* (Minneapolis: University of Minnesota Press, 2011), 132.

7. Derrida, *Specters of Marx*, 126.

8. Derrida, *Specters of Marx*, 125.

9. Derrida, *Spectres de Marx*, 165 (*Specters of Marx*, 125).

10. Derrida, *Specters of Marx*, xviii.

11. Martin Hägglund, *Radical Atheism: Derrida and the Time of Life* (Stanford, CA: Stanford University Press, 2008), 82. For a wider discussion of specters and

spectrality, see Kas Saghafi, *Apparitions—Of Derrida's Other* (New York: Fordham University Press, 2010).

12. Derrida, *Spectres de Marx*, 15 (*Specters of Marx*, xviii).

13. Nussbaum, *Frontiers of Justice*, 355. See also Rasmussen's insightful critique of Nussbaum (and other) somewhat similar approaches to animals and animal rights that "do not challenge the background assumptions about the rights-bearing subject but rather simply assume that animals have been misidentified and therefore can be recategorized under the umbrella of the rights-bearing subject. They repeat the conceit that our categories, like 'human,' 'animal,' or 'rights,' are clear, and that we may alter them simply by arriving at the proper definitions of these terms." Rasmussen, *The Autonomous Animal*, 121.

14. For a wide array of different perspectives on telling animal stories and speaking with and for animals, see Margo DeMello, ed., *Speaking for Animals: Animal Autobiographical Writing* (New York: Routledge, 2013).

15. Derrida, *Specters of Marx*, xviii. For a discussion of justice, rights, and law in Derrida's thinking, see, for example, Theodore W. Jennings, *Reading Derrida/Thinking Paul: On Justice* (Stanford, CA: Stanford University Press, 2006). See also Matthew Leep, "Cosmopolitanism in a Carnivorous World," *Politics and Animals* 3 (2017): 16–30.

16. Derrida, *Specters of Marx*, xviii.

17. Gerard Delanty, *The Cosmopolitan Imagination: The Renewal of Critical Social Theory* (New York: Cambridge University Press, 2009), 3.

18. Walt Whitman, "Sleep-Chasings," in *Leaves of Grass, 1860: The 150th Anniversary Facsimile Edition* (Iowa City: University of Iowa Press, 2009), 429.

19. Derrida, *Specters of Marx*, 6–7. For an insightful discussion of spectrality and the gaze, see Saghafi, *Apparitions—Of Derrida's Other*. For an illuminating discussion of the looking eyes of dead animals, see Oliver, *Technologies of Life and Death*.

20. Bruce Robbins and Paulo Lemos Horta, "Introduction," in *Cosmopolitans*, ed. Bruce Robbins and Paulo Lemos Horta (New York: New York University Press, 2017), 16.

21. Robbins and Horta, "Introduction," 10.

22. Nussbaum, *Frontiers of Justice*, 354.

23. Delanty, *The Cosmopolitan Imagination*, 22.

24. Susan Howe, "Sorting Facts," in *The Quarry* (New York: New Directions, 2015), 112.

25. Noah Webster, *American Dictionary of the English Language*, 1828, http://webstersdictionary1828.com. Susan Howe often made use of Webster's 1828 dictionary, inspiring me to look to it frequently. For Howe, it helped her make sense of the expressions of writers such as Henry David Thoreau and Emily Dickinson. See Susan Howe, *The Birth-mark: Unsettling the Wilderness in American Literary*

History (Middletown: Wesleyan University Press, 1993). The 1828 definitions also provide another way of thinking about these words today.

26. Delanty, *The Cosmopolitan Imagination*.
27. Delanty, *The Cosmopolitan Imagination*, 14, 53.
28. Derrida, *Specters of Marx*, 126.
29. Derrida, *Specters of Marx*, 245.
30. Derrida, *The Beast and the Sovereign Volume II*, 169.
31. Derrida, S*pectres de Marx*, 17 (*Specters of Marx*, xix).

32. See, for example, the insightful work of Lauren B. Wilcox, *Bodies of Violence: Theorizing Embodied Subjects in International Relations* (New York: Oxford University Press, 2015). For an interesting discussion of posthuman bodies, see Alice Cree and Nick Caddick, "Unconquerable Heroes: Invictus, Redemption, and the Cultural Politics of Narrative," *Journal of War & Culture Studies* (2019): 1–21, doi:10.1080/17526272.2019.1615707. For a discussion of dead bodies in relation to notions of security, see Jessica Auchter, "Paying Attention to Dead Bodies: The Future of Security Studies?" *Journal of Global Security Studies* 1, no. 1 (2016): 36–50. Stefanie Fishel suggests that we might reimagine bodies in terms of their connections to other (human and nonhuman) bodies, and she also argues for rethinking bodies in terms of microrelationships within bodies. See Stefanie R. Fishel, *The Microbial State: Global Thriving and the Body Politic* (Minneapolis: University of Minnesota Press, 2017).

33. Jacques Derrida, "A Certain Impossible Possibility of Saying the Event," *Critical Inquiry* 33, no. 2 (2007): 460.

34. Derrida, "A Certain Impossible Possibility," 460. For a discussion of Derrida's use of the term *singularity* in relation to representation and cosmopolitanism, see Matthew C. Watson, "Derrida, Stengers, Latour, and Subalternist Cosmopolitics," *Theory, Culture & Society* 31, no. 1 (2014): 75–98.

35. This focus on moments also shares similarities with what Ty Solomon and Brent Steele introduce as "micro-moves" or "micropolitical perspectives" in global politics. Ty Solomon and Brent J. Steele, "Micro-Moves in International Relations Theory," *European Journal of International Relations* 23, no. 2 (2017): 267–291.

36. Derrida, *Specters of Marx*, xviii.

37. Here I am reminded of Christine Sylvester's claim that "IR is historically disinterested in probing the vast expanse of war's ordinary. It has not usually shown much interest in the fate of everyday people at all, for the reason that they are not seen as the true stake-holders in international relations." Animals are also persons with "ordinary" experiences of war. If war and global violence are "personal, experiential, and complex," as Sylvester writes, an important ambition is thinking with the personal and experiential (animal) moments of war. See Christine Sylvester, "Experiencing War: A Challenge for International Relations," *Cambridge Review of International Affairs* 26, no. 4 (2013): 671.

38. The term "collateral damage" is certainly problematic. Uwe Steinhoff favors the expression "concomitant slaughter and mutilation of innocents" or "concomitant slaughter," because the term "collateral damage" obscures the suffering of innocent lives. See Uwe Steinhoff, "Debate: Jeff McMahan on the Moral Inequality of Combatants," *Journal of Political Philosophy* 16, no. 2 (2008): 220–226.

39. Derrida, *The Beast and the Sovereign Volume II*, 58.

40. Derrida, *The Beast and the Sovereign Volume II*, 9.

41. Derrida, *Specters of Marx*, 174.

42. Derrida, *The Animal*, 7. Others understand Derrida to mean animal thinking is poetic, and poetry emerges when we have thoughts like animals. See Peter Dayan, "The Time for Poetry," *Oxford Literary Review* 31, no. 1 (2009): 1–14. See also Ruth Parkin-Gounelas, "Poetry, Automaticity and the Animal Body: Jacques Derrida with Emily Dickinson," *Textual Practice* 32, no. 5 (2018): 841–858.

43. Derrida, *The Animal*, 7.

44. I wish to call attention to an insightful fragment in Timothy Clark's discussion of Derrida and the question of poetry. Poetry, he notes, "works at the limits of the sayable, not in the sense of the sublime (the representation of the infinite, etc.) but as saying something unsubstitutably singular . . . It produces the possibility, simultaneously, of both a surplus of meaning or of mere obscurity and nonsense." Timothy Clark, *The Poetics of Singularity: The Counter-Culturalist Turn in Heidegger, Derrida, Blanchot and the Later Gadamer* (Edinburgh: Edinburgh University Press, 2005), 141. This passage highlights an interesting difference from Bleiker's important work on the relationship between poetry, politics, the sublime, and the subliminal. See Bleiker, *Aesthetics and World Politics*.

45. Jacques Derrida, "Passages—From Traumatism to Promise," in *Points*, 373.

46. James Henle, "Is (some) Mathematics Poetry?" *Journal of Humanistic Mathematics* 1, no. 1 (2011): 94–100.

47. Derrida, "*Che cos'è la poesia?*" in *Points*, 299.

48. Derrida, "*Che cos'è la poesia?*" in *Points*, 295.

49. Derrida, "*Che cos'è la poesia?*" in *Points*, 299.

50. Derrida, "*Che cos'è la poesia?*" in *Points*, 295.

51. Derrida, "*Che cos'è la poesia?*" in *Points*, 297.

52. Derrida, *Echographies*, 122.

53. Derrida, *Echographies*, 123–124.

54. Derrida, *Echographies*, 123–124.

55. For a discussion of Derrida's ideas on poetry, including poetry in relation to animals, see Nicholas Royle, "Poetry, Animality, Derrida," in *A Companion to Derrida*, ed. Zeynep Direk and Leonard Lawlor (Oxford: Wiley Blackwell, 2014), 524–536.

56. Bleiker, *Aesthetics and World Politics*, 4.

57. John Felstiner, *Can Poetry Save the Earth? A Field Guide to Nature Poems* (New Haven, CT: Yale University Press, 2009), 13–14.

58. Felstiner, *Can Poetry Save the Earth?*, 15.

59. Felstiner, *Can Poetry Save the Earth?*, 357.

60. But to insist on a poetic move is to claim a kind of closure, which defeats the very notion of such a move. Poetry is always open to opening itself to something else, something beyond or beside.

61. Meghana Nayak and Eric Selbin, *Decentering International Relations* (New York: Zed Books, 2013), 86, 88–89.

62. Roland Bleiker, *Aesthetics and World Politics*, 141.

63. Jacques Derrida *On Touching—Jean-Luc Nancy*, trans. Christine Irizarry (Stanford, CA: Stanford University Press, 2005), 290.

64. See, for example, Anthony Burke, "Poetry Outside Security," *Alternatives* 25, no. 3 (2000): 307–321; Anna M. Agathangelou, "Making Anew an Arab Regional Order? On Poetry, Sex, and Revolution," *Globalizations* 8, no. 5 (2011): 581–594; Nevzat Soguk, "Splinters of Hegemony: Ontopoetical Visions in International Relations," *Alternatives* 31, no. 4 (2006): 377–404; Roland Bleiker, *Aesthetics and World Politics*; Roland Bleiker, "'Give it the Shade': Paul Celan and the Politics of Apolitical Poetry," *Political Studies* 47, no. 4 (1999): 661–676; Roland Bleiker, "Learning from Art: A Reply to Holden's 'World Literature and World Politics,'" *Global Society* 17, no. 4 (2003): 415–428. For a discussion of reliance on literature in international relations, see Paul Sheeran, *Literature and International Relations: Stories in the Art of Diplomacy* (New York: Routledge, 2016). For an important assessment of understanding war experiences, including moments of joy, through reading novels, see Julia Welland, "Joy and War: Reading Pleasure in Wartime Experiences," *Review of International Studies* 44, no. 3 (2018): 438–455. For a discussion of literature, war, IR, and cruelty, see Cerwyn Moore, "On Cruelty: Literature, Aesthetics and Global Politics," *Global Society* 24, no. 3 (2010): 311–329.

65. While images and art are also part of this turn, Roland Bleiker claims that "we ultimately need to make sense of our visual experiences, and we can do so only through language." Bleiker, *Aesthetics and World Politics*, 86. However, there might certainly be other ways of "making sense" outside of language. For example, "making sense" can emerge both cognitively and bodily, however we might define these terms (and their inseparableness, such as the ways in which cognition is embodied and the body is cognitized). Moreover, we might also think of "language" itself in its many different forms, including nonlinguistic forms. I am also thinking of Walter Benjamin's expansive sense of language, which emerges in terms of expression, both human and nonhuman, linguistic and nonlinguistic. See Walter Benjamin, "On Language as Such and on the Language of Man," in *Walter Benjamin: Selected Writings Volume 1, 1913–1926*, ed. Marcus Bullock and Michael W. Jennings (Cambridge, MA: Harvard University Press, 2003).

66. Prem Kumar Rajaram, "Disruptive Writing and a Critique of Territoriality," *Review of International Studies* 30, no. 2 (2004): 201–229.

67. As Bleiker mentions, this is not necessarily "for lack of trying," as "even prose comments on poetics and world politics" have often been rejected by the discipline. Bleiker "Learning from Art," 425.

68. Roxanne Doty, "Writing from the Edge," in *The Ashgate Research Companion to Modern Theory, Modern Power, World Politics: Critical Investigations*, ed. Scott G. Nelson and Nevzat Soguk (New York: Routledge, 2016), 152. For an example of creative writing in political science, see Timothy Pachirat, *Among Wolves: Ethnography and the Immersive Study of Power* (New York: Routledge, 2017). I thank Sarah Wiebe, with whom I discussed my completed book draft at the April, 2019, WPSA meeting, for pointing me to *Among Wolves*.

69. Roxanne Lynn Doty, "Maladies of Our Souls: Identity and Voice in the Writing of Academic International Relations," *Cambridge Review of International Affairs* 17, no. 2 (2004): 390. Importantly, Doty has begun experimenting with creative writing about global politics.

70. Catherine Malabou and Jacques Derrida, *Counterpath: Traveling with Jacques Derrida*, trans. David Wills (Stanford, CA: Stanford University Press, 2004), 266.

71. Doty, "Maladies of Our Souls," 381.

72. Jacques Derrida, *The Gift of Death*, 2nd edition, trans. David Wills (Chicago: University of Chicago Press, 2008), 68.

73. Jacques Derrida, *Paper Machine*, trans. Rachel Bowlby (Stanford, CA: Stanford University Press, 2005), 168.

74. Derrida, *The Animal*, 105.

75. Derrida, *The Animal*, 59.

76. Derrida, *The Animal*, 135.

77. Derrida, *The Animal*, 89.

78. Doty, "Writing from the Edge," 150.

79. Derrida, *The Beast and the Sovereign Volume II*, 115.

80. Derrida, *The Beast and the Sovereign Volume II*, 194.

81. Derrida, *The Beast and the Sovereign Volume II*, 194–195.

82. Derrida, *The Beast and the Sovereign Volume II*, 196–197.

83. Jacques Derrida and Elisabeth Roudinesco, *For What Tomorrow . . . A Dialogue*, trans. Jeff Fort (Stanford, CA: Stanford University Press, 2004), 66.

84. Derrida, *The Beast and the Sovereign Volume II*, 306–307.

85. Derrida, *Adieu*, 92.

86. Derrida, *The Beast and the Sovereign Volume II*, 197.

87. Derrida, *The Beast and the Sovereign Volume II*, 198.

88. Derrida, *The Beast and the Sovereign Volume II*, 198.

89. Rafi Youatt, *Counting Species: Biodiversity in Global Environmental Politics* (Minneapolis: University of Minnesota Press, 2015).

90. Francesco Mazzini et al., "Wolf Howling Is Mediated by Relationship Quality Rather Than Underlying Emotional Stress," *Current Biology* 23, no. 17 (2013): 1678–1679.

91. Arik Kershenbaum et al., "Disentangling Canid Howls Across Multiple Species and Subspecies: Structure in a Complex Communication Channel," *Behavioural Processes* 124 (2016): 149–157.

92. Vicente Palacios, Enrique Font, and Rafael Márquez, "Iberian Wolf Howls: Acoustic Structure, Individual Variation, and a Comparison with North American Populations," *Journal of Mammalogy* 88, no. 3 (2007): 606–613.

93. Youatt, "Interspecies Relations," 212.

94. Youatt, "Interspecies Relations," 220.

95. Other human worlds are also *unworldly* islands. Derrida notes that no "two human beings, you and I for example, inhabit the same world, that the world is one and the same thing for both of us." Furthermore, he claims that human worlds are so different to the point of the "monstrosity of the unrecognizable . . . the non-resembling or resemblable, the non-assimilable, the untransferable, the incomparable, the absolutely unshareable . . . the abyssal unshareable—I mean separated, like one island from another by an abyss beyond which no shore [rive] is even promised." Derrida, *The Beast and the Sovereign Volume II*, 266.

96. John Simons, *Animal Rights and the Politics of Literary Representation* (New York: Palgrave, 2002), 139.

97. Simons, *Animal Rights*, 139.

98. Derrida, *The Animal*, 37.

99. Charles Goodrich, "Entries into the Forest," in *Forest Under Story: Creative Inquiry in an Old-Growth Forest*, ed. Nathaniel Brodie, Charles Goodrich, and Frederick J. Swanson (Seattle: University of Washington Press, 2016), 6.

100. Garrett Wallace Brown, "Bringing the State back into Cosmopolitanism: The Idea of Responsible Cosmopolitan States," *Political Studies Review* 9, no. 1 (2011): 53–66. Andrew Dobson, "Thick Cosmopolitanism," *Political Studies* 54, no. 1 (2006): 165–184.

101. Dobson, "Thick Cosmopolitanism." For astute discussions about cosmopolitan motivation, responsibilities, and solidarities, see Eilís Ward, "Human Suffering and the Quest for Cosmopolitan Solidarity: A Buddhist Perspective," *Journal of International Political Theory* 9, no. 2 (2013): 136–154.

102. Dobson, "Thick Cosmopolitanism," 171.

103. Derrida, *The Gift of Death*, 68.

104. Derrida, *The Gift of Death*, 69.

105. Derrida, *The Gift of Death*, 69.

106. Of course, as Derrida reminds us "it is always me who says 'we'; it is always an 'I' who utters 'we' . . . The one signs for the other." It is "I," "a sole person who has the gall to say" and to speak of this "we." Jacques Derrida, *Resistances of Psychoanalysis*, trans. Pascale-Anne Brault and Michael Naas (Stanford, CA: Stanford University Press, 1998), 43.

107. Derrida, *Adieu*, 23.

108. Brandon Wolfe-Hunnicutt, "Embracing Regime Change in Iraq: American Foreign Policy and the 1963 Coup d'etat in Baghdad," *Diplomatic History* 39, no. 1 (2015): 98–125.

109. Alise Alousi, "What Every Driver Must Know," in *We Are Iraqis: Aesthetics and Politics in a Time of War*, ed. Nadje Al-Ali and Deborah Al-Najjar

(Syracuse, NY: Syracuse University Press, 2013), 1–3. Dunya Mikhail, "The War Works Hard," in *The War Works Hard*, trans. Elizabeth Winslow (New York: New Directions, 2005), 6–7.

110. I am thinking of the recent murals on Sadoun Street. Alissa J. Rubin, "In Iraq, Where Beauty Was Long Suppressed, Art Flowers Amid Protests," *New York Times*, February 3, 2020, www.nytimes.com/2020/02/03/world/middleeast/iraq-protests-art.html?searchResultPosition=15

111. See, for example, Dunya Mikhail, ed., *Fifteen Iraqi Poets* (New York: New Directions, 2013).

112. Soheil Najm, "Interview with Soheil Najm," *Silk Routes*, https://iwp.uiowa.edu/silkroutes/interview-soheil-najm. In addition to a cosmopolitan perspective, we should also be reminded of nationalistic poetics and poetry. See Juliana Spahr, "Contemporary US Poetry and its Nationalisms," *Contemporary Literature* 52, no. 4 (2011): 684–715.

113. Malabou and Derrida, *Counterpath*, 240.

114. Derrida, *The Beast and the Sovereign Volume II*, 169. This comment is in relation to a line in a Paul Celan poem: "The world is gone, I have to carry you." Paul Celan, *Breathturn*, trans. Pierre Joris (Los Angeles: Sun & Moon Press, 1995), 232–233.

115. Sarah Manguso, *Ongoingness: The End of a Diary* (Minneapolis: Graywolf Press, 2015), 43.

116. For a discussion of poetic bearing witness, see Jacques Derrida, *Sovereignties in Question: The Poetics of Paul Celan* (New York: Fordham University Press, 2005).

117. Gillian Brock, *Global Justice: A Cosmopolitan Account* (New York: Cambridge University Press, 2009), 315.

118. Derrida, *Specters of Marx*, xviii.

119. Judith Butler, *Frames of War: When is Life Grievable?* (New York: Verso, 2009), 36.

120. Butler, *Frames of War*, 34.

121. Butler, *Frames of War*, 36.

122. I sense Butler coming close to this perspective on responsibility when she offers observations on the voice of Guantanamo detainees in terms of their poetry, writing that these poems "express a sense of solidarity" and tell us "of interconnected lives that carry on each others' words, suffer each others' tears." Butler, *Frames of War*, 62.

123. Derrida, *The Work of Mourning*, 44.

124. Here I am thinking of Derrida's discussion of responsibility in "Passages—From Traumatism to Promise," in *Points*.

125. Pierre Joris is writing about Paul Celan's poetics. Paul Celan, *Selections*, ed. Pierre Joris (Berkeley: University of California Press), 6.

126. Derrida, *Archive Fever*, 76.

127. Derrida, *Archive Fever*, 77.

Chapter Two

1. Trump, "On the Death of ISIS Leader Abu Bakr al-Baghdadi."

2. Donald Trump and Mike Pence, "Remarks by President Trump and Vice President Pence Recognizing Special Operations Military Working Dog from 1st SFOD-D," *The White House*, November 25, 2019, www.whitehouse.gov/briefings-statements/remarks-president-trump-vice-president-pence-recognizing-special-operations-military-working-dog-1st-sfod-d

3. Donna Haraway, *The Haraway Reader*, 330.

4. Adam Weinstein, "Iraq's Slumdog Massacre: One Million Dogs Face Death," *Mother Jones*, June 2010, www.motherjones.com/politics/2010/06/iraq-kbr-one-million-dogs-death

5. Csaba Molnár et al., "Dogs Discriminate Between Barks: The Effect of Context and Identity of the Caller," *Behavioural Processes* 82, no. 2 (2009): 198.

6. Matthew E. Gompper, "One Billion Dogs? What Does That Mean?" *Oxford University Press*, March 24, 2014, https://blog.oup.com/2014/03/one-billion-dogs-wildlife-conservation

7. Christine Dell'Amore, "Stray Dogs in Sochi: What Happens to the World's Free-Roaming Canines?" *National Geographic*, February 8, 2014, news.nationalgeographic.com/news/2014/02/140206-stray-dogs-russia-sochi-olympics-killing-animals-world. *600 Million Dogs*. Available at https://600milliondogs.org

8. Luigi Boitani, "Forward," in Matthew Gompper (ed.), *Free-Ranging Dogs and Wildlife Conservation* (New York: Oxford University Press, 2014), v.

9. Matthew Gompper, "The Dog-Human-Wildlife Interface: Assessing the Scope of the Problem," in Matthew Gompper (ed.) *Free-Ranging Dogs and Wildlife Conservation* (New York: Oxford University Press, 2014), 28.

10. Gompper, "The Dog-Human-Wildlife Interface," 42.

11. Noah Webster, *American Dictionary of the English Language*, 1828, http://webstersdictionary1828.com/Dictionary/wanderer

12. Haraway, *The Haraway Reader*, 330. The rest of this quote is "although not necessarily around the word 'domestication.'" Domestication often signals power and desire to change animals to fit human needs. But it is often devoid of the cultural complexities of so-called domestication within Upper Paleolithic societies, the different paths through which it emerges, how it might work both ways, and perhaps how "domestication" is still happening.

13. Boitani, "Forward," v.

14. Haraway, *The Haraway Reader*, 331.

15. Dell'Amore, "Stray Dogs in Sochi."

16. Adam Mikolsi, *Dog Behavior, Evolution, and Cognition* (New York: Oxford University Press, 2009), 173.

17. Rafi Youatt, "Sovereignty and the Wolves of Isle Royale," in *Political Theory and the Animal/Human Relationship*, ed. Judith Grant and Vincent G. Jungkunz (Albany, NY: SUNY Press, 2016), 124.

18. Haraway, *The Haraway Reader*, 331.

19. Sam Dagher, "In Hard-Bitten Baghdad, Tough Tactics on Strays," *New York Times*, March 14, 2009, www.nytimes.com/2009/03/15/world/middleeast/15strays.html

20. For a recent discussion of variation and trends regarding dogs within Muslim societies, see Jenny Berglund, "Princely Companion or Object of Offense? The Dog's Ambiguous Status in Islam," *Society and Animals* 22, no. 6 (2014): 545–559.

21. Peter Schwartzstein, "Iraq's Unlikely Love Affair with Cuddly Canines," *Newsweek*, 18 April 2017, www.newsweek.com/dogs-iraq-security-585522

22. For an excellent analysis of the multiple meanings of the dog of the Sūrat al-Kahf and the interpretation of the name Qiṭmīr, see George Archer, "The Hellhound of the Qur'an: A Dog at the Gate of the Underworld," *Journal of Qur'anic Studies* 18, no. 3 (2016): 1–33.

23. Mohammed Hanif, "Of Dogs, Faith and Imams," *New York Times*, July 26, 2015, SR6.

24. Bushra Juhi, "58,000 Dogs Killed in Baghdad in Campaign to Curb Attacks by Strays," *Washington Post*, July 11, 2010, www.washingtonpost.com/wp-dyn/content/article/2010/07/10/AR2010071002235.html

25. Arwa Damon, "Stray Dogs being Killed in Baghdad," *CNN*, 12 February 2009, www.cnn.com/2009/WORLD/meast/02/12/baghdad.dogs

26. Damon, "Stray Dogs."

27. Damon, "Stray Dogs."

28. Weinstein, "Iraq's Slumdog Massacre."

29. Aseel Kami, "In Security, Baghdad Tackles 1 Million Stray Dogs," *Reuters*, June 10, 2010, www.reuters.com/article/idINIndia-49201920100610

30. Weinstein, "Iraq's Slumdog Massacre."

31. Reuters, June 10, 2010, https://pictures.reuters.com/archive/IRAQ-DOGS-GM1E66A1MP101.html

32. Bushra Juhi, "Baghdad Kills 58,000 Stray Dogs in 3-Month Span," *San Diego Tribune*, July 10, 2010, www.sandiegouniontribune.com/sdut-baghdad-kills-58000-stray-dogs-in-3-month-span-2010jul10-story.html

33. Bushra Juhi, "Baghdad Kills 58,000 Stray Dogs."

34. Dagher, "In Hard-Bitten Baghdad, Tough Tactics on Strays."

35. Kareem, "Shooting Stray Dogs in Iraq."

36. We need to be reminded of Claire Rasmussen's point about how treatment of animals can problematically be seen or used as "a marker of civilization" and "a sign of moral development." Claire Rasmussen, "Domesticating Bodies: Race, Species, Sex, and Citizenship," in *Political Theory and the Animal/Human Relationship*, ed. Judith Grant and Vincent G. Jungkunz (Albany, NY: SUNY Press, 2016), 90.

37. Alina Lilova, *Insight Hound*, insighthound.wordpress.com

38. Army Staff Sgt. Curt Cashour, "Vector Control Keeps Tabs on Pests" *United States Army Central Defense Video Imagery Distribution System*, June 16, 2007, www.dvidshub.net/news/10851/vector-control-keeps-tabs-pests

39. Weinstein, "Iraq's Slumdog Massacre."

40. "The 'Cat Lady of Baghdad' Battles On, Saving Strays of Iraq," *NBC News*, April 29, 2008, www.nbcnews.com/id/24373120/ns/world_news-mideast_n_africa/t/cat-lady-baghdadsaves-strays/#.Wc0ttEyZORs

41. United States Central Command General Order Number 1B, 13 March 2006, http://img.slate.com/media/42/061101_Exp_GO-1B.pdf

42. Jay Kopelman, *From Baghdad to America: Life after War for a Marine and His Rescued Dog* (New York: Skyhorse Publishing, 2010), viii.

43. Derrida, *Of Hospitality*, 27.

44. Jacques Derrida, *On Cosmopolitanism and Forgiveness*, trans. Mark Dooley and Michael Hughes (New York: Routledge Press, 2001), 15.

45. Consider "Ratchet," a dog that a soldier met in Iraq and later brought back to the United States. Deborah Haynes, "Stray Dog Gets His Ticket to US as Senators Rally Round and Army Relents," *The Times*, October 17, 2008. Available at: lexisnexis.com

46. Derrida, *Sovereignties in Question*, 140.

47. Jacques Derrida, *Béliers, le Dialogue Interrompu: Entre Deux Infinis, le Poéme* (Paris: Galilée, 2003), 23.

48. See, for example, Harris Bechtol's argument that "each person contributes to the meaningful whole of the one world. In this way, each of us opens the one world as a world. So when the other dies, the death of her worlds marks, on account of their relation to the one world, a death of the world." Harris B. Bechtol, "Event, Death, and Poetry: The Death of the Other in Derrida's 'Rams,'" *Philosophy Today* 62, no. 1 (2018): 258.

49. Kelly Oliver, "The Poetic Axis of Ethics," *Derrida Today* 7, no. 2 (2014): 127. For other interpretations, see Kas Saghafi, "The World After the End of the World," *Oxford Literary Review* 39, no. 2 (2017) 265–276.

50. Derrida, *Echographies*, 123.

51. Miho Nagasawa et al., "Oxytocin-Gaze Positive Loop and the Coevolution of Human–Dog Bonds," *Science* 348, no. 6232 (2015): 334.

52. Jacques Derrida, "'Force of Law,'" in *Acts of Religion* (New York: Routledge, 2002), 250.

53. Chloé Taylor, "Hard, Dry Eyes and Eyes That Weep: Vision and Ethics in Levinas and Derrida," *Postmodern Culture* 16, no. 2 (2006).

54. Jill Robbins, "Visage, Figure: Reading Levinas's Totality and Onfinity," *Yale French Studies* 79 (1991): 138.

55. Jacques Derrida, "Violence and Metaphysics," in *Writing and Difference*, trans. Alan Bass (Chicago: University of Chicago Press, 1978).

56. Larry Diamond, "Lessons from Iraq," *Journal of Democracy* 16, no. 1 (2005): 10.

57. Thomas Ricks, *Fiasco: The American Military Adventure in Iraq* (New York: Penguin, 2006), 3.

58. Michael Luo, "Even Picking Up Trash Is a High Risk in Baghdad," *New York Times*, October 13, 2006, A8.

59. The notion of the United States as "capable and culpable" comes from Alise Coen, "Capable and Culpable? The United States, RtoP, and Refugee Responsibility-Sharing," *Ethics and International Affairs* 31, no. 1 (2017): 71–92.

60. Neta Crawford, "U.S. Budgetary Costs of Wars through 2016," *Watson Institute*, September 2016, http://watson.brown.edu/costsofwar/files/cow/imce/papers/2016/Costs%20of%20War%20through%202016%20FINAL%20final%20v2.pdf

61. Such efforts would of course undoubtedly necessitate Iraqi decision makers' coordination and agreement.

62. United Nations, "Restoration of Veterinary Services in Iraq," November 2009, 4, www.fao.org/fileadmin/user_upload/oed/docs/OSROIRQ406UDG_2009_ER.pdf.

63. United Nations, "Restoration of Veterinary Services in Iraq," 11.

64. American Veterinary Medical Foundation, www.avma.org/News/JAVMANews/Pages/061015k.aspx

65. Daniel L. Horton et al., "Rabies in Iraq: Trends in Human Cases 2001–2010 and Characterisation of Animal Rabies Strains from Baghdad," *PLoS Neglected Tropical Diseases* 7, no. 2 (2013): e2075.

66. Horton et al., "Rabies in Iraq," e2075.

67. Horton et al., "Rabies in Iraq," e2075.

68. Jakob Zinsstag et al., "Transmission Dynamics and Economics of Rabies Control in Dogs and Humans in an African City," *Proceedings of the National Academy of Sciences* 106, no. 5 (2009): 14996–15001, www.ncbi.nlm.nih.gov/pmc/articles/PMC2728111

69. U. Kayali et al., "Cost-Description of a Pilot Parenteral Vaccination Campaign against Rabies in Dogs in N'Djaména, Chad," *Tropical Medicine and International Health* 11, no. 7 (2006): 1058–1065.

70. Nowzad, "Our Mission," www.nowzad.com/home/our-mission

71. Rachel Nuwer, "Syria's Cat Calamity: War is Hell for Pets, Too," *Newsweek*, December 16, 2015, www.newsweek.com/2015/12/25/abandoned-house-cats-aleppo-405528.html

72. Much of the funding for rabies projects in parts of Africa come from private donations, such as the Bill and Melinda Gates Foundation. See Erik Stokstad, "Inside the Global Campaign to Get Rid of Rabies," *Science*, January 19, 2017, www.sciencemag.org/news/2017/01/inside-global-campaign-get-rid-rabies

73. Nuwer, "Syria's Cat Calamity."

74. For an example of drone delivery of rabies vaccinations, see Stokstad, "Inside the Global Campaign to Get Rid of Rabies."

75. Derrida, *Paper Machine*, 67.

76. Michael Walzer, *Just and Unjust wars: A Moral Argument with Historical Illustrations*, 4th edition (New York: Basic Books, 2006), 4.

77. Emmanuel Levinas, *Difficult Freedom: Essays on Judaism*, trans. Sean Hand (Baltimore: Johns Hopkins University Press, 1990), 153.

78. Levinas, *Difficult Freedom*, 153.

79. Derrida, *The Animal*, 117.

80. Jacques Derrida, *Of Hospitality: Anne Dufourmantelle Invites Jacques Derrida to Respond*, trans. Rachel Bowlby (Stanford, CA: Stanford University Press, 2000), 47.

81. Derrida, *The Gift of Death*, 68.

82. Derrida, *The Gift of Death*, 70.

83. Derrida, *Paper Machine*, 91.

Chapter Three

1. Abigail Levin, "Zoo Animals as Specimens, Zoo Animals as Friends: The Life and Death of Marius the Giraffe," *Environmental Philosophy* 12, no. 1 (2015): 21–44.

2. Susan Howe, *The Quarry* (New York: New Directions, 2015), 198.

3. Venn Couze, "The Collection," *Theory, Culture & Society* 23, no. 2–3 (2006): 35–40.

4. Mary Quirk, "Zoo Tigers Succumb to Avian Influenza," *The Lancet Infectious Diseases* 4, no. 12 (2004): 716.

5. Alex Halberstadt, "Zoo Animals and Their Discontents," *New York Times*, July 3, 2014, www.nytimes.com/2014/07/06/magazine/zoo-animals-and-their-discontents.html

6. Rainer Maria Rilke, "The Panther: In Jardin des Plantes, Paris," in *Selected Poems*, trans. Stanley Appelbaum (Mineola: Dover Publications, 2011), 83.

7. John M. Kinder, "Zoo Animals and Modern War: Captive Casualties, Patriotic Citizens, and Good Soldiers" in Ryan Hediger, *Animals and War: Studies of Europe and North America* (Boston: Brill, 2013), 47. For an overview of zoos in Japan during World War II, see Mayumi Itoh, *Japanese Wartime Zoo Policy: The Silent Victims of World War II* (New York: Palgrave Macmillan, 2010).

8. Kelly Milner Halls and Major William Sumner, *Saving the Baghdad Zoo* (New York: Greenwillow Books/Harper Collins, 2010), 19–20.

9. Eric Schmitt and Thom Shanker, "Water and Electricity in Baghdad Are Still Below Prewar Levels, Officials Say," *New York Times*, July 8, 2003, www.nytimes.com/2003/07/08/world/after-war-services-water-electricity-baghdad-are-still-below-prewar-levels.html

10. Lawrence Anthony and Graham Spence, *Babylon's Ark: The Incredible Wartime Rescue of the Baghdad Zoo* (New York: Thomas Dunne Books, 2007), 121.

11. Anthony and Spence, *Babylon's Ark*, 26–27.

12. Pamela Constable, "The Cats of War," *Washington Post*, July 21, 2003, www.washingtonpost.com/archive/politics/2003/07/21/the-cats-of-war/d3a9de55-7da4-4e41-9a2c-e71f542cc2ec/?utm_term=.a81c3334d416

13. Jim Garamone, "Baghdad Zoo Recovering From War, Looting," *Department of Defense*, May 12, 2003, http://archive.defense.gov/news/newsarticle.aspx?id=28993

14. Howell and Neal, "Human Interest and Humane Governance in Iraq," 222.

15. Anthony and Spence, *Babylon's Ark*, 65.

16. Douglas Martin, "Lawrence Anthony, Baghdad Zoo Savior, Dies at 61," *New York Times*, March 11, 2012, www.nytimes.com/2012/03/12/world/africa/lawrence-anthony-baghdad-zoo-savior-dies-at-61.html

17. Attention to the choices made within this structure—including those of the looters—helps us understand the unspooling of violence. However, such attention might neglect the experiential effects of these structures and choices. To take seriously the experiences of animals requires more than explanatory frameworks used to decipher choices or to locate and place blame for harm. It also requires moving beyond attention to the complexity of human motives for actions related to these animal experiences. Attending to the moments of animal experiences demands imagining their experiences along the edges of war.

18. Hillary Mayell, "Struggling to Save Baghdad Zoo Animals," *National Geographic*, June 4, 2003.

19. Michael Holmes "Baghdad Zoo: A Different Battle," *CNN*, April 17, 2003, www.cnn.com/2003/WORLD/meast/04/16/sprj.nilaw.baghdad.zoo

20. Jason G. Goldman, "Let them Eat Carcass," *Slate*, January 3, 2014, https://slate.com/technology/2014/01/food-for-pets-and-zoo-animals-they-should-eat-real-meat.html

21. Brad Haynes, "Zoos in a Pickle over Horse Meat," *The Seattle Times*, August 14, 2007, www.seattletimes.com/seattle-news/zoos-in-a-pickle-over-horse-meat

22. Rafi Youatt, "Power, Pain, and the Interspecies Politics of Foie Gras," *Political Research Quarterly* 65, no. 2 (2012): 346–358.

23. Derrida, *Specters of Marx*, 14 (*Spectres de Max*, xvii).

24. Donald M. Broom, Hilana Sena, and Kiera L. Moynihan, "Pigs Learn What a Mirror Image Represents and use it to Obtain Information," *Animal Behaviour* 78, no. 5 (2009): 1037–1041.

25. Kristina Horback, "Nosing Around: Play in Pigs," *Animal Behavior and Cognition* 1, no. 2 (2014): 186–196.

26. Adriana S. Souza et al., "A Novel Method for Testing Social Recognition in Young Pigs and the Modulating Effects of Relocation," *Applied Animal Behaviour Science* 99, no. 1–2 (2006): 77–87.

27. David Judd and James Rocha, "Autonomous Pigs," *Ethics and the Environment* 22, no. 1 (2017): 1–18.

28. Illmann Gudrun et al., "Acoustical Mother-Offspring Recognition in Pigs (Sus scrofa domestica)," *Behaviour* 139, no. 4 (2002): 487–505.

29. David G.M. Wood-Gush and Klaus Vestergaard, "Exploratory Behavior and the Welfare of Intensively Kept Animals," *Journal of Agricultural Ethics* 2, no. 2 (1989): 161–169.

30. Merete Studnitz, Margit Bak Jensen, and Lene Juul Pedersen, "Why Do Pigs Root and in What Will They Root?: A Review on the Exploratory Behaviour of Pigs in Relation to Environmental Enrichment," *Applied Animal Behaviour Science* 107, no. 3–4 (2007): 183–197.

31. "Meet the Animals: Pigs," *Farm Sanctuary*, www.farmsanctuary.org/learn/the-someone-project/pigs

32. Derrida, "Passages—From Traumatism to Promise," in *Points*, 373.

33. "The Struggle for Iraq; U.S. Soldier Kills Tiger in Baghdad Zoo," *New York Times*, September 21, 2003, www.nytimes.com/2003/09/21/world/the-struggle-for-iraq-us-soldier-kills-tiger-in-baghdad-zoo.html. According to *Newsweek*, the Army conducted investigations but did not find evidence that the soldier was intoxicated, although the soldier admitted to drinking. See Rod Nordland, "Tigers Return to Baghdad," *Newsweek*, August 7, 2008, www.newsweek.com/tigers-return-baghdad-88163. This tiger's experience was the subject of the 2009 play "Bengal Tiger at the Baghdad Zoo" by playwright Rajiv Joseph.

34. Anthony and Spence, *Babylon's Ark*, 27.

35. Garamone, "Baghdad Zoo Recovering from War, Looting."

36. Holmes "Baghdad Zoo."

37. "US troops kill Baghdad Lions" *BBC*, April 22, 2003, http://news.bbc.co.uk/2/hi/middle_east/2966107.stm

38. Natalia Borrego and Brian Dowling, "Lions (Panthera Leo) Solve, Learn, and Remember a Novel Resource Acquisition Problem," *Animal Cognition* 19, no. 5 (2016): 1019.

39. One of the more interesting stories about the deaths of these lions is a fictional account. *Pride of Baghdad* envisions the inner lives of these lions, exploring their violent vulnerabilities and struggles before and after explosions at the zoo led to their freedom and eventual death. Brian K. Vaughan and Niko Henrichon, *Pride of Baghdad* (New York: DC Comics, 2006).

40. George B. Schaller, *The Serengeti Lion: A Study of Predator-Prey Relations* (Chicago: University of Chicago Press, 2009), 85.

41. Holmes "Baghdad Zoo."

42. Anthony and Spence, *Babylon's Ark*, 67.

43. Lawrence Rothfield, *The Rape of Mesopotamia: Behind the Looting of the Iraq Museum* (Chicago: University of Chicago Press, 2009), 35.

44. Scott Conroy, "Rescuing The Baghdad Zoo," *CBS*, April 29, 2007, www.cbsnews.com/news/rescuing-the-baghdad-zoo/2

45. Rothfield, *The Rape of Mesopotamia*, 36.

46. Garamone, "Baghdad Zoo Recovering from War, Looting." See also Anthony and Spence, *Babylon's Ark*, 108–109.
47. Anthony and Spence, *Babylon's Ark*, 127.
48. Halls and Sumner, *Saving the Baghdad Zoo*, 20–22.
49. Halls and Sumner, *Saving the Baghdad Zoo*, 30–39.
50. Halls and Sumner, *Saving the Baghdad Zoo*.
51. Carol Morello, "Baghdad's Needs Extend to Zoo Residents," *Washington Post*, April 30, 2003, www.washingtonpost.com/archive/politics/2003/04/30/baghdads-needs-extend-to-zoo-residents/9a250963-8424-4d4b-8240-c1c22ccb4b59/?utm_term=.0ca10e16d731
52. Howell and Neal, "Human Interest and Humane Governance in Iraq," 219.
53. Howell and Neal, "Human Interest and Humane Governance in Iraq," 228.
54. Derrida, *The Animal*, 63.
55. Derrida, *The Animal*, 62.
56. Halls and Sumner, *Saving the Baghdad Zoo*, 41.
57. David Rising, "Iraq's Wildlife Trade Anything but Tame," *NBC News*, May 27, 2010, www.nbcnews.com/id/37372231/ns/world_news-mideast_n_africa/t/iraqs-wildlife-trade-anything-tame/#.XDY4hi3MxPV
58. Usama Redha, "Baghdad's Pet Shop Owners are Back in Business," *LA Times*, March 20, 2009, http://articles.latimes.com/2009/mar/20/world/fg-iraq-pets20
59. Tracey Shelton, "Iraq: Dante's Hell for Animals?" *PRI*, May 30, 2010, www.pri.org/stories/2010-05-22/iraq-dantes-hell-animals
60. Shelton, "Iraq: Dante's Hell for Animals?"
61. Elisa Norelli, "Iraq, Kurdistan: Glkand Zoo Closed. It was the Second Worst Zoo of the World," *International Organization for Animal Protection*, February 11, 2014, www.oipa.org/international/2014/kurdistan.html
62. Robin Wright, "Rescuing the Last Two Animals at the Mosul Zoo," *The New Yorker*, April 24, 2017, www.newyorker.com/news/news-desk/rescuing-the-last-two-animals-at-the-mosul-zoo
63. Morgan Winsor, "Animals Rescued from Mosul's Abandoned Zoo Arrive Safely in Jordan," *ABC News*, April 13, 2017, http://abcnews.go.com/International/animals-rescued-mosuls-abandonned-zoo-arrive-safely-jordan/story?id=46748723
64. Wright, "Rescuing the Last Two Animals at the Mosul Zoo."
65. Wright, "Rescuing the Last Two Animals at the Mosul Zoo."
66. Wright, "Rescuing the Last Two Animals at the Mosul Zoo."
67. Sally Williams, "The Man Who Risks his Life to Rescue Zoo Animals from War Zones," *The Telegraph*, December 8, 2017, www.telegraph.co.uk/news/2017/12/08/man-risks-life-rescue-zoo-animals-war-zones
68. Williams, "The Man Who Risks his Life to Rescue Zoo Animals from War Zones."

69. "How Lula Bear and Simba Lion were Saved from the Mosul Zoo," April 13, 2017, www.youtube.com/watch?v=bjigyQzBN8c

70. Al Ma'wa Wildlife Reserve, www.almawajordan.org

71. Jacques Derrida, *On Cosmopolitanism and Forgiveness*, 22.

72. Nigel Rothfels, *Savages and Beasts: The Birth of the Modern Zoo* (Baltimore: Johns Hopkins University Press, 2002), 12.

73. Youatt, *Counting Species*, 135.

74. Derrida, *The Work of Mourning*, 50.

75. Here I am reminded of Rafi Youatt's remark that we might shift the "human moral and political frameworks that orient our relations with other species." Youatt, "Interspecies Relations," 210.

Chapter Four

1. Derrida, *Specters of Marx*, 136.

2. Peter Schwartzstein, "The Islamic State's Scorched-Earth Strategy," *Foreign Policy*, April 6, 2016, http://foreignpolicy.com/2016/04/06/the-islamic-states-scorched-earth-strategy

3. Schwartzstein, "The Islamic State's Scorched-Earth Strategy."

4. Bronwyn Leebaw, "Scorched Earth: Environmental War Crimes and International Justice," *Perspectives on Politics* 12, no. 4 (2014): 770. For a discussion of how harming nature has been both an unplanned consequence of war and a direct military strategy, see also Julie Andrzejewski, "War: Animals in the Aftermath," in *Animals and War: Confronting the Military-Animal Industrial Complex*, ed. Colin Salter, Anthony J. Nocella II, and Judy K.C. Bentley (New York: Lexington Books, 2013), 73–99.

5. Leebaw, "Scorched Earth," 772.

6. Timothy Morton, *Ecology without Nature: Rethinking Environmental Aesthetics* (Cambridge, MA: Harvard University Press, 2007), 18.

7. Morton, *Ecology without Nature*, 18. There are many different ways to conceptualize nature. For some, nature might be understood as a "person"—legally, psychologically, and morally. See Rafi Youatt's work on nature personhood and the varying perspectives on nature in terms of rights, politics, and ontology. Rafi Youatt, "Personhood and the Rights of Nature: The New Subjects of Contemporary Earth Politics," *International Political Sociology* 11, no. 1 (2017): 39–54.

8. See, for example, Kenneth R. Rutherford, "The Evolving Arms Control Agenda: Implications of the Role of NGOS in Banning Antipersonnel Landmines," *World Politics* 53, no. 1 (2000): 74–114. For an overview of the effects of landmines on the environment, see Asmeret Asefaw Berhe, "The Contribution of Landmines to Land Degradation," *Land Degradation & Development* 18, no. 1 (2007): 1–15.

9. David Zierler, *The Invention of Ecocide: Agent Orange, Vietnam, and the Scientists Who Changed the Way We Think about the Environment* (Athens: University of Georgia Press, 2011).

10. Fawaz A. Gerges, *Isis: A History* (Princeton, NJ: Princeton University Press, 2017), 8.

11. Gerges, *Isis*, 8.

12. Hal Brands and Peter Feaver, "Was the Rise of ISIS Inevitable?," *Survival* 59, no. 3 (2017): 7–54.

13. Gerges, *Isis*, 12.

14. Hamdi Alkhshali, "Iraqi Forces Retake Last ISIS-Held Town," *CNN*, November 17, 2017, www.cnn.com/2017/11/17/middleeast/iraq-isis-rawa/index.html

15. Nick Cumming-Bruce, "U.N. Urges Iraq and Allies to Rethink Tactics as Airstrikes Kill Civilians," *New York Times*, March 28, 2017, www.nytimes.com/2017/03/28/world/middleeast/un-iraq-airstrikes.html

16. Tamer El-Ghobashy and Joby Warrick, "The Islamic State's Toxic Farewell: Environmental Sabotage and Chronic Disease," *Washington Post*, February 4, 2018, www.washingtonpost.com/world/the-islamic-states-toxic-farewell-environmental-sabotage-and-chronic-disease/2018/02/04/927ff2b6-05c8-11e8-ae28-e370b74ea9a7_story.html?utm_term=.efba8aeb5942

17. John Loretz, "The Animal Victims of the Gulf War," *Physicians for Social Responsibility* 1, no. 4 (1991): 221.

18. Loretz, "The Animal Victims of the Gulf War," 224.

19. Michael Parrish, "The Spoils of War: A Report on the Eco-Disaster in the Persian Gulf," *L.A. Times*, June 23, 1991, http://articles.latimes.com/print/1991-06-23/magazine/tm-1752_1_persian-gulf

20. Derrida, *Specters of Marx*, 168 (*Spectres de Marx*, 214).

21. Geoffrey Bennington and Jacques Derrida, *Jacques Derrida*, trans. Geoffrey Bennington (Chicago: University of Chicago Press, 1993), 297.

22. Rachel Mundy, "Museums of Sound: Audio Bird Guides and the Pleasures of Knowledge," *Sound Studies* 2, no. 1 (2016): 61.

23. Thom Van Dooren, *Flight Ways: Life and Loss at the Edge of Extinction* (New York: Columbia University Press, 2014), 27.

24. ISIS is also known by other names, such as the Islamic State of Iraq and Syria, the Islamic State, and also the Arabic acronym *Daesh*. I refer to the group as "ISIS" throughout this chapter.

25. Laris Karklis, "How the Islamic State is Using Scorched Earth Tactics as it Retreats," *Washington Post*, October 25, 2016, www.washingtonpost.com/graphics/world/islamic-state-oil-fire

26. Erika Solomon, Robin Kwong, and Steven Bernard, "Inside Isis Inc: The Journey of a Barrel of Oil," February 29, 2016, *Financial Times*, https://ig.ft.com/sites/2015/isis-oil

27. Azmat Khan and Anand Gopal, "The Uncounted," *New York Times*, November 16, 2017, www.nytimes.com/interactive/2017/11/16/magazine/uncounted-civilian-casualties-iraq-airstrikes.html

28. Atheer Al-Yaseen and Chris Niles, "A New Day in Qayyarah, Iraq," *UNICEF*, September 13, 2016, https://blogs.unicef.org/blog/newly-liberated-qayyarah-iraq

29. Chris Fitch, "Extinguishing Iraq's Burning Oil Wells," *Geographical*, April 6, 2017, http://geographical.co.uk/people/development/item/2193-extinguishing-iraq-s-burning-oil-wells

30. For a discussion of individuals involved in putting out the fires in Qayyarah, see Chris Shearer, "What It's Like Putting Out Oil Fires Lit by Retreating ISIS Fighters," *VICE*, February 1, 2017, www.vice.com/en_us/article/kbgzkv/what-its-like-putting-out-oil-fires-lit-by-retreating-is-fighters

31. An important exception is an Oxfam study about youth in and around Qayyarah after ISIS's exit. Antonio Massella, "We Have Forgotten What Happiness Is: Youth Perspectives Of Displacement And Return In Qayyarah Subdistrict, Mosul," *Oxfam*, October 2017, https://oxfamilibrary.openrepository.com/bitstream/handle/10546/620351/rr-youth-perspectives-displacement-iraq-191017-en.pdf?sequence=1

32. Derrida, *The Animal*, 9.

33. Doug Weir, "The Environmental Consequences of Iraq's Oil Fires are Going Unrecorded," *Conflict and Environment Observatory*, November 30, 2016, https://ceobs.org/the-environmental-consequences-of-iraqs-oil-fires-are-going-unrecorded

34. El-Ghobashy and Warrick, "The Islamic State's Toxic Farewell."

35. Chris Shearer, "What It's Like Putting Out Oil Fires Lit by Retreating ISIS Fighters," *VICE*, February 1, 2017, www.vice.com/en_us/article/kbgzkv/what-its-like-putting-out-oil-fires-lit-by-retreating-is-fighters

36. Weir, "The Environmental Consequences of Iraq's Oil Fires are Going Unrecorded."

37. Namak Khoshnaw and Daniel Silas Adamson, "Desert on Fire," *BBC*, April 5, 2017, www.bbc.co.uk/news/resources/idt-sh/desert_on_fire

38. Khoshnaw and Adamson, "Desert on Fire."

39. Khoshnaw and Adamson, "Desert on Fire."

40. Ellen Meloy, *Eating Stone: Imagination and the Loss of the Wild* (New York: Vintage Books, 2005), 328.

41. Derrida, *The Beast and the Sovereign Volume II*, 104–105.

42. Derrida, *The Animal*, 12.

43. Derrida, *The Animal*, 12.

44. Keith M. Kendrick et al., "Sheep Don't Forget a Face," *Nature* 414, no. 6860 (2001): 165–166.

45. Helen Briggs, "Amazing Powers of Sheep," *BBC*, November 7, 2001, http://news.bbc.co.uk/2/hi/sci/tech/1641463.stm

46. El-Ghobashy and Warrick, "The Islamic State's Toxic Farewell."

47. El-Ghobashy and Warrick, "The Islamic State's Toxic Farewell." The 2003 fire produced more sulfur dioxide than most volcanic eruptions. Measurements from the NASA satellite instrument TOMS (Total Ozone Mapping Spectrometer) indicated that sulfur dioxide emissions from the 2003 Mishraq fire would rank among the largest instances of volcanic sulfur dioxide emissions since 1978. It was the largest human-caused release of sulfur dioxide in history. See S.A. Carn et al., "Fire at Iraqi Sulfur Plant Emits SO2 Clouds Detected by Earth Probe TOMS," *Geophysical Research Letters* 31, no. 19 (2004): L19105.

48. Robert Miller, "Respiratory Disorders Following Service in Iraq," Nashville, TN: Vanderbilt University, Vanderbilt Medical Center (2013).

49. Mark Peplow, "Iraqi Fire Pollution Rivalled Volcano," *Nature*, October 25, 2004, www.nature.com/news/2004/041025/full/news041025-5.html

50. "Sulfur Dioxide Spreads Over Iraq," *NASA Earth Observatory*, October 24, 2016, https://earthobservatory.nasa.gov/NaturalHazards/view.php?id=88994

51. Miller, "Respiratory Disorders."

52. Carole Bartoo, "Home Sick: Vanderbilt Physicians Champion for Veterans with Lung Illness," *Vanderbilt Medicine*, July 2010, www.mc.vanderbilt.edu/vm-archive/?article=9117

53. Miller, "Respiratory Disorders."

54. Schwartzstein, "The Islamic State's Scorched-Earth Strategy."

55. Schwartzstein, "The Islamic State's Scorched-Earth Strategy."

56. Peter Schwartzstein, "Iraq's Unique Wildlife Pushed to Brink by War, Hunting," *National Geographic*, February 6, 2017, http://news.nationalgeographic.com/2017/02/iraq-wildlife-islamic-state-species-war

57. There can also be positive effects of landmines on animal life. See Peter Schwartzstein, "For Leopards in Iran and Iraq, Land Mines Are a Surprising Refuge," *National Geographic*, December 12, 2014, https://news.nationalgeographic.com/news/2014/12/141219-persian-leopard-iran-iraq-land-mine

58. "Four Military Dogs Killed in Action in Afghanistan," *The Telegraph*, October 25, 2013, www.telegraph.co.uk/news/10399699/Four-military-dogs-killed-in-action-in-Afghanistan.html

59. For a discussion of mine detection dogs, see Meiches, "Non-Human Humanitarians," and Janet M. Alger and Steven F. Alger, "Canine Soldiers, Mascots, and Stray Dogs in U.S. Wars: Ethical Considerations," in ed. Ryan Hediger, *Animals and War: Studies of Europe and North America* (Boston: Brill, 2013), 77–104. For a discussion of other animals used for mine detection and other military purposes, see Cudworth and Hobden, "The Posthuman Way of War."

60. Alan Taylor, "Afghanistan: Dogs of War," *The Atlantic*, June 3, 2014, www.theatlantic.com/photo/2014/06/afghanistan-dogs-of-war/100750

61. Jacques Derrida, "Passages—From Traumatism to Promise," in *Points*, 389.

62. Jacques Derrida, *The Animal*, 20.

63. "Yemen: Houthi-Saleh Forces Using Landmines," *Human Rights Watch*, April 20, 2017, www.hrw.org/news/2017/04/20/yemen-houthi-saleh-forces-using-landmines

64. Seth Mydans, "Mines Maim the Ultimate Civilians: Animals," *New York Times*, March 5, 2001, www.nytimes.com/2001/03/05/world/mines-maim-the-ultimate-civilians-animals.html

65. See Andrzejewski, "War: Animals in the Aftermath" for a brief discussion of these elephants and the effects of mines on animals.

66. "Tracing the Supply of Components Used in Islamic State IEDs: Evidence from a 20-month Investigation in Iraq and Syria," *Conflict Armament Research*, February 2016, www.conflictarm.com/wp-content/uploads/2016/02/Tracing_The_Supply_of_Components_Used_in_Islamic_State_IEDs.pdf

67. Hannah Bryce, "It Is No Longer Possible to Ignore the Threat of IEDs," *Chatham House*, April 4, 2017, www.chathamhouse.org/expert/comment/it-no-longer-possible-ignore-threat-ieds

68. Schwartzstein, "Iraq's Unique Wildlife."

69. "I Knew There Were Landmines There, But I Had To Get My Sheep Back," *Mines Advisory Group*, September 26, 2014, www.maginternational.org/our-impact/news/i-knew-there-were-landmines-there-but-i-had-to-get-my-sheep-back

70. Derrida, *Echographies*, 77.

71. Charles Lister, "Trump Says ISIS Is Defeated. Reality Says Otherwise," *Politico*, March 18, 2019, www.politico.com/magazine/story/2019/03/18/trump-isis-terrorists-defeated-foreign-policy-225816

72. Robin Wright, "Baghdadi Is Back—and Vows That ISIS Will Be, Too," *The New Yorker*, April 29, 2019, www.newyorker.com/news/news-desk/baghdadi-is-backand-vows-that-isis-will-be-too

73. This line is inspired by a discussion of vision and tears in Jacques Derrida's, *Memoirs of the Blind: The Self-Portrait and Other Ruins*, trans. Pascale-Anne Brault and Michael Naas (Chicago: University of Chicago Press, 1993).

(In)Conclusion(s)

1. Derrida, *The Beast and the Sovereign Volume II*, 290.
2. Derrida, *Specters of Marx*, 221.
3. Derrida, *The Beast and the Sovereign Volume II*, 263.
4. Derrida, *The Beast and the Sovereign Volume II*, 264.
5. Oliver, *Technologies of Life and Death*, 153.
6. Derrida, *The Beast and the Sovereign Volume II*, 73.
7. Derrida, *The Beast and the Sovereign Volume II*, 73.

8. Paul Celan, *Collected Prose*, trans. Rosmarie Waldrop (Manchester: Carcanet Press, 1986), quoted in Celan, *Breathturn into Timestead*, 516.

9. Derrida, *Spectres de Marx*, 214 (*Specters of Marx*, 168).

10. Derrida, *The Beast and the Sovereign Volume II*, 62.

11. For a detailed discussion of these themes, see David Farrell Krell, *Derrida and Our Animal Others: Derrida's Final Seminar, "The Beast and the Sovereign"* (Bloomington: Indiana University Press, 2013).

12. Derrida, *The Beast and the Sovereign Volume II*, 62.

13. Derrida, *The Beast and the Sovereign Volume II*, 112.

14. Derrida, *Spectres de Marx*, 15 (*Specters of Marx*, xviii).

15. Derrida, *The Beast and the Sovereign Volume II*, 62.

16. Derrida, *The Beast and the Sovereign Volume II*, 62.

17. Derrida, *The Beast and the Sovereign Volume II*, 62.

18. Derrida, "A 'Madness' Must Watch Over Thinking," in *Points*, 355.

19. Derrida, "A 'Madness' Must Watch Over Thinking," in *Points*, 355.

20. Derrida, *The Beast and the Sovereign Volume II*, 169.

21. Derrida, *The Beast and the Sovereign Volume II*, 169. Carrying the dead in our hearts is "both the greatest fidelity and the utmost betrayal," writes Derrida. To interiorize the other is necessary but always a kind of betrayal. One way to think of Derrida's comments is that this "keeping in our hearts" makes the other our own, which involves idealizing, consuming, appropriating, silencing, but also involves listening. Derrida, *The Beast and the Sovereign Volume II*, 169.

22. Derrida, *The Work of Mourning*, 209.

23. Derrida, *On Touching*, 108.

24. Derrida, *Memoires*, 34.

25. Derrida, *Memoires*, 35. As Saghafi notes, success "would amount to reconciling with death and the complete incorporation of the other—a denial or effacement of his alterity." Saghafi, *Apparitions*, 73.

26. Derrida, *Specters of Marx*, xx.

27. Derrida, *Specters of Marx*, 134.

28. Derrida, *Paper Machine*, 169.

Works Cited

"600 Million Dogs." https://600milliondogs.org

Agathangelou, Anna M. "Making Anew an Arab Regional Order? On Poetry, Sex, and Revolution." *Globalizations* 8, no. 5 (2011): 581–594.

Åhäll, Linda. "Feeling Everyday IR: Embodied, Affective, Militarising Movement as Choreography of War." *Cooperation and Conflict* 54, no. 2 (2019): 149–166.

Alger, Janet M., and Steven F. Alger. "Canine Soldiers, Mascots, and Stray Dogs in U.S. Wars: Ethical Considerations." In *Animals and War: Studies of Europe and North America*, ed. Ryan Hediger. Boston: Brill, 2013, 77–104.

Alkhshali, Hamdi. "Iraqi Forces Retake Last ISIS-Held Town," *CNN* (November 17, 2017), www.cnn.com/2017/11/17/middleeast/iraq-isis-rawa/index.html

Al Ma'wa Wildlife Reserve, www.almawajordan.org

Alousi, Alise. "What Every Driver Must Know." In *We Are Iraqis: Aesthetics and Politics in a Time of War*, ed. Nadje Al-Ali and Deborah Al-Najjar. Syracuse, NY: Syracuse University Press, 2013, 1–3.

Al-Yaseen, Atheer, and Chris Niles, "A New Day in Qayyarah, Iraq." *UNICEF* (September 13, 2016), https://blogs.unicef.org/blog/newly-liberated-qayyarah-iraq

Andrzejewski, Julie. "War: Animals in the Aftermath." In *Animals and War: Confronting the Military-Animal Industrial Complex*, ed. Colin Salter, Anthony J. Nocella II, and Judy K.C. Bentley. Lanham, MD: Lexington Books, 2013, 73–99.

Anthony, Lawrence, and Graham Spence. *Babylon's Ark: The Incredible Wartime Rescue of the Baghdad Zoo*. New York: Thomas Dunne Books, 2007.

Appiah, Kwame Anthony. "Global Citizenship." *Fordham Law Review* 75, no. 5 (2007): 2375–2391.

Archer, George. "The Hellhound of the Qur'an: A Dog at the Gate of the Underworld." *Journal of Qur'anic Studies* 18, no. 3 (2016): 1–33.

Auchter, Jessica. *The Politics of Haunting and Memory in International Relations*. New York: Routledge, 2014.

Auchter, Jessica. "Paying Attention to Dead Bodies: The Future of Security Studies?" *Journal of Global Security Studies* 1, no. 1 (2016): 36–50.

Bartoo, Carole. "Home Sick: Vanderbilt Physicians Champion for Veterans with Lung Illness." *Vanderbilt Medicine* (July 2010), www.mc.vanderbilt.edu/vm-archive/?article=9117

Bechtol, Harris B. "Event, Death, and Poetry: The Death of the Other in Derrida's 'Rams.'" *Philosophy Today* 62, no. 1 (2018): 253–268.

Benhabib, Seyla. "Defending a Cosmopolitanism without Illusions. Reply to my Critics." *Critical Review of International Social and Political Philosophy* 17, no. 6 (2014): 697–715.

Benjamin, Walter. *Selected Writings Volume 1, 1913–1926*. Edited by Marcus Bullock and Michael W. Jennings. Cambridge, MA: Harvard University Press, 2003.

Bennington, Geoffrey, and Jacques Derrida. *Jacques Derrida*. Translated by Geoffrey Bennington. Chicago: University of Chicago Press, 1993.

Berger, John. *About Looking*. New York: Vintage Books, 1992.

Berglund, Jenny. "Princely Companion or Object of Offense? The Dog's Ambiguous Status in Islam." *Society and Animals* 22, no. 6 (2014): 545–559.

Berhe, Asmeret Asefaw. "The Contribution of Landmines to Land Degradation." *Land Degradation & Development* 18, no. 1 (2007): 1–15.

Bleiker, Roland. "'Give it the Shade:' Paul Celan and the Politics of Apolitical Poetry." *Political Studies* 47, no. 4 (1999): 661–676.

Bleiker, Roland. "Learning from Art: A Reply to Holden's 'World Literature and World Politics.'" *Global Society* 17, no. 4 (2003): 415–428.

Bleiker, Roland. *Aesthetics and World Politics*. New York: Palgrave Macmillan, 2009.

Bleiker, Roland. "In Search of Thinking Space: Reflections on the Aesthetic Turn in International Political Theory." *Millennium* 45, no. 2 (2017): 258–264.

Boitani, Luigi. "Forward." In *Free-Ranging Dogs and Wildlife Conservation*, ed. Matthew Gompper. New York: Oxford University Press, 2014.

Borrego, Natalia, and Brian Dowling. "Lions (Panthera Leo) Solve, Learn, and Remember a Novel Resource Acquisition Problem." *Animal Cognition* 19, no. 5 (2016): 1019–1025.

Brands, Hal, and Peter Feaver. "Was the Rise of ISIS Inevitable?" *Survival* 59, no. 3 (2017): 7–54.

Briggs, Helen. "Amazing Powers of Sheep." BBC (November 7, 2001), http://news.bbc.co.uk/2/hi/sci/tech/1641463.stm

Brock, Gillian. *Global Justice: A Cosmopolitan Account*. New York: Cambridge University Press, 2009.

Broom, Donald M., Hilana Sena, and Kiera L. Moynihan. "Pigs Learn What a Mirror Image Represents and use it to Obtain Information." *Animal Behaviour* 78, no. 5 (2009): 1037–1041.

Brown, Garrett Wallace. "Bringing the State back into Cosmopolitanism: The Idea of Responsible Cosmopolitan States." *Political Studies Review* 9, no. 1 (2011): 53–66.

Bryce, Hannah. "It Is No Longer Possible to Ignore the Threat of IEDs." *Chatham House* (April 4, 2017), www.chathamhouse.org/expert/comment/it-no-longer-possible-ignore-threat-ieds

Bump, Philip. "15 Years after the Iraq War Began, the Death Toll Is Still Murky." *Washington Post* (March 20, 2018), www.washingtonpost.com/news/politics/wp/2018/03/20/15-years-after-it-began-the-death-toll-from-the-iraq-war-is-still-murky

Burke, Anthony. "Poetry Outside Security." *Alternatives* 25, no. 3 (2000): 307–321.

Burke, Anthony. "Security Cosmopolitanism." *Critical Studies on Security* 1, no. 1 (2013): 13–28.

Butler, Judith. *Frames of War: When Is Life Grievable?* New York: Verso, 2009.

Calarco, Matthew. *Zoographies: The Question of the Animal from Heidegger to Derrida.* New York: Columbia University Press, 2008.

Caney, Simon. *Justice beyond Borders: A Global Political Theory.* New York: Oxford University Press, 2005.

Carn, S.A., A.J. Krueger, N.A. Krotkov, and M.A. Gray. "Fire at Iraqi Sulfur Plant Emits SO2 Clouds Detected by Earth Probe TOMS." *Geophysical Research Letters* 31, no. 19 (2004): L19105.

Cashour, Army Staff Sgt. Curt. "Vector Control Keeps Tabs on Pests" *United States Army Central Defense Video Imagery Distribution System* (June 16, 2007), www.dvidshub.net/news/10851/vector-control-keeps-tabs-pests

"The 'Cat Lady of Baghdad' Battles On, Saving Strays of Iraq." *NBC News* (April 29, 2008), www.nbcnews.com/id/24373120/ns/world_news-mideast_n_africa/t/cat-lady-baghdadsaves-strays/#.Wc0ttEyZORs

Celan, Paul. *Breathturn.* Translated by Pierre Joris. Los Angeles: Sun & Moon Press, 1995.

Celan, Paul. *Selections.* Edited by Pierre Joris. Berkeley: University of California Press, 2005.

Clark, Timothy. *The Poetics of Singularity: The Counter-Culturalist Turn in Heidegger, Derrida, Blanchot and the Later Gadamer.* Edinburgh: Edinburgh University Press, 2005.

Coen, Alise. "Capable and Culpable? The United States, RtoP, and Refugee Responsibility-Sharing." *Ethics and International Affairs* 31, no. 1 (2017): 71–92.

Conroy, Scott. "Rescuing The Baghdad Zoo." *CBS* (April 29, 2007), www.cbsnews.com/news/rescuing-the-baghdad-zoo/2

Constable, Pamela. "The Cats of War." *Washington Post* (July 21, 2003), www.washingtonpost.com/archive/politics/2003/07/21/the-cats-of-war/d3a9de55-7da4-4e41-9a2c-e71f542cc2ec/?utm_term=.a81c3334d416

Crawford, Neta. "US Budgetary Costs of Wars through 2016." *Watson Institute* (September 2016), http://watson.brown.edu/costsofwar/files/cow/imce/papers/2016/Costs%20of%20War%20through%202016%20FINAL%20final%20v2.pdf

Cree, Alice, and Nick Caddick. "Unconquerable Heroes: Invictus, Redemption, and the Cultural Politics of Narrative." *Journal of War & Culture Studies* (2019): 1–21. doi:10.1080/17526272.2019.1615707

Cudworth, Erika, and Stephen Hobden. *Posthuman International Relations: Complexity, Ecologism and Global Politics.* New York: Zed Books, 2013.

Cudworth, Erika, and Stephen Hobden. "The Posthuman Way of War." *Security Dialogue* 46, no. 6 (2015): 513–529.

Cudworth, Erika, and Stephen Hobden. *The Emancipatory Project of Posthumanism.* New York: Routledge, 2018.

Cumming-Bruce, Nick. "U.N. Urges Iraq and Allies to Rethink Tactics as Airstrikes Kill Civilians." *New York Times* (March 28, 2017), www.nytimes.com/2017/03/28/world/middleeast/un-iraq-airstrikes.html

Dagher, Sam. "In Hard-Bitten Baghdad, Tough Tactics on Strays." *New York Times* (March 14, 2009), www.nytimes.com/2009/03/15/world/middleeast/15strays.html

Damon, Arwa. "Stray Dogs being Killed in Baghdad." CNN (February 12, 2009), www.cnn.com/2009/WORLD/meast/02/12/baghdad.dogs

Dayan, Peter. "The Time for Poetry." *Oxford Literary Review* 31, no. 1 (2009): 1–14.

Dell'Amore, Christine. "Stray Dogs in Sochi: What Happens to the World's Free-Roaming Canines?" *National Geographic* (February 8, 2014), http://news.nationalgeographic.com/news/2014/02/140206-stray-dogs-russia-sochi-olympics-killing-animals-world

DeMello, Margo, ed. *Speaking for Animals: Animal Autobiographical Writing.* New York: Routledge, 2013.

Derrida, Jacques. "A Certain Impossible Possibility of Saying the Event." *Critical Inquiry* 33, no. 2 (2007): 441–461.

Derrida, Jacques. *Acts of Religion.* New York: Routledge, 2002.

Derrida, Jacques. *Adieu to Emmanuel Levinas.* Translated by Pascale-Anne Brault and Michael Naas. Stanford, CA: Stanford University Press, 1999.

Derrida, Jacques. *Athens, Still Remains: The Photographs of Jean-François Bonhomme.* Translated by Pascale-Anne Brault and Michael Naas. New York: Fordham University Press, 2010.

Derrida, Jacques. *Béliers, le Dialogue Interrompu: Entre Deux Infinis, le Poéme.* Paris: Galilée, 2003.

Derrida, Jacques. *Echographies of Television: Filmed Interviews.* With Bernard Stiegler. Translated by Jennifer Bajorek. Cambridge: Polity Press, 2002.

Derrida, Jacques. *Memoires for Paul de Man,* revised edition. Translated by Cecile Lindsay, Jonathan Culler, Eduardo Cadava, and Peggy Kamuf. New York: Columbia University Press, 1989.

Derrida, Jacques. *Memoirs of the Blind: The Self-Portrait and Other Ruins.* Translated by Pascale-Anne Brault and Michael Naas. Chicago: University of Chicago Press, 1993.

Derrida, Jacques. *Of Hospitality: Anne Dufourmantelle Invites Jacques Derrida to Respond*. Translated by Rachel Bowlby. Stanford, CA: Stanford University Press, 2000.
Derrida, Jacques. *On Cosmopolitanism and Forgiveness*. Translated by Mark Dooley and Michael Hughes. New York: Routledge Press, 2001.
Derrida, Jacques. *On the Name*. Translated by David Wood, John P. Leavey, Jr., and Ian McLeod. Stanford, CA: Stanford University Press, 1995.
Derrida, Jacques. *On Touching—Jean-Luc Nancy*. Translated by Christine Irizarry. Stanford, CA: Stanford University Press, 2005.
Derrida, Jacques. *Paper Machine*. Translated by Rachel Bowlby. Stanford, CA: Stanford University Press, 2005.
Derrida, Jacques. *Points . . . Interviews, 1974–1994*. Stanford, CA: Stanford University Press, 1995.
Derrida, Jacques. *Resistances of Psychoanalysis*. Translated by Pascale-Anne Brault and Michael Naas. Stanford, CA: Stanford University Press, 1998.
Derrida, Jacques. *Sovereignties in Question: The Poetics of Paul Celan*. New York: Fordham University Press, 2005.
Derrida, Jacques. *Specters of Marx: The State of Debt, the Work of Mourning and the New International*. Translated by Peggy Kamuf. New York: Routledge, 1994.
Derrida, Jacques. *Spectres de Marx: L'etat de la dette, le travail du deuil et la nouvelle Internationale*. Paris: Galilée, 1993.
Derrida, Jacques. *The Animal that Therefore I Am*. Translated by David Wills. New York: Fordham University Press, 2008.
Derrida, Jacques. *The Beast and the Sovereign Volume I*. Translated by Geoff Bennington. Chicago: University of Chicago Press, 2009.
Derrida, Jacques. *The Beast and the Sovereign Volume II*. Translated by Geoff Bennington. Chicago: University of Chicago Press, 2011.
Derrida, Jacques. *The Gift of Death*, 2nd edition. Translated by David Wills. Chicago: University of Chicago Press, 1995.
Derrida, Jacques. *The Politics of Friendship*. Translated by George Collins. New York: Verso, 2005.
Derrida, Jacques. *The Work of Mourning*. Chicago: University of Chicago Press, 2003.
Derrida, Jacques. *Writing and Difference*. Translated by Alan Bass. Chicago: University of Chicago Press, 1978.
Derrida, Jacques and Elisabeth Roudinesco, *For What Tomorrow . . . A Dialogue*. Translated by Jeff Fort. Stanford, CA: Stanford University Press, 2004.
Diamond, Larry. "Lessons from Iraq." *Journal of Democracy* 16, no. 1 (2005): 9–23.
Dobson, Andrew. "Thick Cosmopolitanism." *Political Studies* 54, no. 1 (2006): 165–184.
Doty, Roxanne Lynn. "Maladies of our Souls: Identity and Voice in the Writing of Academic International Relations." *Cambridge Review of International Affairs* 17, no. 2 (2004): 377–392.

Doty, Roxanne Lynn. "Writing from the Edge," in *The Ashgate Research Companion to Modern Theory, Modern Power, World Politics: Critical Investigations*, ed. Scott G. Nelson and Nevzat Soguk. New York: Routledge, 2016, 149–160.

El-Ghobashy, Tamer, and Joby Warrick. "The Islamic State's Toxic Farewell: Environmental Sabotage and Chronic Disease," *Washington Post* (February 4, 2018), www.washingtonpost.com/world/the-islamic-states-toxic-farewell-environmental-sabotage-and-chronic-disease/2018/02/04/927ff2b6-05c8-11e8-ae28-e370b74ea9a7_story.html?utm_term=.efba8aeb5942

Fabre, Cécile. *Cosmopolitan War*. New York: Oxford University Press, 2012.

Felstiner, John. *Can Poetry Save the Earth: A Field Guide to Nature Poems*. New Haven, CT: Yale University Press, 2009.

Fishel, Stefanie R. *The Microbial State: Global Thriving and the Body Politic*. Minneapolis: University of Minnesota Press, 2017.

Fitch, Chris. "Extinguishing Iraq's Burning Oil Wells," *Geographical* (April 6, 2017), http://geographical.co.uk/people/development/item/2193-extinguishing-iraq-s-burning-oil-wells

"Four Military Dogs Killed in Action in Afghanistan." *The Telegraph* (October 25, 2013), www.telegraph.co.uk/news/10399699/Four-military-dogs-killed-in-action-in-Afghanistan.html

Frankel, Rebecca. *War Dogs: Tales of Canine Heroism, History, and Love*. New York: St. Martin's Press, 2014.

Fritsch, Matthias. *The Promise Of Memory: History and Politics in Marx, Benjamin, and Derrida*. Albany, NY: SUNY Press, 2005.

Garamone, Jim. "Baghdad Zoo Recovering From War, Looting." *Department of Defense* (May 12, 2003), http://archive.defense.gov/news/newsarticle.aspx?id=28993

Gerges, Fawaz A. *Isis: A History*. Princeton, NJ: Princeton University Press, 2017.

Gibran, Khalil. *The Prophet*. New York: Alfred A. Knopf, 1923.

Gilmore, Jonathan. "Protecting the Other: Considering the Process and Practice of Cosmopolitanism." *European Journal of International Relations* 20, no. 3 (2014): 694–719.

Goldman, Jason G. "Let them Eat Carcass." *Slate* (January 3, 2014), https://slate.com/technology/2014/01/food-for-pets-and-zoo-animals-they-should-eat-real-meat.html

Gompper, Matthew. "The Dog-Human-Wildlife Interface: Assessing the Scope of the Problem." In *Free-Ranging Dogs and Wildlife Conservation*, ed. Matthew Gompper. New York: Oxford University Press, 2014.

Gompper Matthew E. 2014. "One Billion Dogs? What Does That Mean?" *Oxford University Press*, March 24. https://blog.oup.com/2014/03/one-billion-dogs-wildlife-conservation

Goodrich, Charles. "Entries into the Forest." In *Forest Under Story: Creative Inquiry in an Old-Growth Forest*, ed. Nathaniel Brodie, Charles Goodrich, and Frederick J. Swanson. Seattle: University of Washington Press, 2016, 5–14.

Gudrun, Illmann, Marek Špinka, Lars Schrader, and Pavel Šustr. "Acoustical Mother-Offspring Recognition in Pigs (Sus scrofa domestica)." *Behaviour* 139, no. 4 (2002): 487–505.

Hägglund, Martin. *Radical Atheism: Derrida and the Time of Life*. Stanford, CA: Stanford University Press, 2008.

Halberstadt, Alex. "Zoo Animals and Their Discontents." *New York Times* (July 3, 2014), www.nytimes.com/2014/07/06/magazine/zoo-animals-and-their-discontents.html

Halls, Kelly Milner, and Major William Sumner. *Saving the Baghdad Zoo*. New York: Greenwillow Books/Harper Collins, 2010.

Hanif, Mohammed. "Of Dogs, Faith and Imams." *New York Times* (July 26, 2015), SR6.

Haraway, Donna. *The Haraway Reader*. New York: Routledge, 2004.

Haslanger, Andrea. "The Cynic as Cosmopolitan Animal." In *Cosmopolitan Animals*, ed. Kaori Nagai, Karen Jones, Donna Landry, Monica Mattfeld, Caroline Rooney, and Charlotte Sleigh. New York: Palgrave Macmillan, 2015, 29–42.

Haynes, Brad. "Zoos in a Pickle over Horse Meat." *The Seattle Times* (August 14, 2007), www.seattletimes.com/seattle-news/zoos-in-a-pickle-over-horse-meat

Haynes, Deborah. "Stray Dog Gets His Ticket to US as Senators Rally Round and Army Relents." *The Times* (October 17, 2008). Available at lexisnexis.com

Hediger, Ryan. "Dogs of War: The Biopolitics of Loving and Leaving the US Canine Forces in Vietnam." *Animal Studies Journal* 2, no. 1 (2013): 55–73.

Holmes Michael. "Baghdad Zoo: A Different Battle." *CNN* (April 17, 2003) www.cnn.com/2003/WORLD/meast/04/16/sprj.nilaw.baghdad.zoo

Horback, Kristina. "Nosing Around: Play in Pigs." *Animal Behavior and Cognition* 1, no. 2 (2014): 186–196.

Horta, Oscar. "Expanding Global Justice: The Case for the International Protection of Animals." *Global Policy* 4, no. 4 (2013): 371–380.

Horton, Daniel L., Mashair Z. Ismail, Eman S. Siryan, Abdul Raheem A. Wali, Husam E. Abdulla, Emma Wise, Katja Voller, Graeme Harkess, Denise A. Marston, Lorraine M. McElhinney, Salah F. Abbas, and Anthony R. Fooks, "Rabies in Iraq: Trends in Human Cases 2001–2010 and Characterisation of Animal Rabies Strains from Baghdad." *PLoS Neglected Tropical Diseases* 7, no. 2 (2013): e2075.

"How Lula Bear and Simba Lion were Saved from the Mosul Zoo" (April 13, 2017), www.youtube.com/watch?v=bjigyQzBN8c

Howe, Susan. "The Difficulties Interview." *The Difficulties* 3, no. 2 (1989).

Howe, Susan. *The Birth-mark: Unsettling the Wilderness in American Literary History*. Middletown, CT: Wesleyan University Press, 1993.

Howe, Susan. "An Open Field: Susan Howe in Conversation." *The Academy of American Poets* (September 7, 2011), www.poets.org/poetsorg/text/open-field-susan-howe-conversation

Howe, Susan. *The Quarry*. New York: New Directions, 2015.

Howell, Alison, and Andrew W. Neal. "Human Interest and Humane Governance in Iraq: Humanitarian War and the Baghdad Zoo." *Journal of Intervention and Statebuilding* 6, no. 2 (2012): 213–232.

"I Knew There Were Landmines There, But I Had To Get My Sheep Back." *Mines Advisory Group*, September 26, 2014, www.maginternational.org/our-impact/news/i-knew-there-were-landmines-there-but-i-had-to-get-my-sheep-back

Iraq Body Count. www.iraqbodycount.org

Itoh, Mayumi. *Japanese Wartime Zoo Policy: The Silent Victims of World War II*. New York: Palgrave Macmillan, 2010.

Jackson, Holly. "Perverse International: Modern War and World Imaginings in Pablo de la Torriente Brau's Aventuras del Soldado Desconocido Cubano." *Symposium: A Quarterly Journal in Modern Literatures* 71, no. 3 (2017): 128–139.

Jennings, Theodore W. *Reading Derrida/Thinking Paul: On Justice*. Stanford, CA: Stanford University Press, 2006.

Johnston, Steven. "Animals in War: Commemoration, Patriotism, Death." *Political Research Quarterly* 65, no. 2 (2012): 359–371.

Judd, David, and James Rocha. "Autonomous Pigs." *Ethics and the Environment* 22, no. 1 (2017): 1–18.

Juhi, Bushra. "Baghdad Kills 58,000 Stray Dogs in 3-Month Span." *San Diego Tribune* (July 10, 2010), www.sandiegouniontribune.com/sdut-baghdad-kills-58000-stray-dogs-in-3-month-span-2010jul10-story.html

Juhi, Bushra. "Baghdad Kills More than 58,000 Stray Dogs." *Toronto Star* (July 10, 2010), www.thestar.com/news/world/2010/07/10/baghdad_kills_more_than_58000_stray_dogs.html.

Juhi, Bushra. "58,000 Dogs Killed in Baghdad in Campaign to Curb Attacks by Strays." *Washington Post* (July 11, 2010), www.washingtonpost.com/wp-dyn/content/article/2010/07/10/AR2010071002235.html

Kami, Aseel. "In Security, Baghdad Tackles 1 Million Stray Dogs." *Reuters* (June 10, 2010), www.reuters.com/article/idINIndia-49201920100610

Kamuf, Peggy. "Teleiopoetic World." *SubStance* 43, no. 2 (2014): 10–19.

Kareem, Ali. "Shooting Stray Dogs in Iraq." *Denver Post* (July 21, 2010), www.denverpost.com/2010/07/21/kareem-shooting-stray-dogs-in-iraq

Karklis, Laris. "How the Islamic State is Using Scorched Earth Tactics as it Retreats." *Washington Post* (October 25, 2016), www.washingtonpost.com/graphics/world/islamic-state-oil-fire

Kayali, U., R. Mindekem, G. Hutton, A. G. Ndoutamia, and J. Zinsstag, "Cost-Description of a Pilot Parenteral Vaccination Campaign against Rabies in Dogs in N'Djaména, Chad." *Tropical Medicine and International Health* 11, no. 7 (2006): 1058–1065.

Kendrick, Keith M., Ana P. da Costa, Andrea E. Leigh, Michael R. Hinton, and Jon W. Peirce. "Sheep Don't Forget a Face." *Nature* 414, no. 6860 (2001): 165–166.

Kershenbaum, Arik, Holly Root-Gutteridge, Bilal Habib, Janice Koler-Matznick, Brian Mitchell, Vicente Palacios, and Sara Waller. "Disentangling Canid Howls Across Multiple Species and Subspecies: Structure in a Complex Communication Channel." *Behavioural Processes* 124 (2016): 149–157.

Khan, Azmat, and Anand Gopal. "The Uncounted." *New York Times* (November 16, 2017), www.nytimes.com/interactive/2017/11/16/magazine/uncounted-civilian-casualties-iraq-airstrikes.html

Khoshnaw, Namak, and Daniel Silas Adamson. "Desert on Fire." BBC (April 5, 2017), www.bbc.co.uk/news/resources/idt-sh/desert_on_fire

Kinder, John M. "Zoo Animals and Modern War: Captive Casualties, Patriotic Citizens, and Good Soldiers." In *Animals and War: Studies of Europe and North America*, ed. Ryan Hediger. Boston: Brill, 2013, 45–76.

Kopelman, Jay. *From Baghdad to America: Life after War for a Marine and His Rescued Dog*. New York: Skyhorse Publishing, 2010.

Krell, David Farrell. *Derrida and Our Animal Others: Derrida's Final Seminar, "The Beast and the Sovereign."* Bloomington: Indiana University Press, 2013.

Leebaw, Bronwyn. "Scorched Earth: Environmental War Crimes and International Justice." *Perspectives on Politics* 12, no. 4 (2014): 770–788.

Leep, Matthew Coen. "(Ac)Counting (for) their Dead: Responsiveness to Iraqi Civilian Casualties in the US House of Representatives." *International Politics* 52, no. 1 (2015): 45–65.

Leep, Matthew. "Cosmopolitanism in a Carnivorous World." *Politics and Animals* 3 (2017): 16–30.

Leep, Matthew. "Stray Dogs, Post-Humanism and Cosmopolitan Belongingness: Interspecies Hospitality in Times of War." *Millennium: Journal of International Studies* 47, no. 1 (2018): 45–66.

Levin, Abigail. "Zoo Animals as Specimens, Zoo Animals as Friends: The Life and Death of Marius the Giraffe." *Environmental Philosophy* 12, no. 1 (2015): 21–44.

Levinas, Emmanuel. *Difficult Freedom: Essays on Judaism*. Translated by Sean Hand. Baltimore: Johns Hopkins University Press, 1990.

Lilova, Alina. *Insight Hound*, insighthound.wordpress.com

Lister, Charles. "Trump Says ISIS Is Defeated. Reality Says Otherwise." *Politico* (March 18, 2019), www.politico.com/magazine/story/2019/03/18/trump-isis-terrorists-defeated-foreign-policy-225816

Loretz, John. "The Animal Victims of the Gulf War." *Physicians for Social Responsibility* 1, no. 4 (1991): 221–225.

Lowell, Robert. *Day by Day*. New York: Farrar, Straus and Giroux, 1977.

Luo, Michael. "Even Picking Up Trash Is a High Risk in Baghdad." *New York Times* (October 13, 2006), A8.

Malabou, Catherine, and Jacques Derrida. *Counterpath: Travelling with Jacques Derrida*. Translated by David Wills. Stanford, CA: Stanford University Press, 2004.

Manguso, Sarah. *Ongoingness: The End of a Diary*. Minneapolis: Graywolf Press, 2005.
Martin, Douglas. "Lawrence Anthony, Baghdad Zoo Savior, Dies at 61." *New York Times* (March 11, 2012), www.nytimes.com/2012/03/12/world/africa/lawrence-anthony-baghdad-zoo-savior-dies-at-61.html
Massella, Antonio. "We Have Forgotten What Happiness Is: Youth Perspectives of Displacement and Return in Qayyarah Subdistrict, Mosul." *Oxfam* (October 2017), https://oxfamilibrary.openrepository.com/bitstream/handle/10546/620351/rr-youth-perspectives-displacement-iraq-191017-en.pdf?sequence=1
Mayell, Hillary. "Struggling to Save Baghdad Zoo Animals." *National Geographic* (June 4, 2003).
Mazzini, Francesco, Simon W. Townsend, Zsófia Virányi, and Friederike Range. "Wolf Howling Is Mediated by Relationship Quality Rather Than Underlying Emotional Stress." *Current Biology* 23, no. 17 (2013): 1678–1679.
"Meet the Animals: Pigs." Farm Sanctuary, www.farmsanctuary.org/learn/the-someone-project/pigs
Meiches, Benjamin. "Non-Human Humanitarians." *Review of International Studies* 45, no. 1 (2019): 1–19.
Meloy, Ellen. *Eating Stone: Imagination and the Loss of the Wild*. New York: Vintage Books, 2005.
Mendieta, Eduardo. "Interspecies Cosmopolitanism: Towards a Discourse Ethics Grounding of Animal Rights." *Philosophy Today* 54 Supplement (2010): 208–216.
Menely, Tobias. "Zoöphilpsychosis: Why Animals Are What's Wrong with Sentimentality." *symplokē* 15, no. 1/2 (2007): 244–267.
Merleau-Ponty, Maurice. *The Visible and the Invisible*. Translated by Alphonso Lingis. Evanston, IL: Northwestern University Press, 1968.
Mikhail, Dunya. *The War Works Hard*. Translated by Elizabeth Winslow. New York: New Directions, 2005.
Mikhail, Dunya, ed. *Fifteen Iraqi Poets*. New York: New Directions, 2013.
Mikolsi, Adam. *Dog Behavior, Evolution, and Cognition*. New York: Oxford University Press.
Miller, David. *National Responsibility and Global Justice*. New York: Oxford University Press, 2007.
Miller, Robert. "Respiratory Disorders Following Service in Iraq." Nashville, TN: Vanderbilt University, Vanderbilt Medical Center (2013).
Moe, Aaron M. *Zoopoetics: Animals and the Making of Poetry*. Lanham, MD: Lexington Books, 2014.
Moellendorf, Darrel. *Cosmopolitan Justice*. Boulder, CO: Westview Press, 2002.
Molnár, Csaba, Péter Pongrácz, Tamás Faragó, Antal Dóka, and Ádám Miklósi, "Dogs Discriminate Between Barks: The Effect of Context and Identity of the Caller," *Behavioural Processes* 82, no. 2 (2009): 198–201.

Moore, Cerwyn. "On Cruelty: Literature, Aesthetics and Global Politics." *Global Society* 24, no. 3 (2010): 311–329.
Morello, Carol. "Baghdad's Needs Extend to Zoo Residents." *Washington Post* (April 30, 2003), www.washingtonpost.com/archive/politics/2003/04/30/baghdads-needs-extend-to-zoo-residents/9a250963-8424-4d4b-8240-c1c22ccb4b59/?utm_term=.0ca10e16d731
Morton Timothy. *Ecology Without Nature: Rethinking Environmental Aesthetics.* Cambridge, MA: Harvard University Press, 2007.
Morton, Timothy. *Humankind: Solidarity with Non-Human People.* London: Verso, 2017.
Mundy, Rachel. "Museums of Sound: Audio Bird Guides and the Pleasures of Knowledge." *Sound Studies* 2, no. 1 (2016): 52–68.
Mydans, Seth. "Mines Maim the Ultimate Civilians: Animals." *New York Times* (March 5, 2001), www.nytimes.com/2001/03/05/world/mines-maim-the-ultimate-civilians-animals.html
Naas, Michael. *Derrida from Now On.* New York: Fordham University Press, 2008.
Naas, Michael. *The End of the World and Other Teachable Moments: Jacques Derrida's Final Seminar.* New York: Fordham University Press, 2014.
Nagasawa, Miho, Shouhei Mitsui, Shiori En, Nobuyo Ohtani, Mitsuaki Ohta, Yasuo Sakuma, Tatsushi Onaka, Kazutaka Mogi, and Takefumi Kikusui. "Oxytocin-Gaze Positive Loop and the Coevolution of Human-Dog Bonds." *Science* 348: 6232 (2015): 333–336.
Najm, Soheil. "Interview with Soheil Najm." *Silk Routes.* https://iwp.uiowa.edu/silkroutes/interview-soheil-najm
Narayanan, Yamini, and Sumanth Bindumadhav. "'Posthuman Cosmopolitanism' for the Anthropocene in India: Urbanism and Human-Snake Relations in the Kali Yuga." *Geoforum* 106 (2019): 402–410.
Nava, Mica. *Visceral Cosmopolitanism: Gender, Culture and the Normalisation of Difference.* Oxford: Berg, 2007.
Nayak, Meghana, and Eric Selbin. *Decentering International Relations.* New York: Zed Books, 2013.
Nayar, Pramod K. "'Novel Globalism,' The Transnational Exotic and Spectral Cosmopolitanism: David Mitchell's Fiction," *The Grove* 18 (2011): 69–86.
Nordland, Rod. "Tigers Return to Baghdad." *Newsweek* (August 7, 2008), www.newsweek.com/tigers-return-baghdad-88163
Norelli, Elisa. "Iraq, Kurdistan: Glkand Zoo Closed. It was the Second Worst Zoo of the World." *International Organization for Animal Protection* (February 11, 2014), www.oipa.org/international/2014/kurdistan.html
Nowzad, "Our Mission." www.nowzad.com/home/our-mission
Nussbaum, Martha C. "Kant and Stoic Cosmopolitanism." *Journal of Political Philosophy* 5, no. 1 (1997): 1–25.
Nussbaum, Martha C. *Frontiers of Justice: Disability, Nationality, Species Membership.* Cambridge, MA: Belknap, 2006.

Nuwer, Rachel. "Syria's Cat Calamity: War is Hell for Pets, Too." *Newsweek* (December 16, 2015), www.newsweek.com/2015/12/25/abandoned-house-cats-aleppo-405528.html

Oliver, Kelly. *Animal Lessons: How They Teach us to be Human.* New York: Columbia University Press, 2009.

Oliver, Kelly. *Technologies of Life and Death: From Cloning to Capital Punishment.* New York: Fordham University Press, 2013.

Oliver, Kelly. "The Poetic Axis of Ethics." *Derrida Today* 7, no. 2 (2014): 121–136.

Pachirat, Timothy. *Among Wolves: Ethnography and the Immersive Study of Power.* New York: Routledge, 2017.

Palacios, Vicente, Enrique Font, and Rafael Márquez. "Iberian Wolf Howls: Acoustic Structure, Individual Variation, and a Comparison with North American Populations." *Journal of Mammalogy* 88, no. 3 (2007): 606–613.

Parkin-Gounelas, Ruth. "Poetry, Automaticity and the Animal Body: Jacques Derrida with Emily Dickinson." *Textual Practice* 32, no. 5 (2018): 841–858.

Parrish, Michael. "The Spoils of War: A Report on the Eco-Disaster in the Persian Gulf." *L.A. Times* (June 23, 1991), http://articles.latimes.com/print/1991-06-23/magazine/tm-1752_1_persian-gulf

Pearson, Chris. " 'Four-Legged Poilus:' French Army Dogs, Emotional Practices and the Creation of Militarized Human-Dog Bonds, 1871–1918." *Journal of Social History* 52, no. 3 (2019): 731–760.

Peplow, Mark. "Iraqi Fire Pollution Rivalled Volcano." *Nature* (October 25, 2004), www.nature.com/news/2004/041025/full/news041025-5.html

Rajaram, Prem Kumar. "Disruptive Writing and a Critique of Territoriality." *Review of International Studies* 30, no. 2 (2004): 201–229.

Rasmussen, Claire E. *The Autonomous Animal: Self-Governance and the Modern Subject.* Minneapolis: University of Minnesota Press, 2011.

Rasmussen, Claire. "Domesticating Bodies: Race, Species, Sex, and Citizenship." In *Political Theory and the Animal/Human Relationship*, ed. Judith Grant and Vincent G. Jungkunz. Albany, NY: SUNY Press, 2016, 75–101.

Redha, Usama. "Baghdad's Pet Shop Owners are Back in Business." *LA Times* (March 20, 2009), http://articles.latimes.com/2009/mar/20/world/fg-iraq-pets20

Reuters. (June 10, 2010). https://pictures.reuters.com/archive/IRAQ-DOGS-GM1E-66A1MP101.html

Ricks, Thomas. *Fiasco: The American Military Adventure in Iraq.* New York: Penguin, 2006.

Rilke, Rainer Maria. *Selected Poems.* Translated by Stanley Appelbaum. Mineola, NY: Dover Publications, 2011.

Rising, David. "Iraq's Wildlife Trade Anything but Tame." *NBC News* (May 27, 2010), www.nbcnews.com/id/37372231/ns/world_news-mideast_n_africa/t/iraqs-wildlife-trade-anything-tame/#.XDY4hi3MxPV

Robbins, Bruce, and Paulo Lemos Horta, eds. *Cosmopolitans.* New York: New York University Press, 2017.

Rothfels, Nigel. *Savages and Beasts: The Birth of the Modern Zoo*. Baltimore: Johns Hopkins University Press, 2002.

Rothfield, Lawrence. *The Rape of Mesopotamia: Behind the Looting of the Iraq Museum*. Chicago: University of Chicago Press, 2009.

Rubin, Alissa J. "In Iraq, Where Beauty Was Long Suppressed, Art Flowers Amid Protests." *New York Times* (February 3, 2020), www.nytimes.com/2020/02/03/world/middleeast/iraq-protests-art.html?searchResultPosition=15

Rutherford, Kenneth R. "The Evolving Arms Control Agenda: Implications of the Role of NGOS in Banning Antipersonnel Landmines." *World Politics* 53, no. 1 (2000): 74–114.

Saghafi, Kas. *Apparitions—Of Derrida's Other*. New York: Fordham University Press, 2010.

Saghafi, Kas. "The World after the End of the World." *Oxford Literary Review* 39, no. 2 (2017) 265–276.

Salgado, Sebastião. "Exposures: When the Oil Fields Burned." *New York Times* (April 8, 2016), www.nytimes.com/interactive/2016/04/08/sunday-review/exposures-kuwait-salgado.html

Sandburg, Carl. "Buffalo Dusk." *Poetry Foundation* (1970), www.poetryfoundation.org/poems/53232/buffalo-dusk

Schaller, George B. *The Serengeti Lion: A Study of Predator-Prey Relations*. Chicago: University of Chicago Press, 2009.

Schott, Robin May. "Just War and the Problem of Evil." *Hypatia* 23, no. 2 (2008): 122–140.

Schmitt Eric, and Thom Shanker, "Water and Electricity in Baghdad Are Still Below Prewar Levels, Officials Say." *New York Times* (July 8, 2003), www.nytimes.com/2003/07/08/world/after-war-services-water-electricity-baghdad-are-still-below-prewar-levels.html

Schwartzstein, Peter. "For Leopards in Iran and Iraq, Land Mines Are a Surprising Refuge." *National Geographic* (December 12, 2014), https://news.nationalgeographic.com/news/2014/12/141219-persian-leopard-iran-iraq-land-mine

Schwartzstein, Peter. "The Islamic State's Scorched-Earth Strategy." *Foreign Policy* (April 6, 2016), http://foreignpolicy.com/2016/04/06/the-islamic-states-scorched-earth-strategy

Schwartzstein, Peter. "Iraq's Unique Wildlife Pushed to Brink by War, Hunting." *National Geographic* (February 6, 2017), http://news.nationalgeographic.com/2017/02/iraq-wildlife-islamic-state-species-war

Schwartzstein, Peter. "Iraq's Unlikely Love Affair with Cuddly Canines." *Newsweek* (April 18, 2017), www.newsweek.com/dogs-iraq-security-585522

Shea, Louisa. *The Cynic Enlightenment: Diogenes in the Salon*. Baltimore: Johns Hopkins University Press, 2010.

Shearer, Chris. "What It's Like Putting Out Oil Fires Lit by Retreating ISIS Fighters." *VICE* (February 1, 2017), www.vice.com/en_us/article/kbgzkv/what-its-like-putting-out-oil-fires-lit-by-retreating-is-fighters

Sheeran, Paul. *Literature and International Relations: Stories in the Art of Diplomacy*. New York: Routledge, 2016.

Shelton, Tracey. "Iraq: Dante's Hell for Animals?" *PRI* (May 30, 2010), www.pri.org/stories/2010-05-22/iraq-dantes-hell-animals

Simons, John. *Animal Rights and the Politics of Literary Representation*. New York: Palgrave, 2002.

Soguk, Nevzat. "Splinters of Hegemony: Ontopoetical Visions in International Relations." *Alternatives* 31, no. 4 (2006): 377–404.

Solomon, Erika, Robin Kwong, and Steven Bernard. "Inside Isis Inc: The Journey of a Barrel of Oil." (February 29, 2016), *Financial Times*, https://ig.ft.com/sites/2015/isis-oil

Solomon, Ty, and Brent J. Steele. "Micro-Moves in International Relations Theory." *European Journal of International Relations* 23, no. 2 (2017): 267–291.

Souza, Adriana S., Jarno Jansen, Robert J. Tempelman, Michael Mendl, and Adroaldo J. Zanella. "A Novel Method for Testing Social Recognition in Young Pigs and the Modulating Effects of Relocation." *Applied Animal Behaviour Science* 99, no. 1–2 (2006): 77–87.

Spahr, Juliana. "Contemporary US Poetry and its Nationalisms." *Contemporary Literature* 52, no. 4 (2011): 684–715.

Steiner, Gary. "Toward a Non-Anthropocentric Cosmopolitanism." In *Anthropocentrism: Humans, Animals, Environments*, ed. Rob Boddice (Leiden: Brill, 2011): 81–114;

Steinhoff, Uwe. "Debate: Jeff McMahan on the Moral Inequality of Combatants." *Journal of Political Philosophy* 16, no. 2 (2008): 220–226.

Stokstad, Erik. "Inside the Global Campaign to Get Rid of Rabies." *Science* (January 19, 2017), www.sciencemag.org/news/2017/01/inside-global-campaign-get-rid-rabies

"The Struggle for Iraq; U.S. Soldier Kills Tiger in Baghdad Zoo." *New York Times* (September 21, 2003), www.nytimes.com/2003/09/21/world/the-struggle-for-iraq-us-soldier-kills-tiger-in-baghdad-zoo.html

Studnitz, Merete, Margit Bak Jensen, and Lene Juul Pedersen. "Why Do Pigs Root and in What Will They Root? A Review on the Exploratory Behaviour of Pigs in Relation to Environmental Enrichment." *Applied Animal Behaviour Science* 107, no. 3–4 (2007): 183–197.

"Sulfur Dioxide Spreads Over Iraq." *NASA Earth Observatory* (October 24, 2016), https://earthobservatory.nasa.gov/NaturalHazards/view.php?id=88994

Sylvester, Christine. "War, Sense, and Security." In *Gender and International Security: Feminist Perspectives*, ed. Laura Sjoberg. New York: Routledge, 2010, 24–37.

Sylvester, Christine. "The Forum: Emotion and the Feminist IR Researcher." *International Studies Review* 13, no. 4 (2011): 687–708.

Sylvester, Christine. "Experiencing War: a Challenge for International Relations." *Cambridge Review of International Affairs* 26, no. 4 (2013): 669–674.

Taylor, Alan. "Afghanistan: Dogs of War." *The Atlantic* (June 3, 2014), www.theatlantic.com/photo/2014/06/afghanistan-dogs-of-war/100750
Taylor, Chloé. "Hard, Dry Eyes and Eyes That Weep: Vision and Ethics in Levinas and Derrida." *Postmodern Culture* 16, no. 2 (2006).
"Tracing the Supply of Components used in Islamic State IEDs: Evidence from a 20-month Investigation in Iraq and Syria." *Conflict Armament Research* (February 2016), www.conflictarm.com/wp-content/uploads/2016/02/Tracing_The_Supply_of_Components_Used_in_Islamic_State_IEDs.pdf
Trump, Donald. "Remarks by President Trump on the Death of ISIS Leader Abu Bakr al-Baghdadi." The White House (October 27, 2019), www.whitehouse.gov/briefings-statements/remarks-president-trump-death-isis-leader-abu-bakr-al-baghdadi
Trump, Donald, and Mike Pence. "Remarks by President Trump and Vice President Pence Recognizing Special Operations Military Working Dog from 1st SFOD-D." The White House (November 25, 2019), www.whitehouse.gov/briefings-statements/remarks-president-trump-vice-president-pence-recognizing-special-operations-military-working-dog-1st-sfod-d
United Nations, "Restoration of Veterinary Services in Iraq" (November 2009), www.fao.org/fileadmin/user_upload/oed/docs/OSROIRQ406UDG_2009_ER.pdf
Van Dooren, Thom. *Flight Ways: Life and Loss at the Edge of Extinction*. New York: Columbia University Press, 2014.
Vaughan, Brian K., and Niko Henrichon. *Pride of Baghdad*. New York: DC Comics, 2006.
Venn, Couze. "The Collection." *Theory, Culture & Society* 23, no. 2–3 (2006): 35–40.
Walzer, Michael. *Just and Unjust wars: A Moral Argument with Historical Illustrations*, 4th edition. New York: Basic Books, 2006.
Ward, Eilís. "Human Suffering and the Quest for Cosmopolitan Solidarity: A Buddhist Perspective." *Journal of International Political Theory* 9, no. 2 (2013): 136–154.
The Watson Institute for International and Public Affairs, https://watson.brown.edu/costsofwar/costs/human/civilians
Watson, Matthew C. "Derrida, Stengers, Latour, and Subalternist Cosmopolitics." *Theory, Culture & Society* 31, no. 1 (2014): 75–98.
Webster, Noah. *American Dictionary of the English Language*, 1828, http://webstersdictionary1828.com
Weinstein, Adam. "Iraq's Slumdog Massacre: One Million Dogs Face Death." *Mother Jones* (June 2010), www.motherjones.com/politics/2010/06/iraq-kbr-one-million-dogs-death
Weir, Doug. "The Environmental Consequences of Iraq's Oil Fires are Going Unrecorded." *Conflict and Environment Observatory* (November 30, 2016), https://ceobs.org/the-environmental-consequences-of-iraqs-oil-fires-are-going-unrecorded

Welland, Julia. "Joy and War: Reading Pleasure in Wartime Experiences." *Review of International Studies* 44, no. 3 (2018): 438–455.

Whitman, Walt. *Leaves of Grass, 1860: The 150th Anniversary Facsimile Edition.* Iowa City: University of Iowa Press, 2009.

Wilcox, Lauren B. *Bodies of Violence: Theorizing Embodied Subjects in International Relations.* New York: Oxford University Press, 2015.

Willett, Cynthia. *Interspecies Ethics.* New York: Columbia University Press, 2014.

Williams, Sally. "The Man Who Risks his Life to Rescue Zoo Animals from War Zones." *The Telegraph* (December 8, 2017), www.telegraph.co.uk/news/2017/12/08/man-risks-life-rescue-zoo-animals-war-zones

Winsor, Morgan. "Animals Rescued from Mosul's Abandoned Zoo Arrive Safely in Jordan." *ABC News* (April 13, 2017), http://abcnews.go.com/International/animals-rescued-mosuls-abandonned-zoo-arrive-safely-jordan/story?id=46748723

Wolfe-Hunnicutt, Brandon. "Embracing Regime Change in Iraq: American Foreign Policy and the 1963 Coup d'etat in Baghdad." *Diplomatic History* 39, no. 1 (2015): 98–125.

Wolfe, Cary. *What Is Posthumanism?* Minneapolis: University of Minnesota Press, 2010.

Wood-Gush, David G.M., and Klaus Vestergaard. "Exploratory Behavior and the Welfare of Intensively Kept Animals." *Journal of Agricultural Ethics* 2, no. 2 (1989): 161–169.

Wright, Robin. "Rescuing the Last Two Animals at the Mosul Zoo." *The New Yorker* (April 24, 2017), www.newyorker.com/news/news-desk/rescuing-the-last-two-animals-at-the-mosul-zoo

Wright, Robin. "Baghdadi Is Back—and Vows That ISIS Will Be, Too." *The New Yorker* (April 29, 2019), www.newyorker.com/news/news-desk/baghdadi-is-backand-vows-that-isis-will-be-too

"Yemen: Houthi-Saleh Forces Using Landmines." *Human Rights Watch* (April 20, 2017), www.hrw.org/news/2017/04/20/yemen-houthi-saleh-forces-using-landmines

Youatt, Rafi. "Power, Pain, and the Interspecies Politics of Foie Gras." *Political Research Quarterly* 65, no. 2 (2012): 346–358.

Youatt, Rafi. "Interspecies Relations, International Relations: Rethinking Anthropocentric Politics." *Millennium: Journal of International Studies* 43, no. 1 (2014): 207–223.

Youatt, Rafi. *Counting Species: Biodiversity in Global Environmental Politics.* Minneapolis: University of Minnesota Press, 2015.

Youatt, Rafi. "Sovereignty and the Wolves of Isle Royale." In *Political Theory and the Animal/Human Relationship*, ed. Judith Grant and Vincent G. Jungkunz. Albany, NY: SUNY Press, 2016, 103–128.

Youatt, Rafi. "Personhood and the Rights of Nature: The New Subjects of Contemporary Earth Politics." *International Political Sociology* 11, no. 1 (2017): 39–54.

Youatt, Rafi. *Interspecies Politics: Nature, Borders, States*. Ann Arbor: University of Michigan Press, 2020.
Zierler, David. *The Invention of Ecocide: Agent Orange, Vietnam, and The Scientists Who Changed the Way We Think About the Environment*. Athens: University of Georgia Press, 2011.
Zinsstag, J., Durr, S., Penny, M.A., Mindekem, R., Roth, F., Gonzalez, S.M., Naissengar, S., and Hattendorf, J. "Transmission Dynamics and Economics of Rabies Control in Dogs and Humans in an African City." *Proceedings of the National Academy of Sciences* 106, no. 5 (2009): 14996–15001.

About the Author

Matthew Leep is an instructor of political science at Western Governors University.

Index

absence, 5, 20–21, 36, 97–99
affective solidarities, 15
Afghanistan, 58, 61, 94–95
agency, 23, 35–36, 46, 111n40
al-Baghdadi, Abu Bakr, 45, 97
Al Ma'wa Wildlife Reserve, 80
Alousi, Alise, 40
al-Qaeda, 85
Andrzejewski, Julie, 129n4
animal experiences of war, 4, 6, 10–16, 20, 24, 27–28, 52–55, 58, 63, 67, 71, 96–104
animality/animalities, 9, 62
Anthony, Lawrence, 69, 74, 76
anthropocentrism, 6, 34–35, 108–109
anthropomorphism, 38, 65
apparitional presence, 21–22. See also *fantômes*; ghost(s)
Arendt, Hannah, 53
army: investigations, 127n33; veterinarians, 75
Auchter, Jessica, 113n6, 115n32
avian influenza, 67. See also H5N1; viruses

Baghdad: electricity, 68; litter in, 50–51; municipal government, 46; stray dog killings, 50–52, 58, 60; street dogs, 5, 51; and trash collection, 4–5, 50, 58; zoo, 66–69, 71–74, 76–78
Barthes, Roland, 29
bear(s): Knut, 65; Lula, 79–80; Saedia, 74–76; and zoos, 65, 69
belonging: beyond-human, 32, 84; debt of, 6; and hearts, 104; and identifiable connection(s), 39; and justice, 2; and lost animals, 23; poetic, 9; and possibilities of, 10; and responsibility, 41; and spectral strata, 6; time and, 25; to the world, 8. See also belongingness
belongingness: across time, 23; beyond-human, 22–23, 25, 43, 59, 76; boundaries of, 17; cosmopolitan/cosmopolitanism and, 3–10, 16; and culpability, 58; and difference, 35; and dogs, 55–56, 58; elegiac space of, 16; human and animal, 6; interspecies, 27, 35, 62; and the never-known, 105; and poetry, 100; possibilities of, 35, 52; multispecies, 35, 60; searching for, 102; spectral, 8, 101. See also belonging
Benjamin, Walter, 117n65
Bentham, Jeremy, 10
Berger, John, 20

birds, 72, 78, 87, 93
bison: extermination, 20; and poetry, 20. *See also* buffaloes
Bleiker, Roland, 30–31, 116n44, 117nn62, 64–65
Bobby, 62. *See also* Levinas
body/bodies: animal, 20, 26; camel, 19–20; counts, 14, 26, 50–51, 70, 79; dead sheep and cows, 92; decomposing, 79; dog, 51, 95; pig, 69–70, 92; theorizing, 25; and violence, 26
Bolton, John, 97
bomb(s), 28, 61, 68, 70, 95
bombing, 13, 67–68
border(s), 1–3, 8, 11, 15, 19–20, 29, 32, 42, 67, 71, 77, 81, 86, 96
borderless responsibility, 13, 102
boundaries: between life forms, 70; cosmopolitanism and 1–3; of emotional and political attachments, 15; human-animal, 34, 62; of moral difference, 17; of poetry and poetic thinking, 29, 34; temporal, 22
Brock, Gillian, 41
buffaloes, 20. *See also* bison
Burke, Anthony, 6, 117n64
Butler, Judith, 41, 120n122.

camel(s), 19–20, 25, 72, 76, 87, 101
canine, 47, 49, 113n63. *See also* dog(s)
captivity, 67, 73, 81
casualties, 25–26, 94
cat(s), 52, 55, 61
cattle, 87. *See also* cow(s)
Celan, Paul, 100, 110n36, 120n114
Che cos'è la poesia? (Derrida), 29
cheetahs, 76–77
children and war, 52, 90, 94

civilians: and landmines, 96; Iraqi, 107n3; targeting of, 13; and U.S. airstrikes, 78, 86, 88; and war, 1
Clark, Timothy, 116n44
collateral damage, 4–5, 12, 26–27, 89, 116n38
community: global, 2, 103–104; human, 15; political, 9, 37; world, 9, 103–104
compassion, 10–11, 59, 111n40
Conan, 45. *See also* dog(s)
The Conflict and Environment Observatory, 90
constrictive bronchiolitis, 93. *See also* respiratory illnesses
cosmopolis, 9
cosmopolitan: approaches to war, 2–4, 13–14, 21–24, 99, 112n52; belongingness, 6, 8, 10, 16; Diogenes, 9; elegies, 1, 14, 43, 98, 101; and International Relations, 3; justice, 1–2, 22, 103; literature on war, 12–14; memory, 2; poetics, 40; responsibilities, 11, 13, 38, 40–41, 102; spectral, 21; text/writing, 5, 10, 12, 14, 23–24, 27; tradition and animals, 111n40. *See also* responsibility/responsibilities
cosmopolitanism, 2–3, 5, 8–9, 11–15, 17, 19, 21–24, 28, 30–32, 34, 36–39, 41–43, 53, 65, 67, 99, 101–105, 108n13, 111n40, 112n50
cosmopolitans: and analytic philosophy, 13; and belonging to the world, 8; and global responsibilities, 11, 38; and poetry, 5, 23, 31, 33; and war, 12, 14
cow(s), 84, 92. *See also* cattle
culpability, 17, 32, 39–40, 57–61, 85–86

Index

Dada, 29
Daesh, 130n24. *See also* ISIS; Islamic State of Iraq and al-Sham
death, 1, 3–4, 6, 9–10, 12–14, 16, 20–21, 25, 28, 32, 34–35, 39–40, 42, 45, 50, 52–54, 58, 63, 69–70, 73, 76, 79, 83, 88–89, 95–97, 100–101, 103, 107n2, 110n38, 114n19, 123n48, 127n39, 134n25
de-Baathification, 85
Delanty, Gerard, 24
Derrida, Jacques, 1–2, 5–6, 8–12, 15–16, 18–19, 21–22, 24–30, 33–36, 38–43, 53–57, 61–63, 69, 71, 77, 81, 83, 87, 91, 95, 99–105, 107n1, 109n27, 110nn36, 38, 111n49, 112n50
Diogenes, 8–9, 110n31
distance, 2–3, 6, 8–11, 14–15, 20–21, 23, 28, 33, 37, 51–52, 54, 64, 71, 76, 89, 96, 99, 101–104
distant others, 2, 10–12, 23, 29, 31, 39, 54, 104
Dobson, Andrew, 39
dog(s), 5, 7, 9, 17, 45–64, 94–96, 100, 104–105; bark(s), 46, 60, 63, 105; and belongingness, 55–56, 58; companionship, 17, 49; Conan, 45; Drak, 95; and ecological flexibility, 48; free-ranging, 46; free-roaming, 60; and human relations, 47; and Islam/Muslim societies, 49, 122n20; military, 17, 95, 113n63; mine-detecting/mine-sniffing, 17, 95; misfit, 17; patriotic, 95; shelters, 61; stray, 16–17, 45–59, 61, 63–65, 95, 104; street, 16–17, 45–48, 50–52, 60, 102, 105; wandering, 47–49, 51–52, 62–63, 104. *See also* canine; stray dog(s); street dog(s); wanderer(s); wandering dog(s)
Doty, Roxanne, 32, 34, 118n69

Drak, 95. *See also* dog(s)
dream(s), 7, 9, 30, 33, 37, 60, 63, 72, 74, 77, 79, 105

Echographies (Derrida), 5
ecological: dogs and ecological flexibility, 48; fates, 20; harm, 84–87, 94
elegiac: accounting, 6; articulation, 102; assessments, 42; connection, 17, 21; fragments, 5, 32; space, 1–3, 8, 12, 14, 16, 18, 21, 25–27, 41, 46, 97, 99, 104–105; turn, 3, 84
elegy/elegies, 1, 8, 11, 14, 32, 43, 81–82, 97, 99, 101, 103
elephant(s), 96, 100. *See also* Mosha and Motala
entanglements, 2–3, 84
environmental devastation, 83, 88
Erbil, 78
ethology, 16, 23, 33–34. *See also* zoological knowledge
event, 3–4, 6, 22, 24–27, 63, 89, 97, 99
experience, 2, 4–6, 8–10, 13–14, 16, 20, 23–30, 33–35, 38, 52–54, 62–63, 65–67, 69, 71, 76, 81, 100–101, 108n9, 117n64, 126n17, 127n33
explosive devices, 94, 96–97. *See also* IEDs; improvised explosive devices

Fabre, Cécile, 13–14
fantômes, 21. *See also* ghosts
Felstiner, John, 31
finitude, 9–10
fire(s), 17, 19, 73, 83–85, 87–90, 92–94
forests, 17, 38, 83–84, 94
Four Paws International, 80
future(s), 2, 8, 15–18, 20–21, 24–25, 27, 39, 41–43, 52, 58, 62, 75–76, 82, 91, 94, 96, 98, 105

gaze, 16, 22–23, 38, 40, 54–56, 65, 67, 69, 91, 98, 101, 105, 114n19
Gerges, Fawaz, 85
ghost(s), 2–3, 5–6, 11, 16, 21–22, 28, 38, 40–41, 83, 95, 99–100, 102–103, 107. See also *fantômes*
ghostly, 4–6, 8, 12, 17, 21–22, 32, 41–42, 76, 103–105, 113n6
giraffe(s), 27, 65, 72, 102, 105
Glkand Zoo, 78
global pandemics, 20. See also pandemics; trans-species infections
global politics: and creative writing, 118n69; as ghostly, 21, 113n6; as interspecies politics, 3; and poetry, 31; sensory focus on, 3. See also International Relations (IR)
global community, 2, 103–104. See also community
Goodrich, Charles, 38
grief, 42
grievable, 41

H5N1, 67. See also avian influenza; viruses
Hägglund, Martin, 21
Halliburton, 49
Hanif, Mohammed, 49
Harambe, 65
Haraway, Donna, 45, 47, 49, 121n12
haunt/haunting, 7, 12, 17, 22, 76, 84, 113n6
hauntology, 8
heart(s): beats, 22; of others, 1, 18, 23, 32, 40; and poetry, 29, 31–32, 40, 43, 100; memory, 29, 31–32; unknowable, 21; and the world, 8
Hediger, Ryan, 113n63
Heidegger, Martin, 33–36, 102
herons, 93
horse(s), 70, 94
Horta, Paulo Lemos, 23

hospitable, 12, 57, 80
hospitality, 9, 35, 53, 56, 61, 81, 112n50
Houthi, 96
Howe, Susan, 5, 15, 24, 65, 102, 114n25
Howell, Alison, 17, 68–69, 76–77
howl(s), 36. See also wolf/wolves
human–animal boundaries, 34, 62
human–animal politics, 59
human–animal relations, 16, 34–35, 47–48, 59, 113n6
humanity, 9, 62–63, 77
Hussein, Saddam, 49, 57–58, 112n52
Hussein, Uday, 76–77

IEDs, 84, 90, 94, 96. See also explosive devices; improvised explosive devices
Ijhala, 92
illegal pet markets, 78
imagination, 4, 8, 12, 15, 25, 28, 30–31, 43, 64, 82, 91, 101–102, 104
imaginative, 2, 4, 11, 17, 22, 24, 26, 28, 31, 40, 42, 76, 100, 102–103
imperialism, 12
improvised explosive devices, 84, 90, 94, 96. See also explosive devices; IEDs
inhumanity, 62
interconnectedness: global, 23; interspecies/international, 9; 23; multispecies, 23
interiority/interiorities, 1–2, 10, 20, 24, 67, 78, 81, 99–101
International Fund for Animal Welfare, 76
International Relations (IR): aesthetic, 3, 31; animals and, 108n11; creativity and, 32; poetry and, 31–32, 34, 117n64; and war, 25. See also global politics

interspecies, 3, 6, 9–11, 20, 27, 32–37, 55, 58–63, 66, 102–103, 105, 111n40
invasion of Iraq, 39–41, 49–52, 57, 68–69, 75, 85, 99. See also Iraq War; occupation of Iraq
Iraq War, 1–3, 7–8, 16–17, 23, 25–26, 28 32, 35, 40, 61, 63, 66—67, 69, 85, 87–89, 92, 99, 107n3. See also invasion of Iraq
Iraqi(s), 17, 40, 49, 51–52, 57, 59, 68, 72–82, 74, 77–79, 82, 86–88, 92, 107n3, 124n61
ISIS, 16–17, 45, 78–79, 83–89, 92, 94, 96–97. See also Daesh; Islamic State of Iraq and al-Sham
Islamic State of Iraq and al-Sham, 16. See also Daesh; ISIS
island(s) 8–11, 15, 27–28, 30, 34–38, 40, 71, 96, 101, 103–104, 119n95. See also world(s)

jihad, 97
Joris, Pierre, 42
justice: animals as subjects of, 22; civilian casualties and measures of, 25; cosmopolitan, 1–2, 22, 103; dogs and the demands of, 46; elegies and, 43; the face and, 56; ghostly, 12; hospitable, 57; poetry and, 22; remains of justice, 22–23; of remembrance of the unknown and nameless, 57; theories of, 14; where it is no longer, 22
just war theory, 12–14, 25, 62, 112n52

Kabul, 67
Khalil, Amir, 80
kill/killed/killing: Abu Bakr al-Baghdadi, 45; bison, 20; and civilians, 13, 78, 86, 107n3; and cosmopolitanism, 13–14; and

improvised explosives, 84, 94, 96; and just war theory, 13–14; language of, 40; Native Americans, 20; sheep, 92, 96; stray dogs, 5, 46, 48–49, 50–52, 57–58, 60, 69–70; zoo animals, 66, 68–69, 71–72, 77, 79
Kinder, John, 67
knowability, 35, 65
knowledge, 7, 14, 26, 29–30, 33–35, 37–38, 42, 76, 91, 100–101
Kurdistan, 78
Kuwait, 87, 112n52

Lacan, Jacques, 33
landmine(s), 84, 94, 96
Leebaw, Bronwyn, 83
Levinas, Emmanuel, 33, 55–56, 62. See also Bobby
lion(s), 17, 58, 65, 72–73, 76–80
listening, 3, 6, 9, 12, 18–19, 21, 23, 26, 29, 43, 46, 64, 82–83, 99, 104–105, 134n21
literary, 23, 31, 82. See also writing
looters, 17, 68–70, 72, 74–75
looting, 17, 59, 67, 69, 74
loss, 1–6, 9, 11–13, 15–16, 18, 20–29, 32–33, 39–42, 57–59, 64, 67, 71, 83–84, 86–87, 96–97, 99–104, 107n3
losses, 1, 4, 8, 16, 39, 43, 54, 76, 100, 102, 107n3
lost, 1–12, 14–29, 31–33, 39–43, 46, 55, 57–58, 61–63, 67–68, 71, 73, 82–86, 91, 94, 96–97, 99–105, 107
love, 80
Lowell, Robert, 20
Lula, 79–80. See also bear(s)
Luna Park, 76

Mahmudiyah, 50
Mansour district, 67

market(s): animal, 78; black, 72; and dogs, 7, 50
memory/memories, 1–2, 4–6, 12, 17, 19–20, 29, 31, 39, 43, 53, 57, 63, 71, 86, 89, 91, 94, 96, 98–99, 103–105, 107n2
menagerie, 17, 65, 101
Mikhail, Dunya, 40
military dogs, 17, 95, 113n63. *See also* dog(s)
Miller, Robert, 93. *See also* constrictive bronchiolitis
Mines Advisory Group, 96
Mishraq, 92–93
Moellendorf, Darrel, 112n52
moment(s), 1, 3–7, 9–12, 14–17, 19–31, 33, 35–38, 40–43, 48, 50, 52, 55, 58, 60, 62–65, 69, 71–73, 76–77, 84–85, 87, 89, 91, 97–101, 102, 104–105, 115n35, 126n17
Montazah al-Morour Zoo, 78–79
Morton, Timothy, 84, 109–110n27
Mosha and Motala, 96. *See also* elephants; landmine(s)
mourning, 100, 105
multispecies: battleground, 67; belongingness, 35; cosmopolitanism, 2; experiences, 5, 17; histories, 82; inquiry, 6, 8; interconnectedness, 23; living and dying, 59; pasts and futures, 20; political relations, 60; storytelling, 22; world, 1, 36; writing about, 1, 23, 31

Najm, Soheil, 40, 120n112
name(s), 1, 4–6, 20, 22, 47, 53, 57, 63, 65, 71, 84, 95–96, 107, 109
named, 20, 45, 49, 62, 65–66, 79, 95–96
nameless, 1–2, 6, 20, 43, 46, 51, 53, 57, 71, 96, 104
nature, 9, 31, 38, 83–84, 87, 129n7

Nava, Mica, 108n13
Nayak, Meghana, 31
Neal, Andrew, 17, 68–69, 76–77
neighbor: dog as, 62–63; and lions, 73
neural circuits and mechanisms, 91
nonhuman(s), 1, 4–5, 15, 17, 22, 31–32, 36, 38, 58, 64, 77, 93, 104, 109n27, 111n40, 115n32, 117n65
Nowzad, 61
Nussbaum, Martha, 22–23, 114n13
N'Djamena, 60–61

occupation of Iraq, 4, 39, 57, 67, 72–73, 76, 78, 85. *See also* invasion of Iraq
oil, 17, 19, 84–85, 87–90
Oliver, Kelly, 54, 100n38, 114n19
ongoingness of war, 4, 27, 63, 82
ontology/ontological, 6, 8, 17, 49, 110n27, 129n7
openness, 5, 24, 104
orientalist, 17, 69
oxytocin, 55

panda, 65
pandemics, 20. *See also* global pandemics; trans-species infections
Pence, Mike, 45
personhood, 35–36, 47
pets, 49, 52–53, 78
pig(s), 17, 69–71, 76, 102. *See also* root
poem(s), 1–2, 4–5, 8, 10, 14, 29–33, 38–42, 48, 67, 97, 100, 105, 120n122
poetic, 1–6, 8–11, 14–18, 21–22, 26, 28–38, 40–43, 46, 56, 58, 64, 81–82, 100–105, 109n17, 116n42, 117n60, 120nn112, 116
poetics, 34, 40, 116, 117n67, 120n112
poetry, 3, 5–6, 10, 12, 14–16, 20, 22–23, 28–35, 37–40, 42–43,

99–101, 104, 109n17, 113, 116nn42, 44, 117n60, 120n112. *See also* literary; writing
poisoned: dogs, 50–51, 92; sheep, 92
political: attachments, 15, community, 9, 37; debt, 80; life, 11, 105; power and multispecies living, 59; responsibility, 11, 60, 77, 80, 120n122; violence, 10, 41, 102
politics: human-animal, 59; interspecies, 3, 11, 33, 37. *See also* global politics; International Relations (IR)
posthuman/posthumanism, 108–109, 111, 115n32, 132n59
posthumanist, 1–2, 17, 33, 103, 108n9. *See also* responsibility/responsibilities
power: and animals, 10–11, 20, 59, 70; coercive/military, 20, 69, 74
primatological, 33
Princess Alia Foundation, 80

Qarqar, 19
Qayyarah, 17, 83, 87–90, 92, 95, 97
Qitmīr, 49, 58, 122n22
Qur'an, 49, 122n22

rabies, 45, 48, 50–53, 59–61, 124n74. *See also* vaccination(s)
Rajaram, Prem, 31
Rasmussen, Claire, 113n6, 114n13, 122n36
relational/relationality, 4, 8, 36, 47–48, 77
requiem, 16
respiratory illnesses, 67, 87, 93. *See also* constrictive bronchiolitis
responsibility/responsibilities: to animals, 5, 39, 57, 77; borderless, 13, 102; cosmopolitan, 11, 13, 38, 40–41, 102; and culpability, 38–39,

60, 86; and elegies, 41, 81–82; and grief, 42; to imagine, 81; infinite, 39, 42, 53, 56; interspecies, 11, 34, 76; material, 41, 60, 80–81; and names, 65; and poetry, 33, 39–41; political, 11, 60, 77, 80, 120n122; posthumanist, 17, 33; to remember, 20, 41, 53, 57, 105; spectral, 2, 6, 12, 33, 40–41, 64, 76, 81, 102
rights, 22, 78, 112n52, 114n13, 129n7
Riley, 66. *See also* tiger(s)
Rilke, Rainer Maria, 67
river(s), 84, 88, 93–94
Robbins, Bruce, 23
root, 71. *See also* pig(s)
Rothfels, Nigel, 81

Saedia, 74–76. *See also* bear(s)
Saghafi, Kas, 114n11, 123n49, 134n25
Sandburg, Carl, 20
Schott, Robin May, 14
Scott-Heron, Gil, 20
sectarianism, 85
Selbin, Eric, 31
self-reflexive/self-reflexivity, 3, 21, 24–25, 28, 30–31, 99, 101–102
sensory, 3–4, 34, 108n11
sentimentality, 15
sheep, 17, 27, 35, 83–84, 90–92, 96–98, 101–102, 104–105
Shia, 85
silenced/silencing, 5, 53, 81–82, 134n21
Simba, 79–80
singular, 4, 7, 9, 11, 19, 24, 26–27, 36, 39–40, 56, 63, 76, 80, 97, 100, 104
singularity/singularities, 25, 32–33, 36, 53, 65, 89, 97, 115n34
soldier(s), 17, 45, 52–53, 55, 61, 66, 71–73, 93
solidarities, 15. *See also* affective solidarities
Solomon, Ty, 115n35

species, 9, 23, 36, 38, 66, 69, 129n75
speciesist, 35
specter(s), 1–2, 10, 19, 21, 24–25, 27–28, 83–84, 87, 99, 101, 104–105. See also *spectre/spectres*
Specters of Marx (Derrida), 19, 21, 24, 28, 99, 109n27
spectral, 2–3, 5–6, 8–9, 11–12, 15–17, 19–23, 25, 27–31, 39–43, 46, 48, 54, 56, 58, 62–64, 72, 76, 81–84, 91, 98–99, 101–105
spectralité, 21. See also spectrality
spectrality, 8, 12, 16, 18, 21, 99, 109–10. See also *spectralité*
spectral-poetic, 1–5, 7–10, 15–18, 21–23, 28, 30, 32–33, 38, 41–42, 64, 84, 96–97, 99, 101–105
spectre/spectres, 10, 87. See also specter(s)
strangeness, 28, 73
strangers, 24, 47, 53
stray dog(s), 5, 16–17, 45–59, 61, 63–65, 95, 104. See also dog(s); street dog(s)
Steele, Brent, 115n35
Steinhoff, Uwe, 116n38
Stiegler, Bernard, 29
storytelling, 22
street dog(s), 5, 16–17, 45–48, 50–52, 60, 102, 105. See also dog(s); stray dog(s)
subhuman, 62
sublime, 116n44
suffering, 9–11, 17, 66, 110n38
sulfur, 88, 90, 92–93, 132. See also sulphur
sulphur, 90. See also sulfur
Sumner, William, 74, 76–77
Sunni, 85–86
Sūrat al-Kahf, 49, 122n22
Sylvester, Christine, 3, 108n11, 115n37

sympathy, 15
Syria, 80, 86, 96

Tanzania, 60
theorizing: grief, 42; and poetry, 31; war, 3, 5, 13–14, 38
theory: and calculations of loss, 13; and distance, 14; just war, 12–14, 62, 112n52; and poetry, 31
tiger(s), 66–67, 69–71, 80, 96, 101, 104
Tigris, 88, 93
time: belongingness across, 23; and death, 53–54, 97; dogs un-named by, 53; of experience, 24; imaginative, 76; inexpressible, 40; of loss/becoming lost, 2, 24, 99; lost, 19; and memory, 5, and moments, 24–27; and the ongoingness of war, 27; of the other, 3, 5, 6, 26, 29; past, 24, 69; 76; predatory, 96; and sheep, 91; and specters, 25, 46, 100; spectral-poetic, 5, 16, 42, 96; strange, 4; time/timelines between us, 16, 25; travel, 49; war, 4–6, 8, 11–12, 15–16, 26, 45, 58, 67, 76, 94, 96, 100–101
toxic, 50, 84–85, 89–93, 132n47
toxins, 50, 84
trafficked animals, 78
transborder, 66
trans-species infections, 20. See also global pandemics; pandemics
trash, 4, 7, 50–51, 57–59, 79
Trump, Donald, 45, 97

uncountable, 20–21, 84, 89, 96
unknowability, 101, 105
unknowable, 3, 10, 20–22, 24, 41, 46, 54, 58, 62–63, 87, 97, 100, 105
unnamable, 30, 53, 63, 65, 101
unnamed, 30, 95–96, 101

vaccination(s), 58–61, 124n74. *See also* rabies
Van Dooren, Thom, 87
vector(s), 16, 45, 52–56, 58–59
veterinarian(s), 50, 59, 75, 80
veterinary, 59, 61
violence, 3, 5, 7, 9–10, 12, 15, 17, 22, 24, 26, 28, 41, 43, 45, 48–52, 56–57, 60–61, 67–68, 71, 74–75, 78–81, 85–86, 92, 96, 99, 102, 107n3, 112n50
viruses, 59, 67. *See also* avian influenza; H5N1
voice(s), 1, 3–6, 11–12, 15, 18, 21–23, 28–29, 31–32, 36–38, 41–43, 46, 53, 62–64, 70–71, 78, 82–84, 95, 98–100, 102–105, 109n17, 120n122
vulnerability/vulnerabilities, 10–11, 32, 41–42, 47–48, 52, 63, 110n 38, 111n40

Walzer, Michael, 62
wanderer(s), 45–47, 54, 63. *See also* dog(s); stray dog(s); street dog(s); wandering dog(s)
wandering dog(s), 47–49, 51–52, 62–63, 104. *See also* dog(s); stray dog(s); street dog(s); wanderer(s)
wartime, 4–6, 12, 14, 67, 100–101
Watson Institute, 124n60
WildAid, 74
Willett, Cynthia, 109n15, 111n40
witness(es) 20, 40, 42, 51, 62–65, 71–72, 84, 120n116
witnessing: imaginative, 17, 40; and spectral responsibility, 64

wolf/wolves, 36–37, 54, 69–70
Wolfe, Cary, 108n9, 111n40
world(s): alternative ways of inhabiting, 61; animal, 103; conception of, 28, 35–36, 63, 76; community, 9, 103; and cosmopolitanism, 8–10, 24, 27, 114n15; cow, 92; and the dead, 25, 41, 54; end of, 53–54; human, 47, 119n95; interconnectivity of, 2; of multiplicities, 36; multispecies, 1, 36; of pigs, 71; and poetry, 31–32, 34, 38, 40, 43; responsibility to, 33–34, 40, 76; sense of, 91; spectral/spectrality and, 20, 22, 27, 41; of street dogs, 60; of wolves, 37. *See also* island(s)
writing: about animals, 3–4, 12, 18, 27, 81; and being-with others, 27; and cosmopolitanism, 3, 12, 14, 23–24; creativity and International Relations, 118n69; disruptive, 32; and distance, 14; and imagination, 4, 12; and justice, 22; and listening, 3, 18, 82; and multispecies interconnectedness, 23; about war, 3, 14, 24. *See also* literary; poetry

Yemen, 96
Youatt, Rafi, 36–37, 48, 70, 81, 129nn7, 75

zoo(s), 16–17, 65–82, 104, 125n7, 127n39
zoological knowledge, 33–38. *See also* ethology

www.ingramcontent.com/pod-product-compliance
Lightning Source LLC
Chambersburg PA
CBHW030827230426
43667CB00008B/1420